MINORITY GOVERNMENT AND MAJORITY RULE

STUDIES IN RATIONALITY AND SOCIAL CHANGE

Editors: Jon Elster and Michael Macpherson

Editorial Board:
Fredrik Barth
Amartya Sen
Arthur Stinchcombe
Amos Tversky
Bernard Williams

Kaare Strom

MINORITY GOVERNMENT AND MAJORITY RULE

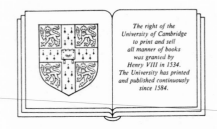

The right of the
University of Cambridge
to print and sell
all manner of books
was granted by
Henry VIII in 1534.
The University has printed
and published continuously
since 1584.

Cambridge University Press

Cambridge

New York   Port Chester   Melbourne   Sydney

Published by the Press Syndicate of the University of Cambridge
The Pitt Building, Trumpington Street, Cambridge CB2 1RP
40 West 20th Street, New York, NY 10011, USA
10 Stamford Road, Oakleigh, Melbourne 3166, Australia

© Cambridge University Press 1990

First published 1990

Printed in Canada

Library of Congress Cataloging-in-Publication Data
Strom, Kaare.
Minority government and majority rule / by Kaare Strom.
p.   cm. – (Studies in rationality and social change)
ISBN 0-521-37431-6
1. Cabinet system.   2. Coalition governments.   3. Comparative
government.   I. Title.   II. Series.
JF331.S77   1990
321'.043 – dc20   89–17377
                                                               CIP

British Library Cataloguing in Publication Data
Strom, Kaare

Minority government and majority rule. – (Studies in
rationality and social change)
1. Minority governments
I. Title   II. Series
321.8'043

ISBN 0-521-37431-6 hard covers

Contents

Acknowledgments

In a previous incarnation, this book was a doctoral dissertation at Stanford University. My first fledgling efforts to come to grips with the phenomenon of minority governments were supervised by Giovanni Sartori and later by Gabriel Almond. I remain indebted to both for their sage counsel, firm guidance, and friendship. I also thank Marty Lipset and Bob Packenham for their advice and support, which I often sought and always appreciated. Many other individuals at Stanford in the early 1980s helped provide an environment of intellectual stimulation and encouragement from which I benefited enormously. John Chubb, John Ferejohn, Judy Goldstein, Greg Luebbert, Gary Marks, Gary Meyers, Don Share, Kathy Teghtsoonian, and Kim Voss were among them. My fieldwork in Italy was much facilitated by Roberto D'Alimonte, who patiently introduced me to the intriguing world of Italian coalition politics. Henry Valen and Johan P. Olsen were similarly helpful in my work on Norwegian governments.

Over the years a number of individuals have given me thoughtful and constructive comments on various drafts of the book. Paul Abramson, Sam Barnes, Ian Budge, Bruce Bueno de Mesquita, Beppe Di Palma, Geoff Garrett, Bob Jackman, Peter Lange, Arend Lijphart, Jim Morrow, and Bing Powell have all helped improve the manuscript. Jon Elster, Ron Rogowski, and George Tsebelis have read and commented on the manuscript in its entirety. I hope they will recognize their contributions. Finally, I am especially grateful to Mik Laver and Terry Moe, who have continuously challenged me through the incisiveness of their comments and the exacting standards of their own work.

In the various institutions where I have worked on this book, I have invariably been blessed with excellent research and secretarial assistance. Torbjörn Bergman and John Huber have given me research assistance of the most thorough and conscientious kind. Karla

Bellingar, Gisela Lohne, and especially Mary Ellen Otis have helped me greatly with typing and word processing and responded efficiently and cheerfully to my most unreasonable requests. I am particularly delighted to acknowledge my debt to Bruce Bueno de Mesquita for his assistance in typing the manuscript.

My research has been supported financially by the Norwegian Research Council for Science and the Humanities (NAVF), the McKnight Foundation, and the University of Minnesota. I thank all of these institutions for making my research possible.

Finally, I wish to thank my family and friends who have supported and encouraged me throughout the many years this research has taken. This book is dedicated to them and especially to the memory of my father.

1. The problem of minority government

When Edward Heath "went to the country" in the winter of 1974, Britain was facing its worst economic crisis since the Great Depression. The trade deficit was at a record level, inflation was rampant, and industrial production was declining. Industry was on a three-day workweek as a result of the miners' strike, and the conflict between the government and the unions seemed likely only to escalate. But when the results of the general election of February 28 became known, Britain plunged even deeper into political and economic depression. The *Financial Times* industrial (stock market) index fell by a record 24 points. The value of the pound dropped sharply in the currency markets. The winter in the oil- and coal-starved country seemed even gloomier. Heath's Conservative government had just lost its parliamentary majority, but for the first time since 1929 there was no new majority to take its place. Both the Conservatives and Labour were held to less than 40% of the popular vote, and in the House of Commons the Liberals and other minor parties held the balance. The *Times* called it "an election with a result but no government."

On Saturday, March 2, the prime minister invited Jeremy Thorpe, the Liberal leader, to talks in Downing Street. These conversations, whose purpose was to explore the opportunities for a coalition government, continued the next day. On March 4 Heath wrote Thorpe imploring the Liberals to join his government to give the country a "stable and confident" administration. In declining Heath's offer, Thorpe expressed his desire for an even broader coalition: a "government of national unity" including the Labour party. Heath duly tendered his resignation, and Harold Wilson promptly formed Britain's first minority government in 45 years. This outcome, a minority government, was what Heath less than a week before the election had described as the *worst* possible result (Butler and Kavanagh, 1974).

This book is about the kind of cabinet Heath feared and Britain got: minority governments in parliamentary regimes. British observers of Wilson's experiment generally agreed on two observations about minority governments: (1) They represent significant departures from two-party politics, and (2) they are generally unhealthy and ineffective. The main thesis of this book is that these observers were wrong on both counts. As Wilson's government took to its tasks with vigor and notable successes, some people in Britain came to change their view of minority cabinets (see Butler and Kavanagh, 1975; Finer, 1975), but that is another story.

Minority governments are defined by the relationship between the legislative and the executive branches of government in parliamentary democracies, the most common type of democratic regime. Nothing could be more distinctly political than such intragovernmental relations. Yet, the modern science of politics has hardly belabored minority governments to exhaustion. On the contrary, political science has been strangely silent on this phenomenon. This discrepancy has to do with two important developments in modern political science. One is the behavioral revolution in social science, which directed scholarly interest away from political institutions and toward behavior and its social origins. The second factor is the wave of radical activism that hit the discipline in the late 1960s, shifting attention away from institutions and toward social problems and policies. Certainly these developments resulted from both political and scientific dissatisfactions, and just as surely they have had scholarly as well as political consequences.

If political scientists had moved little beyond formal institutional analysis in the past, they soon came to neglect issues at the very core of democratic politics. Then, in recent years, students of behavior and policy alike have rediscovered the importance of institutions. Students of interest groups and corporatism (Berger, 1981; Schmitter and Lehmbruch, 1979), legislative decisions (Shepsle, 1979), social revolutions (Skocpol, 1979), and democratic stability (Lijphart, 1984a; Powell, 1982a) have rediscovered the importance of governmental and other political institutions. There has been a renaissance in the comparative study of governments and electoral systems (Bogdanor and Butler, 1983; Grofman and Lijphart, 1985), as well as of party and government coalitions (Bogdanor, 1983; Browne and Dreijmanis, 1982; Laver and Budge, forthcoming; Luebbert, 1986; Pridham, 1986). This growing recognition of the importance of governmental institutions has not meant a return to the formalism of bygone days. The new institutionalists are innovative and diverse (March and Olsen, 1984).

Executive–legislative relations remain at the core of democratic politics in advanced industrial nations, and the study of comparative politics may be on its way back to its institutionalist basics. But we still lack an adequate understanding of the causes and performance of minority governments in parliamentary democracies. It is to this task we now turn.

Democracy and parliamentary government

In the emergent nation-states of Western Europe, the differentiation between executive and legislative power was an early and critical development. In fact, the protracted struggle between the two has provided the essential constitutional structure of these polities. Through Montesquieu and the Federalists political authority came to be seen as naturally differentiated into legislative, executive, and judicial branches of government. This conception is still very much with us today, in theory as well as in actual institutions.

The constitutional relationship between the legislative and executive branches of government is the basis for the distinction between *unified* (or fused) and *separation-of-powers* forms of government. In the contemporary world of democracies the two forms of government roughly correspond to parliamentary and presidential systems, respectively.[1] This book is confined to parliamentary government, which is the predominant form of government among the democracies of Western Europe and the Commonwealth. The distinguishing characteristics of unified parliamentary systems are that the chief exec-

[1] Parliamentary and presidential systems are not exhaustive categories, and hybrid forms exist (Blondel, 1973; Lijphart, 1984a). The Fifth French Republic, in which the prime minister is responsible to the assembly as well as to the president, represents one such mixed case.

utive is elected by, and responsible to, the legislature (Lijphart, 1984a: 68).

The responsibility of the executive branch to the legislature is often ambiguous. It consists in a relationship of accountability, in which the government (executive) must resign if it no longer enjoys the confidence of the legislative assembly. A defeat on a confidence motion or an "important" bill is typically enough to send the government packing. However, in such polities as the German Federal Republic, Spain, and Switzerland the power of the legislature to retire the cabinet is seriously circumscribed (Laver and Schofield, in press).

But what part of the executive branch is responsible to what part of the legislature? Conventionally, parliamentary responsibility concerns only politically appointed members of government and not career civil servants. And the sanction these incumbents face is the loss of office.[2] A further qualification of the parliamentary principle is that the confidence relation applies only to popularly elected chambers. Parliamentary democracy does not imply cabinet responsibility to unelected chambers, such as the British House of Lords. Nor is the cabinet normally responsible to *indirectly* elected chambers in bicameral systems, such as the French Senate or German Bundesrat. Only in the relatively rare cases of coequal chambers with similar electoral laws (e.g., Italy) can the cabinet be responsible to both chambers of the legislature.[3] The decision rule for the confidence relation between government and legislature is normally simple majority. The counting of abstentions, however, is often ambiguous, and some modern constitutions have decision rules that protect the status quo through such mechanisms as the German *constructive vote of no confidence*.

Majority and minority governments

The application of the majority principle to parliamentary responsibility is not altogether straightforward. In parliamentary regimes, cabinets must at various junctures produce legislative majorities in

[2] We are not concerned here with such constitutional sanctions as impeachment.
[3] The confidence relation between the government and the upper chamber of the legislature may still be a controversial issue. Consider, for example, the Australian constitutional crisis of 1976 (Lijphart, 1984a: 95–105).

order to perform their constitutional functions. In general there are two critical tests of government majorities: (1) confidence motions, and (2) final votes on bills supported by the government.

Parliamentary governments must be able to win votes of confidence. Such votes generally come in three forms, according to their origins. Votes of confidence may be demanded by the government itself or by the opposition, or they may be required by the constitution. Governments are normally free to press confidence motions at any time, although they may not be permitted to dissolve the legislature in the event of a loss. The opposition may be more restricted in its access to confidence motions, as in the Spanish constitution. Constitutionally mandated confidence votes are particularly likely at the time when a new government first presents itself to the legislature. Many constitutions, especially modern and republican ones, require a *vote of investiture* at this juncture (Laver and Schofield, 1989). Let us call the necessity of winning votes of confidence a *viability* requirement, since a defeat on such a vote typically ends the government's "life."

But viability is no guarantee that a government can fulfill its constitutional functions. Parliamentary governments also face the requirement of *effectiveness*. Over anything but the very short run, they must regularly be able to muster legislative majorities for their legislative and budgetary bills, their appointments, etc. Parliamentary governments, then, must be both viable and effective. In studies of coalitions in parliamentary government it is commonly assumed (1) that the legislative coalitions that provide a government's viability and effectiveness are identical, and (2) that these majorities consist of the political parties from which the members of the government are drawn. In coalition-theoretic parlance, the assumptions are that the coalitions over policy and office are identical and that they can be identified as the parties holding cabinet portfolios.

Neither of these assumptions is necessarily true. Parties without cabinet portfolios may well support the government on confidence votes, legislative bills, or both. It is particularly common for parties not in the portfolio coalition to participate in the legislative coalition all or part of the time. Parties not represented in the cabinet may even receive some office payoffs, for example in the form of sub-cabinet offices, legislative chairmanships, or other appointments in the public sector. However, parties in the portfolio coalition are likely to be members of the legislative coalition almost all the time. Members of governing parties are particularly unlikely to get away with frequent departures from the fold on votes of confidence.

Thus, coalitions over policy may well be larger than coalitions over portfolios, and viability coalitions may differ from effectiveness coalitions. These simple points go right to the heart of the problem of minority governments. In short, they problematize the expectation of *majority government*. Let us define a majority cabinet (or government) as

> any cabinet that meets all appropriate constitutional requirements and that is composed of persons acting as representatives of political parties or parliamentary groups that collectively control no less than one half of all seats in the national legislature, or that chamber of the legislature to which the cabinet is constitutionally responsible.[4]

By implication, this definition admits the possibility of cabinets without legislative majorities.[5] Indeed, it is precisely such aberrations that interest us. Minority cabinets (or governments) are cabinets that meet all of the foregoing requirements except the majority clause. However, majority and minority governments do not jointly exhaust

---

[4] The technical distinction between the less inclusive term "cabinet" and the more inclusive term "government" is of little relevance to my concerns here. Unless otherwise specified, I henceforth use both synonymously for that part of the executive branch that is responsible to parliament in parliamentary systems.

[5] Note that I define the majority so as to include the tie vote. The rationale is that most parliaments have rules favoring the status quo in the event of tie votes. In parliamentary regimes this generally means the party or parties in office. Even in the absence of such a bias, the worst predictable outcome for the government would be a stalemate. But under no existing institutional rule would this suffice to bring down the incumbent government. And the crucial property of a minority government is precisely that the composition of parliament appears sufficient to bring down the government at any time. The point is less academic than it may seem. The parties represented in Scelba's Italian government (1954–5) accounted for exactly 295 of 590 seats in the Chamber of Deputies. In Ireland, the third Lemass government (1965–6) likewise controlled exactly half the seats in the Dáil. Moreover, both Sweden and Iceland experienced even splits between their major political blocs during the 1970s. In the course of this decade both Norway and Sweden changed the memberships of their respective parliaments from an even to an odd number purely to avoid such an outcome.

the set of possible cabinet solutions. A further possibility is a non-partisan solution, such as a caretaker or business administration.

One might believe this third category to be indistinct, since we know empirically that many minority and some majority cabinets are precisely caretakers. But the distinguishing characteristic here is non-partisanship and not the caretaker role. If the cabinet members represent parliamentary parties, then we can count the legislative seats controlled by these parties collectively, the government's *parliamentary basis*. This parliamentary basis must logically be either a majority or a minority. On the other hand, if the cabinet members do not act as party representatives (even though they may hold party memberships), then the numerical criterion is inapplicable. We then have a distinct class of cabinets, which I call *nonpartisan*.

The difference between majority and minority governments cross-cuts another important distinction between partisan governments. This is the distinction between *single-party* and *coalition* governments.[6] It is commonly assumed that single-party and coalition governments form under distinct conditions: single-party governments in *majority situations* (i.e., when one party alone controls a majority of the legislators), and coalition governments in *minority situations*, when no party is so advantaged. Political scientists have generally shown much greater interest in coalition governments than in either single-party majority or minority governments.

Both minority and nonpartisan governments deviate from the norms of parliamentary democracy. Nonpartisan governments violate the most fundamental norm, that of party government (Duverger, 1954; Rose, 1974b; Sartori, 1976). However, nonpartisan governments are quite rare, and hence of limited practical interest. The low incidence of such governments will be demonstrated in Chapter 3.

Minority governments violate the expectation that executive and legislative coalitions are identical. Even when the distinction between these two coalitions is recognized, it is difficult to see what would cause them to differ. Why would any party agree to support the government legislatively if it gets no portfolios in exchange? From a

---

[6] Technically, we could refer to single-party governments as coalitions consisting of a single party. However, this usage is unconventional in the literature on party systems and parliamentary government and could easily confuse many readers. I shall therefore refer to governments as coalitions only when they consist of two or more parties.

different perspective, the puzzle is why the opposition, by definition a majority coalition in parliament, does not depose the government and take the spoils of office for itself. These puzzles indicate that minority government is a *counterintuitive* phenomenon in the world of parliamentary democracy. The difficulty of explaining minority government formation presents itself most clearly in the game-theoretic tradition, where the expectation of majority government is conventionally treated as an axiom. Any occurrence of minority governments therefore seems to threaten the entire edifice of deductive coalition theory. Given the counterintuitive nature of minority governments, the question is whether they can be as easily dismissed as nonpartisan administrations.

Minority governments: the record

The answer to the preceding question is an emphatic no. Minority governments are nowhere near as rare as nonpartisan administrations. In fact, existing studies suggest that undersized (minority) cabinets are a surprisingly common occurrence across a number of parliamentary democracies. In a study of 132 governments in 12 parliamentary democracies, Michael Taylor and Michael Laver have found 45, or 34.1%, to be minority governments (1973: 229). Very similar figures have been presented in several other studies. Valentine Herman and John Pope (1973), in an article on minority cabinets, find that this cabinet type accounts for 35.8% of the 207 administrations they studied. Hans Daalder reports an almost identical percentage of 36.5 in his study of 10 smaller European democracies (1971: 288). In a more recent survey, Arend Lijphart reports the proportion as 67 of 218 (30.7%) governments in 20 countries over the period from 1945 to 1980 (1984a: 81). Finally, Gregory Luebbert's (1986) data on 12 parliamentary democracies yield a frequency of 37.2%.

Thus, several independent studies show that in large samples of the world's parliamentary democracies, minority cabinets account for about one-third of all postwar governments. Beyond this basic result the analyses differ, and none can be considered an authoritative account of minority governments. For one thing, the data sets differ in their spatial and temporal parameters. Lijphart's analysis is the most inclusive in both respects. Second, the experts differ in how they define government composition and change. Finally, these authors have widely different theoretical ambitions. Some are mainly interested in descriptions of party systems and patterns of coalition formation. Others are out to test explicit hypotheses of coalition formation. Most important, only Herman and Pope are primarily interested in the phenomenon of minority governments, and their article is dated and mainly descriptive. In all the other studies, minority cabinets are a topic of decidedly secondary importance.

The causes of minority government formation

As we have noted, there is no rich literature on minority governments per se. However, a number of studies bear on this issue. The subject has been approached chiefly from the following perspectives:

1. Traditional comparative analysis of governmental institutions;
2. Deductive coalition theory based on game-theoretic assumptions; and
3. The literature on comparative party systems.

Each body of scholarship has its merits as well as its flaws. The traditional institutional literature is rich in historical detail, but much weaker in explanatory rigor. Coalition theory unquestionably provides the most rigorous explanations and predictions of government formation. But the interest of coalition theorists in *minority* governments has until recently been only tangential, and their assumptions often patently implausible. Students of party systems have provided many valuable empirical surveys, but their explanatory efforts have been weaker and often underdeveloped.

The most striking feature of the literature on minority government formation is the considerable bias against such cabinets. The explanations that are advanced typically reflect an assumption that minority governments represent some political accident or defect. It is often difficult to get a clearer interpretation of the arguments, since they tend to be *ad hoc* and impressionistic. In fairness I should point out that these ambiguities often are caused by the fact that the authors' principal concerns are so far removed from minority governments. Yet some themes recur in explanations of minority cabinet formation. The next few pages review the most widely suggested conditions favoring minority governments.

Political crisis and instability

Some form of political crisis is often taken to be the immediate cause of minority government formation. This is a particularly prevalent explanation in institutionalist scholarship on government formation. Consider, for example, Ernst Friesenhahn's account: "Minority governments, which must seek their majorities from issue to issue, can thus be no more than an emergency measure, and indicate a crisis situation" (1971: 312).[7] Klaus von Beyme concurs in his monumental work on parliamentary government: "According to the basic rules of the parliamentary system, every minority cabinet is an unwanted crisis symptom" (1970: 570).

This association of minority governments with political crisis is hardly ever developed in greater detail. As an explanation it is unsatisfactory on several grounds. Neither the locus nor the magnitude of a crisis sufficient to bring about a minority government is specified. Are such cabinets to be understood as reflections of severe systemic crisis or simply of coalition frictions in otherwise stable party systems? Whereas the former interpretation may reasonably represent Friesenhahn and von Beyme, the latter seems closer to the spirit of party systems theorists Michael Taylor and Valentine Herman:

> Minority governments are often "crisis" governments, coming to power when no majority can be found. In a multi-party system with a dominant party, a general election may deprive the dominant party of its absolute majority after a series of one-party majority governments, and the other parties, finding themselves with an unexpected combined majority, may be unable to agree on the formation of a coalition, in which case the dominant party may continue in office for some time. Its position, however, will be

---

[7] Here as elsewhere I am responsible for translations of quotations from works in languages other than English.

precarious, as it usually will have to rely on the support of a small party to provide a legislative majority. (1971: 31)

The crisis explanation is closely related to a focus on political instability as a precondition or concomitant of minority government formation. According to this view, the less stable the political system, the more common minority governments should be. Again, the type and severity of instability associated with minority governments are commonly left vague. A "strong" interpretation would equate minority governments with severe systemic instability, for example, in the form of civil disorder, riots, and strikes. A weaker interpretation might predict a positive correlation between the level of cabinet instability and the incidence of minority governments.

Political culture and heritage

Scholars of a more historical bent have linked minority governments to historical heritage and political culture. Hans Daalder (1971) holds the relative timing of the introduction of responsible parliamentary government responsible for subsequent patterns of government formation. Historical legacies may also be responsible for present-day cultural patterns that impinge on government formation. Consociational democracy exemplifies such practices. Consociationalism in plural democracies includes reliance on "grand coalitions" (Lijphart, 1977). These coalitions need not always form at the cabinet level, but there should be a tendency toward oversized coalitions and an avoidance of minority governments in consociational democracies (Lijphart, 1984a; Powell, 1982). But although Lijphart identifies conditions under which oversized coalitions form, he is much less sanguine about the possibility of explaining undersized governments in similar ways. Minority cabinets, Lijphart admits, may form under a variety of conditions (Lijphart, 1984a: 62).

Whereas these historical approaches point to the importance of long-standing legacies for cabinet formation, other theories put the stress more directly on contemporary political culture. Gregory Luebbert (1984, 1986) linked minority government formation to macropolitical regime characteristics. Luebbert classified parliamentary systems on the basis of two variables: (1) the degree of regime legitimacy, and (2) the extent to which the opposition parties engage in consensus-building legislation. Regimes with high legitimacy and consensus building were called *consensual*, those without these features *conflictual*. Luebbert found one empirically significant hybrid form, namely, regimes with high legitimacy but without the institutions and norms necessary for consensus building. He called such regimes *competitive*.[8]

Luebbert reported great and systematic differences in patterns of government formation across his three main regime types. Minority governments are most common in consensual regimes and virtually absent in competitive regimes. Conflictual regimes fall somewhere in between. Luebbert explained these differences in terms of the need and ability of political parties to cooperate in government. In consensual polities minority governments form because parties have no great need for government collaboration (although their ability is present). In conflictual regimes, undersized governments result from the inabilities of the parties to cooperate (although the need is there). Thus Luebbert combined cultural and structural factors with strategic considerations in his explanation of minority government formation (1983, 1984, 1986).

Party system fractionalization

Structural properties of the party system enter several explanations of minority governments. Giovanni Sartori (1976) associates minority cabinets with the type of party system he calls *moderate pluralism*. This type of party system is characterized by a moderate number of parties (three to five "relevant" ones) separated by modest ideological distance:

> Vis-à-vis the properties of twopartism, the major distinguishing trait of moderate pluralism is coalition government. This feature follows from the fact that the relevant parties are at least three, that no party generally attains the absolute majority, and that it appears irrational to allow the major or dominant party to govern

[8] The fourth logically possible type, the *unconsolidated* democracy characterized by consensus building without legitimacy, was in Luebbert's opinion of scant empirical importance.

alone when it can be obliged to share its power. Thus minority single party governments do materialize, but they do so either as a result of miscalculated Indian wrestlings, or on the basis of a precise calculus (such as shedding unpopular, if necessary, policies), and otherwise as disguised coalitions and transitional caretaker governments. (Sartori, 1976: 178)

Sartori here suggests several causal factors behind the formation of minority governments, as well as some of the functions such cabinets may have. Note that undersized governments are associated with irrationality and miscalculation. His main message, though, is that it is party system *fractionalization* (or fragmentation) that permits such aberrations. Fractionalization is a function of the number and size of political parties. The more parties, and the more evenly they split the electorate, the greater the degree of fractionalization (see Rae, 1971). It stands to reason that fractionalization could correlate positively with the incidence of minority government formation. The larger the number of parties, the more difficult it may be to build a majority, and the greater the probability of a minority solution. Inversely, the number of undersized cabinets should decline toward zero as we approach a pure two-party system (Budge and Herman, 1978).

Of course, explanations of government formation need not be monocausal. The linkage between fractionalization and minority government formation has occasionally been framed in more complex terms. The most prominent example is found in Lawrence Dodd's coalition-theoretic explanation (Dodd, 1976). According to Dodd, party system fractionalization causes uncertainty for party leaders. The more fractionalized the legislature is, the more difficulty they have in securing reliable information about the commitments and strength of other parties. And the worse informed party leaders are, the more likely they will form cabinets that deviate from minimum winning status (Dodd, 1976: 62–70). Dodd thus provides a micropolitical rationale for the correlation between fractionalization and undersized governments.

But in Dodd's theory fractionalization is only a necessary, and not a sufficient, condition for minority government formation. In addition, high levels of cleavage conflict or polarization are required (see the following section). Moreover, information uncertainty is a function not only of fractionalization but also of party system instability and the interaction of these two factors. Dodd's emphasis on party system instability is akin to arguments surveyed earlier. However, his theory suggests that what matters is incremental, rather than absolute, fractionalization. Minority governments are particularly probable solutions when party systems suddenly become *more* fractionalized. Specifically, the precipitating factor is the occurrence of a minority situation in a country accustomed to majority situations. This contention is not explicated in Dodd's theory, but finds a clearer expression in the article by Taylor and Herman (1971). It is most clearly formulated by G. Bingham Powell:

> In short, where the party and electoral system typically produces majorities, the elites tend to rely on direct election outcomes and orient themselves to the forthcoming election, rather than to legislative bargaining for a coalition. Where the electoral system does not usually produce majorities, the parties respond to the need for coalition-building. (1982a: 143)

Cleavage conflict and polarization

Whereas explanations from fractionalization stress the numerical properties of party systems, other accounts emphasize the ideological character of its members and their interaction. The extent of cleavage conflict, extremism, or polarization becomes the principal cause of minority government formation. The more polarized or divided the party system, the greater the likelihood of minority governments.[9]

Sartori is the preeminent analyst of party system polarization, but he fails to develop the implications of this phenomenon for minority cabinet formation. Dodd is much more explicit. Cleavage conflict or polarization (Dodd uses these two terms interchangeably and in agreement with Sartori) adversely affects the *a priori willingness* of

---

[9] Following Sartori's definition, I use the term "polarization" to refer to the overall ideological distance between the relevant parties (Sartori, 1976: 135). While it is far from obvious how to operationalize this concept, it is clearly distinct from a second prevalent conception of polarization as the extent of party system bipolarity. For a more thorough conceptual analysis, see Putnam, Leonardi, and Nanetti (1981).

political parties to negotiate for government participation. And the less willing parties are to bargain, the more likely they will end up with an undersized (minority) government. This is especially likely when polarization coincides with fractionalization and party system instability (Dodd, 1976: 57–68). But extreme polarization may in itself suffice to bring about minority governments: "Under conditions of extremely high polarization, multi-party parliaments will experience minority cabinets as parties will not consider majority coalitions even with the existence of information certainty" (Dodd, 1976: 69).

Dodd's argument is seconded by Powell: "In some cases the formation of a minority government represents intense legislative conflict. The parties are too deeply divided to agree on a stable coalition capable of positive action, so they accept a minority caretaker" (1982a: 142). Note, however, that Powell's argument concerns only one class of minority governments. Undersized cabinets, he contends, form in three different kinds of situations, of which polarization is a salient characteristic of one.

Proximate conditions

The final explanation we shall consider focuses on the proximate conditions of government formation. In this review, we have moved from causes associated with the structure and culture of the political system as a whole, through party system properties, to circumstances surrounding the particular cabinet crisis. I refer to these processes as the *proximate conditions* of government formation. According to conventional wisdom, minority governments form only when all other options have been exhausted, or when no other options exist. Minority governments accordingly represent failed interparty negotiations.

Such explanations of minority government formation are most common in deductive coalition theories. This literature generally presumes that rationality in government formation entails majority solutions. A minority outcome is hardly ever considered a possible equilibrium. Minority government formation is commonly explained through reference to constraints, limited choice, failure of negotiation, and lower-order preferences, conditions that are often tied to the negotiation process itself (Dodd, 1976: 46; see also von Beyme,

1985: 326; Sartori, 1976). The focus on proximate causes of minority government formation need not be incompatible with structural explanations, as Dodd demonstrates. Note, however, that Dodd's theory is the only rigorous multicausal explanation of this kind.

Summary

This survey has revealed the inadequacy of existing explanations of minority government formation. Although a variety of explanations have been advanced, there has been little serious effort to move beyond simple ad hoc hypotheses. Explanatory efforts have often been superficial and imprecise. Rarely have they been theoretically ambitious. Few have been systematically tested. Institutionalists have occasionally provided less simplistic accounts, but these have tended to be little more than atheoretical post hoc catalogues of parliamentary situations favoring minority governments.

Despite their apparent diversity, existing explanations of minority government formation have many common elements and few incompatibilities. Minority cabinets, it is conventionally held, form in unstable and conflictual political systems, whose party systems may be highly fractionalized. Such cabinets are suboptimal and unstable solutions, which are resorted to only when all else fails. Although specific causal claims are rarely made, minority governments are commonly associated with social and political malaise. I shall refer to this reconstructed characterization as the *conventional theory* (or view) of minority government formation, although it is clearly a theory only in a very loose sense of the word. Rather, this label serves as an umbrella for a variety of explanations with two common characteristics: (1) a failure to relate minority government formation successfully to rational actions by the political parties involved, and (2) an essentially negative evaluation of such governments.

Minority governments in office

Students of party coalitions have come to realize that cabinet formation is only part of the story of parliamentary government. This is particularly true of minority governments, since the viability and effectiveness of such governments seem so obviously threatened. The counterintuitive character of minority cabinets naturally gives rise to questions of how such governments survive and succeed. These are questions of government *performance*. If the literature on the causes of minority government formation is meager, there has been even less research on performance. Partly this is because there are few adequate measures of government performance. Moreover, what operational measures exist have scant theoretical justification.

We shall return to these problems in greater detail in Chapter 4. For the moment, simply note that our knowledge of minority government performance is lacking because the whole literature on government performance is inadequate. However, this larger literature is not entirely unfocused. Studies of government performance (including that of minority cabinets) have generally revolved around two criteria, namely, stability (viability) and legislative effectiveness (D'Alimonte, 1978). These two criteria have not always been kept distinct, as when cabinet durability (a conventional stability measure) is used as an indicator of government effectiveness (e.g., Powell, 1980).

Minority governments have rarely received high marks for either stability or effectiveness. Several empirical studies have shown minority governments to be less durable than others, particularly when compared to single-party majority governments and minimum winning coalitions (Lijphart, 1984b; Warwick, 1979). Dodd argues that minority governments should be nondurable, giving way either to minimum winning coalitions through expansion, or to parliamentary dissolution where broader cooperation fails (Dodd, 1976: 68–9). Indeed, in Dodd's empirical analysis, minority governments turn out to be among the least durable cabinet types (1976: 157–71). Taylor and Herman (1971) come to similar conclusions, although they observe much less dramatic differences. This discrepancy highlights one of the problems of quantitative duration studies, which is that the results depend substantially on the rules by which governments are counted (see Lijphart, 1984b).

There has been no systematic cross-national study of the legislative *effectiveness* of minority governments. The literature is generally restricted to impressionistic evaluations with a largely negative flavor. Klaus von Beyme characterizes the state of the art thus:

Minority governments are not part of the normative concepts of the democracy theory. They are also held to be unstable, and for this reason too incompatible with a properly functioning democracy. But except in the form of a caretaker government, they are not necessarily less efficient than majority governments. However, no comparison has yet been made of the achievements in terms of political decision making by minority governments. (1985: 327)

Note that von Beyme questions the stability more than the effectiveness of minority governments. His argument is in this sense not typical of the conventional view of minority cabinets. Powell (1982a) makes a more negative, though qualified, assessment:

The government is kept in office as long as it remains passive in policy formation. Its retention depends on outside parties who prefer it to other governments as a temporary measure and prefer it to an absence of government, but will not join it in positive policies. . . . Similarly limited in policy capacity is perhaps the largest group of minority governments, the "pre-election caretakers." (142–3)

More sweeping indictments are not uncommon. Nevil Johnson's summary of the disadvantages of minority governments aptly represent many of the misgivings frequently expressed. In Johnson's view, minority governments tend to be:

1. Weak and exposed to the risk of parliamentary defeat;
2. Opportunistic and in search of ways to escape their minority position; and
3. Lacking in the authority and support necessary to handle serious problems (1975: 87).

Minority cabinets (or at least unsupported ones) are conventionally portrayed as governments of lowered effectiveness (Linz, 1978: 66). In some cases, it is argued, decisional paralysis or immobilism may result (von Beyme, 1970: 570–1). The negative consequences of such minority rule need not be confined to the legislative arena. A pervasive erosion of political responsibility may result. This erosion of responsibility, together with a possible loss of control over crucial decision-making processes, introduces extraordinary personal stress on cabinet members. This in turn may cause rapid turnover in personnel (Valen, 1981: 378). These defects may have severe regime ramifications. If cabinet instability sometimes contributes to the breakdown of democratic regimes (Linz, 1978: 110), then minority governments may be partly responsible.

The conventional wisdom about minority government performance adds up to a great deal of gloom – perhaps entirely too much, given the commonness of such cabinets. If minority governments are such poor performers, then why do they form so often? And if these cabinets are so frequent, why have there been so few crises of democracy in postwar Europe? These puzzles call for studies of the incidence as well as the performance of minority governments.

But government performance is a matter not only of *how well*, but also of *how* cabinets attain legislative coalitions. In contrast to most majority governments, the process by which a minority cabinet is formed does not necessarily explain how it stays in power. If we are to understand minority governments properly, we need to grasp the mechanisms by which these cabinets secure whatever viability and effectiveness they can.

Little is known about such legislative strategies. Several students of parliamentary government have emphasized the importance of support agreements between minority governments and parties outside the cabinet. Herman and Pope (1973) distinguish between *supported* and *unsupported* minority cabinets and find the former category to account for a majority of their empirical cases. Daalder harbors a similar suspicion that many minority cabinets are in reality majority governments "in disguise," but finds little supporting evidence (Daalder, 1971: 288; see also De Swaan, 1973: 85). Powell is aware of the problem, as well as the diversity of support agreements:

A third kind of minority government is one in which the governing party has consistent support from one or more parties outside the government, parties that support at least some of its policy initiatives. Arrangements between parties range from informal understandings to written agreements for full consultations and policy vetos (as in the long-lived Communist- and Socialist-supported

Christian Democratic governments in Italy in the late 1970s). (1982a: 143)

Dodd, on the other hand, expresses strong doubts about the pervasiveness of such government arrangements. His argument rests on reason and impression, however, rather than systematic evidence:

> Judging from the comparative literature, supporting parties are not relevant to most parliamentary settings. There appears to be a widespread norm that all parties in the supporting coalition are in the cabinet. This norm results in a large part because parties desire specific ministerial positions: one aspect of policy payoff will normally be control of vital ministries that regulate the policy areas of particular concern to specific parties (the agriculture ministry for Agrarian parties, and so forth). (1976: 214)

This disagreement is most probably due to the lack of an operational definition of what a support agreement is. As Powell points out, there are a number of ways in which a nongoverning party can support the cabinet. Some of these entail explicit and far-reaching commitments; others represent no more than coincidental compatibilities with no long-range implications (see Bogdanor, 1983). A loose definition of support agreements leads to trivial propositions about legislative coalitions. Any coincidence of voting patterns is interpreted as a legislative coalition. But to observe similar voting patterns is not to explain why some pivotal parties consistently tolerate cabinets from which they get no spoils.

An even less rigorous explanation of how minority cabinets function directs our attention to the *effective decision point* in legislatures. A near majority, it is argued, is in many cases as good as a real majority:

> A party, like a government, which controls over 45 percent of the seats in a legislature is likely to receive the support necessary to provide it with a majority on crucial divisions. . . . We are now in a better position to understand the reasons why minority governments form. Governments – whether single- or multi-party in composition – are able to take office in minority situations when they control *almost* a majority of legislative seats. This suggests that the

effective decision point in these parliaments is a number smaller than a simple majority. (Herman and Pope, 1973: 203; see also Blondel, 1968)

It is not clear why these relaxed requirements obtain, and one suspects a case of circular reasoning: If less-than-winning coalitions prevail, then they have in some sense "won," and we must consequently change our definition of "winning." But parliamentary voting rules do not often distinguish between "small" and "big" losses, and pivotal parties are no less pivotal for being small. Almost-winning explanations do not make institutional sense, and they also need to demonstrate that most minority cabinets in fact hover very close to the majority threshold.

The significance of minority governments

Let us sum up the discussion so far. Minority governments deviate significantly from what we expect of governments in parliamentary democracies. We do not well understand why they form or how they operate. Despite some inconsistencies in the literature, it is possible to identify what I have called a conventional wisdom concerning minority cabinets. In this view, minority governments are associated with political malaise, irrationality, and poor performance.

We are now in a position to understand the importance of studying minority governments:

1. Minority governments violate many basic assumptions of how parliamentary democracy works, and they have not been well understood in the literature on party systems and government institutions. They are a counterintuitive phenomenon.
2. Minority governments specifically challenge the most sophisticated body of literature on government formation, namely, game-theoretic coalition theory. From this perspective minority governments are the least expected and explicable cabinet type (Browne, 1982a: 348). This point will be elaborated in the next chapter.
3. The available evidence suggests that minority cabinets are quite common across a large number of parliamentary democracies.

This chapter has summarized the conventional wisdom on minority governments. In Chapter 2 I present an alternative explanation of minority government formation and performance. This explanation takes issue with a number of common assumptions in the study of governments and coalitions. It is tested against more conventional explanations in Chapter 3. Chapter 4 turns our attention to minority governments in office and examines their legislative coalition-building strategies and performance in office. Chapters 5 and 6 are case studies of minority government formation and performance in Italy and Norway, respectively. Finally, Chapter 7 summarizes the results and assesses the implications for our understanding of party systems, coalition theory, and parliamentary democracy.

2. The rationality of minority government formation

The science of politics has left minority governments largely unexplained. In this chapter, I shall present a theoretical framework within which the formation and survival of minority governments can be more fruitfully understood. Initially the exposition will take the form of an explanation of the formation of minority governments. The implications of this explanation for government performance and party systems analysis will be developed later.

My explanation of minority government formation is grounded in what is arguably the most ambitious research program in political science: the rational-choice tradition (see Lakatos, 1970; Riker, 1983). Contrary to the conventional wisdom about minority governments, I shall argue that their formation can be understood as the consequence of rational behavior by the relevant party leaders. Informational uncertainty, unwillingness to bargain, or failures of negotiation need not be invoked to account for the incidence of such cabinet solutions. On the contrary, different patterns of cabinet formation can be explained through structural features of political systems, which make the calculi leading to minority government formation more or less likely.

This explanation of minority governments will depart from a host of common assumptions in the study of political parties and parliamentary governments. Yet the argument should not be taken as a blanket indictment of previous analyses of minority governments. And although I reject many of the operational assumptions game theorists have often made about political parties and their institutional environment, I am fundamentally beholden to the game-theoretic tradition and more generally to rational models of political behavior. My utilization of these models will be developed later. Let us now explore the political phenomenon we must seek to understand, namely, the process of government formation in parliamentary democracies.

The process of government formation

Under parliamentary democracy, government formations perform at least three specific functions:

1. The recruitment of individuals to the highest executive offices of government;
2. The formulation of some sort of governmental policy program; and
3. The structuring of the parliamentary arena into more or less cohesive blocs of legislators. We may roughly identify these blocs as government versus opposition, although we shall see the necessity of finer gradations.

In two-party systems these functions are to a large extent displaced to the electoral arena. Governmental alternatives are presented to the voters at election time, and the outcome monopolizes bargaining power in the hands of one party. In multiparty systems, however, government formation is normally not an automatic response to electoral results, especially if the election results in a minority situation, where no party alone commands a legislative majority. Government formation then requires *coalition building* of some sort. Note that the process of coalition building need not result in formal government coalitions, nor in legislative coalitions with identical memberships across all issue areas. The former assumption, which has been uncritically adopted by many coalition theorists, is neither logically compelling nor universally valid. The second assumption will be explored in Chapter 4.

For present purposes, let us define a coalition as a set of parliamentary political parties that

1. Agree to pursue a common goal or a common set of goals;
2. Pool their resources in pursuit of this goal;
3. Communicate and form binding commitments concerning their goal; and

4. Agree on the distribution of the payoffs to be received on obtaining their goal (Browne, 1982b: 2).

A coalition government consists of two or more parties meeting these criteria.[1] Generally, the simple agreement of two or more different parties to serve in the same government signifies the fulfillment of these conditions.

The process of government formation is hardly anarchic. Cabinets are formed in highly structured institutional settings, and it is often possible to identify distinct phases of the process. Parliamentary democracies vary in the stringency of their regulations concerning the cabinet formation process. Some of these regulations are embedded in the constitution; others are more informal. One of the most important such regulations is the *investiture* requirement. In some parliamentary democracies (such as Italy), the premier-designate and his (or her) entire cabinet are required to gain parliamentary approval (investiture) after their appointment by the head of state. In other systems (such as the Republic of Ireland), the prime minister alone is elected by the legislature. In yet other polities (such as Norway) the incoming head of government need not submit to any parliamentary vote. Countries with long traditions of parliamentary government tend to have less explicit and demanding provisions than nations with more recent constitutions and histories of greater contention regarding constitutional issues.

Investiture requirements restrict the range of governmental options by placing a hurdle at the end of the cabinet formation process. Other regulations impose restrictions at earlier stages of the process. One such stage may be the designation of a candidate for prime minister. The head of state typically plays at least a formal role at this stage.[2] If the person charged with the responsibility of leading negotiations toward cabinet formation is envisioned as a likely prime minister, we speak of him as a *formateur*. Some heads of state (especially directly

---

[1] Technically, we can speak of single-party governments as coalitions of one party. Most of the time this usage is confusing, and I shall therefore avoid it. However, my general references to "coalitional options" should not be understood as excluding single-party alternatives.

[2] The recent Swedish constitution has eliminated even the appearance of royal intervention in the designation of a candidate for prime minister.

elected presidents) may be influential in the selection of formateurs,[3] but particularly in constitutional monarchies the selection is effectively made by the party leaders themselves or by the outgoing prime minister. If the parliamentary situation is highly ambiguous, an *informateur* may be designated in lieu of a formateur. The use of informateurs has been especially common in Belgium and the Netherlands. Informateurs are selected for their access to party leaders, bargaining skills, or personal prestige, but are not necessarily expected to head the government they may help to form. Informateurs may occasionally be formateurs in disguise, preferring the ambiguity of the former role in case negotiations should fail.

For formateurs and informateurs do not always succeed. Not infrequently, the designated person must go back to the head of state and report that the negotiations have failed. In such cases, the latter will either change the mandate of the formateur (informateur) or give the task to another person, normally representing another party or bloc of parties. When a formateur finally succeeds, however, a second stage of negotiations begins. At this point, the parties involved typically have to resolve the distribution of two important payoffs: cabinet portfolios and government policies. A basic agreement or understanding often has been reached before the parties commit themselves to cabinet participation.[4] The sequence in which portfolio and policy agreements are reached may vary from country to country and from government to government. When these issues have been settled, the agreement typically goes back to the participating parties for ratification. Following such approval, the new government must normally be approved formally and inaugurated by the head of state. Then, finally, investiture may be required (see von Beyme, 1970).

Note that after the initial designation of a prime ministerial candidate, the government formation process is almost entirely in the hands of the leaders of the parliamentary parties. Although the third and fifth stages of the formation process (ratification and investiture)

---

[3] The Finnish president Urho Kekkonen is a prime historical example of a strong head of state in this regard.

[4] This description assumes that the government formation process involves several parties and results in a coalition government. Of course the process leading up to the formation of a single-party government is typically simpler and shorter. However, if the party is severely factionalized (as, e.g., the Italian Christian Democrats in the 1960s and 1970s), the process may closely parallel that involving a coalition of parties.

involve somewhat lower echelons of the parties, it is at this point very difficult and costly to tamper with solutions that have been negotiated. Typically, only a handful of party leaders are involved in the crucial negotiations over portfolios and government policies. It is true that these individuals are constrained by previous party policies and commitments, but such constraints rarely go beyond the specification of an acceptable set of coalition partners and a small set of unnegotiable issues. Fundamentally, the process of cabinet formation is a game played by a *very small and select set of party leaders*.

Parties and their choices

Government formations are processes of *choice*. The outcomes of negotiations toward a new government are not structurally determined in a strong sense. The range of possible alternatives is often broad, although many of these options may be very unlikely for reasons of party preference. This is not to say that the relevant players, parliamentary party leaders, are unconstrained in their deliberations. On the contrary, the preceding section has shown that the government formation process is typically highly institutionalized and can impose significant constraints on the range of feasible alternatives, for example, through investiture requirements. Constraints can also be imposed by players outside the parliamentary arena, such as foreign powers or influential interest groups. Moreover, the very structure of the formation process can act as a "soft" constraint to make certain solutions more or less probable. For example, if initially the task of forming a government is always offered to the largest party, its likelihood of participating in government is probably enhanced. Or, if there are severe time constraints on interparty bargaining, previously untried coalitions may be less likely to materialize, since the requisite negotiations would be too difficult and time-consuming.

Yet in multiparty systems, and particularly when the number of parliamentary parties exceeds four or five, the number of possible coalitions rises rapidly. Structural constraints typically only reduce the number of feasible coalitions moderately. Note that the range of feasible governmental alternatives cannot simply be inferred from observed behavior. Such an exercise would be tautological and would seriously underestimate the range of options available. The fact that only coalitions A and B have materialized in a given country does not mean that coalitions C and D have been unfeasible. Perhaps the relevant parties simply found the latter alternatives less desirable.

The process of government formation is best understood as a series of sequential decisions. The players are the parliamentary parties (represented by their respective leaders). There are strong bargaining and electoral incentives for parties to act cohesively, and the act of government formation is one area where the need for party unity is particularly pressing and dissent severely punished. So political parties try hard to behave as unitary actors in this process. Thus when a prime ministerial candidate is designated, he normally acts as a representative of his own party, but at least initially rarely of any other.

The sequential nature of the government formation process lies in subsequent decisions whether to add additional parties to the protocoalition. Initially, the decision may be whether to invite any party other than that of the premier-designate. If this party controls a legislative majority in its own right (in other words, in a majority situation), such an invitation is not likely to be forthcoming. Even if the "core" party does not command majority support,[5] it may decide to try to go it alone, possibly on the basis of ad hoc legislative coalitions. If an invitation is extended to one or several other parties, these may or may not decide to join. The members of the new protocoalition may then decide to invite other parties to participate in the next stage, and so on until no further expansion of the protocoalition is deemed desirable by its members. Any existing member of a protocoalition commonly has veto power over the admission of additional members. Deviations from this general model do of course occur, as when the premier-designate is appointed as a representative of a set of parties (e.g., a pre-electoral coalition), or when the official task of forming a government is explicitly tied to a certain coalition of parties. Yet the conception of government formation as a sequential game is a fair approximation in most cases.

---

[5] The notion of a "core" party here refers to any party (or set of parties) in a protocoalition entrusted with the task of forming a government. In this context I am not using the concept in the strict game-theoretic sense as the set of undominated solutions.

The implication is that at each stage of the government formation process, the outcome depends on the decisions of two sets of players: the "core" parties, which may or may not wish to expand the protocoalition, and the "marginal" or "peripheral" parties, which may or may not decide to join if invited. The protocoalition will continue to grow until either the core or the marginal parties, or both, no longer wish to expand. If this point comes before any party has been added, the outcome is a single-party government. If expansion halts before the majority threshold has been reached, the result is a minority cabinet. Given the obvious advantages of commanding a legislative majority, what needs to be explained is why protocoalitions often cease to grow before they reach this status.

In order to understand the phenomenon of minority governments, then, we need to grasp these party decisions. We need to understand party behavior in parliamentary interaction and therefore to look for the *intentions* behind this behavior. Although political parties are large and complex organizations, their decisions in the game of government formation are, as we have seen, typically made by very small leadership groups. It is therefore not far-fetched to treat the party as if it were an individual and impute reasons and intentions. In so doing, we come to search for the objectives pursued by political parties (or more specifically, their parliamentary leaders) and relate these to the options available in the process of government formation, as well as to the projected consequences of the various courses of action. We need to know what party leaders seek to attain when they decide whether or not to participate in government or whether or not to allow others to do so.

Rational models and party behavior

The upshot of the preceding argument is that the formation of minority governments should be studied through assumptions of *intentional* behavior. In fact, I shall go one step further and analyze minority government formation under assumptions of *rational* party behavior. In the most general conception, rational behavior consists of reasonable and purposeful acts, which can be contrasted with random, unreflected, or purely mechanical acts. But in order to invoke rationality, we must be able to make a number of additional assumptions.

First, rationality requires a set of *players*. Strictly speaking, these players should be individuals or groups whose preference schedules are dictated by single individuals. This is because there is demonstrably no guarantee that collectivities can meet the requirements stipulated later for the arrangement of preferences (see Arrow, 1951). In the case of government formations, I assume that party leaders act as short-term dictators within their respective parties.[6]

Second, the players are faced with a set of optional *actions* and *strategies*, which are causally connected to a set of *outcomes*. Rational analysis makes no sense if the players have no choices, or if the options have no consequences for them. In the case of government formation, the most prominent actions are related to government formation, portfolio distribution, and policy formulation. Strategies tell players what actions to take under what circumstances.

Third, players must have a *preference order* over the various outcomes that are associated with their strategies. This preference ordering must satisfy the criteria of transitivity and completeness; that is, all possible actions must be comparable, and if A is preferred to B and B to C, then A must also be preferred to C. In the context of government formation, this means that party leaders must have such preference orders over all possible government solutions.

Finally, rationality implies the *consistent* choice of strategies associated with more preferred outcomes over less preferred ones. In context, if a majority party prefers governing alone to all possible alternatives, then it must always eschew coalitions in practice (as long as its preference order does not change).

Although these are in some ways exacting conditions, they are not as strict as commonly believed. For example, rationality need not imply narrow self-interest. In the case of government formation, rationality does not necessarily mean that party leaders are only out for themselves, nor even that they are strictly concerned with the interests of their own parties. Moreover, there is no need to assume that players (party leaders) are fully cognizant of their preference

---

[6] Party leaders need not be dictators in the long run. Thus, this assumption is simply a stylized convenience, which does not preclude all forms of intraparty democracy.

orders, as long as such orders can be inferred from their behavior. Hence, rationality is a much less restrictive assumption than is commonly believed, and in many applications an eminently common-sensical one. As Terry Moe (1980: 14) argues, "The assumption of rationality is typically among the least unrealistic a theorist is called upon to make."

In the case of political parties and government formations, the assumption of rationality implies a stylized representation of human behavior, but a plausible one. Party leaders, as representatives of their organizations, make very public, deliberate, and consequential decisions concerning government participation. If these decisions are inconsistent or fail to promote the perceived party interest, there is normally no shortage of individuals willing and able to relieve them of their responsibilities. In other words, since the tenure of party leaders is insecure and their performance easily measured, they are constrained to act rationally.

Even if rationality is a plausible stylization of the behavior of party leaders engaged in coalition formation, one might question the realism of this assumption as a description of their cognitive processes. Three questions in particular indicate potential challenges to the rationality assumption:

1. Are the cost and benefits involved in the process of government formation sufficiently large to motivate rational calculi on the part of party leaders?
2. Are these leaders sufficiently informed and skilled to perform the calculi posited by the rational models?
3. Do intercultural variations make generalizations about utility functions, or the whole concept of instrumental rationality, inapplicable in cross-national research on government formation?

No doubt the first question can be answered in the affirmative. Party leaders generally care a great deal about whether or not they hold office. Indeed, for many, a government portfolio may represent their lives' highest ambition. Information certainty and skills have been a more critical consideration in the study of government coalitions. Riker (1962) and Dodd (1976) both pinpoint uncertainty as a critical cause of deviation from minimum winning size. I believe these concerns are exaggerated. As Gregory Luebbert persuasively argues,

Rationalist theory greatly overstates the role of information uncertainty. It would be difficult to find a bargaining situation in which
the principal actors are more familiar with each other. The party
leaders involved work together almost daily, often for many years,
in parliament; they know each other's constituency interests; they
read each other's speeches; they study each other's political commitments and divisions. It is surely the case that no one observes
the behavior of politicians more closely than other politicians.
(1983: 14)

Dodd contends that party leaders fear being deceived and trapped
in a coalition with undesirable partners (1976: 45–46). Again, this
problem appears overblown. Political parties can hardly be forced to
participate in government against their perceived interest. And for
subsequent government viability and effectiveness, strategies of de-
ception and entrapment would likely have devastating effects.

The possibility of cultural bias is obviously heavily dependent on
the scope of the analysis. It might be problematic to impute similar
preferences and rational behavior to a set of players who differed
vastly within as well as between political systems. However, in the
present case, the assumption applies only to a small set of political
elites in institutionally similar polities. Moreover, the nations involved
are all highly developed, democratic, and capitalist; and all but two
are in Western Europe. I shall discuss the scope of the analysis further
in a later section. Finally, recall that the rationality criterion is only
an "as if" assumption. What is needed is not really that party leaders
perform the kind of calculi implied by the theory, but only that they
behave as if this were the case. In this case the calculus is even
plausible.

Verisimilitude is not the only or even the principal reason to assume
rationality. A more compelling consideration lies in the scientific
status of rational models. Scientific progress depends on the development of fruitful scientific research programs (Lakatos, 1970), of
which the social sciences have few. The rational-choice tradition arguably represents the most viable and progressive research program
in present-day social science (see Elster, 1986). From a core of rig-
orously defined and parsimonious assumptions, rational-choice the-

orists have developed increasingly rich and successful explanations of a variety of social phenomena. From its core in economics, this research program has increasingly been adopted in disciplines such as political science, sociology, and anthropology. The rationalist approach is the most compelling way of giving *choice* its due in political analysis. Among its other prime virtues are parsimony, predictive ability, and the ease with which hypotheses can be tested and if necessary falsified on empirical as well as logical grounds. The rational-choice tradition has also proved powerful in its ability to clarify our thought about social issues, and empirical and normative issues have often been successfully interrelated.

Game theory and coalitions

Rational models come in two basic forms: parametric and strategic (Elster, 1983). Parametric rationality applies if a player can assume that his environment is constant in the sense that it does not adapt to his own actions. An example is the behavior of buyers and sellers in a perfectly competitive market. Strategic rationality applies if the environment is not constant, that is, if the behavior of each player depends on that of every other. Clearly the latter form of rationality is more applicable to the process of government formation, where the decision of one party leader whether or not to participate in government crucially depends on those of other such leaders. The principal analytic tool for the study of strategic rationality is game theory, which was first systematically developed about 40 years ago (Von Neumann and Morgenstern, 1945).

Game theory has dominated the study of parliamentary government formation since the publication of William Riker's (1962) seminal work, *The Theory of Political Coalitions*. According to Riker, in social situations similar to n-person, zero-sum cooperative games where the players have perfect information and side payments are permitted, only minimum winning coalitions (MWCs) will form. Government formations, argues Riker, are among the social situations to which these assumptions are applicable. Minimum winning coalitions are coalitions that have no unnecessary members, that is, members whose defection from the coalition would not cause a loss of "winning" status. Because Riker's theory establishes a size criterion for predicted coalitions, it is commonly referred to as the *size principle*.

The operational meaning of winning has not been extensively discussed in the coalition-theoretic literature on government formation. Intuitively, it is obvious that the requirements for winning are largely institutionally determined. Specifically, the meaning of winning depends on the decision rules in force in each particular legislature. If all important decisions require a two-thirds majority, then a two-thirds majority is the minimum winning size. Most empirical studies have simply assumed a pure-majority decision rule and hence equated winning with majority status. However, this operationalization is arbitrary and far from universally compelling.

Riker's theory builds on a number of critical, and sometimes controversial, assumptions. Besides the fundamental stipulations of rationality and game structure, the following assumptions are among the most important:

1. The game is zero sum or at least constant sum.[7] That is to say, the sum of payoffs to the players is the same regardless of which outcome is reached.
2. In applications to government formation, it has generally been assumed that parties are motivated solely by the desire to gain cabinet portfolios, or more generally governmental power. This is commonly referred to as the *office-seeking* or *power-seeking* assumption, and it is closely related to the conception of the game as constant-sum. It makes sense to think of the distribution of government portfolios as constant sum,[8] whereas this assumption would be less plausible if parties were assumed to be driven by policy motivations, for example.
3. It follows from this that the characteristic function of the game, as it varies by the size of the winning coalition, is nonpositively sloped beyond the point of minimum winning size. In other words, as the coalition gets larger than minimum winning, the

---

[7] Riker makes the more restrictive zero-sum assumption, but it is not necessary for his results, since zero-sum and constant-sum games are strategically equivalent.

[8] Even government portfolios are not necessarily constant sum. The number of portfolios may vary from one government to the next, and different parties may value different portfolios differently.

total payoff to the members declines or stays constant. Hence, the payoff to each member can only decline as coalitions expand their majorities.

4. Existing members effectively control the membership of the coalition. No party can join a coalition without the permission of those who already participate.
5. The players (parties) have *perfect information*. This means that all parties know the rules and the payoff structure of the game, as well as all previous moves made by other players.
6. The admissibility of *side payments* means that the parties can negotiate with each other concerning the distribution of the payoffs (cabinet portfolios).
7. Finally, in Riker's conception, each process of government formation is an isolated event, independent of any previous or future interaction between the players.

Criticism of Riker's theory has been directed against its internal consistency as well as against the plausibility of its assumptions for empirical research. In the former vein, Butterworth (1971) has argued that the minimum winning size principle should be replaced by one of "maximum positive gainers." Oversized coalitions (i.e., coalitions containing unnecessary members) can result if some player who outside the coalition would have suffered a substantial loss can bribe his or her way into the coalition and thereby suffer a lesser loss. Hardin (1976) generalizes this critique and contends that the size principle is valid only for *supersymmetric* games, where the payoff to the winning coalition is equal to the negative sum of the guaranteed minimum payoffs to the members of the losing coalition (see Abrams, 1980).

This internal critique of Riker has not spawned much empirical work on government formations. Instead, the main challenge has come from theorists who have rejected the constant-sum assumption and the related conception of political parties as exclusively office motivated. If one instead assumes that parties are motivated by the desire to influence public policy, the game is more naturally conceived as variable sum, and the size principle no longer applies.

The assumption of policy motivation does indeed form the basis of the most prominent alternative to Riker's theory in the study of government formation. Axelrod (1970) assumes an ordinal and uni-dimensional policy space, and predicts that only coalitions consisting of parties that are *connected* (adjacent) in this space will form. Retaining the majority stipulation, Axelrod predicts the formation of *minimal connected winning coalitions*. Axelrod (1970) and Leiserson (1966) add policy motivation to models that retain the office assumption in a modified form of the size principle. Party preferences are in essence assumed to be *lexicographic*, in the sense that policy preferences only come into play in the choice between coalitions that all satisfy the majority criterion.

De Swaan (1973) and Budge and Laver (1986) have developed "purer" policy-based theories, which depart more radically from Riker's theory. More recent and sophisticated policy-based theories have transcended Axelrod's and De Swaan's limitation to one-dimensional policy space. New solution concepts, such as the *competitive solution*, have also been introduced (McKelvey, Ordeshook, and Winer, 1978; Ordeshook and Winer, 1980). Some theorists have sought to synthesize policy-based theory with bargaining set theory (Schofield, 1982) or spatial voting models (Austen-Smith and Banks, 1988). The latter model, which is based on noncooperative game theory, departs most radically from conventional policy distance theory.

Policy distance theory has been adopted and adapted by a number of other students of government formation (e.g., Budge and Herman, 1978; De Swaan, 1973; Grofman, 1982; Laver, 1981; Luebbert, 1986). Recently, Budge and Laver (1986) have provided a lucid exposition of the different implications of the assumptions of office seeking versus policy pursuit. A number of empirical tests have pitted office-based against policy-based predictions (De Swaan, 1973; Lijphart, 1984a; Schofield and Laver, 1985; Taylor and Laver, 1973). Policy distance theories have generally performed at least as well as size theories in such tests.

Several of Riker's other assumptions have also been challenged in the empirical literature. The assumption of perfect information is relaxed even by Riker (1962), who explains deviation from minimum winning size through information uncertainty. Lawrence Dodd (1974, 1976) has elaborated this argument, as noted in Chapter 1. Since this is the primary explanation of minority governments offered by adherents of the size principle, it is obviously important for present purposes.

Finally, the assumption of government formations as mutually independent events has come under fire. Parties and governments, it has been pointed out, have a history and tend to anticipate interaction well into the future. Interparty commitments are not made and unmade anew for each electoral period or each instance of government formation. Hence it is reasonable to expect choices in the process of government formation to be constrained both by previous patterns of coalition and by expectations of future interaction (see Bueno de Mesquita, 1975, 1979; Franklin and Mackie, 1983; Laver, 1974).

All these critiques and new theoretical developments have not, however, led to a consensus in favor of any office- or policy-based theory. Policy-based theories clearly have gained the support of many scholars in the field. But these theories have so far failed to incorporate many of the other criticisms that have been raised against Riker's original theory. Most important (for present purposes), policy-based theories generally have continued to impose the majority requirement (see, however, Budge and Laver, 1986; Laver and Budge, forthcoming). They are thus no more capable of explaining minority government formation than their office-based counterparts.

The rationality of minority government formation

In this section I shall develop an explanation of minority government formation that on several points challenges the size principle and other conventional explanations of government formation. At the same time, the assumption of rationality in government formation is retained. The main advantages of my explanation are: (1) a more satisfactory account of minority government formation, (2) a more coherent understanding of the rationality of *all* cabinet formation processes, and (3) a more plausible and less rigid set of assumptions about political party behavior generally.

Note that although my assumptions should be more institutionally sensitive, and less heroic, they are nevertheless simplifications of reality, and clearly more plausible in some political contexts than elsewhere. Note also that the enhanced richness and plausibility of my explanation comes at a substantial cost. Whereas the theories of Riker, Axelrod, and their followers yield specific (although not necessarily unique) predictions of coalitions to be formed, my explanation is strictly probabilistic. That is to say, the objective is to specify and motivate conditions that increase or decrease the incentives for minority cabinet formation. However, the theoretical model will not yield specific predictions of cabinet composition in any particular case. In this respect, the exercise is more akin to that of Dodd (1974, 1976).

In brief, the assumptions that underlie my explanation of minority cabinet formation are the following:

1. Majority status is not necessarily the *effective decision point* in parliamentary legislatures. A parliamentary majority need not be a functional requisite for government formation, and the relevant party leaders do not invariably seek such a solution. Legislative and executive coalitions need not coincide.
2. In the process of government formation, political parties are not motivated solely by office (power) considerations, but also to a significant extent by opportunities for *policy influence.*
3. To the extent that policy motivation is an important determinant of party behavior, government participation is not a *necessary condition for payoff.* One need not hold government office in order to gain policy influence, much less pleasing policy outcomes.
4. Party leaders are not concerned exclusively with immediate objectives. Their behavior must be understood in a *temporal perspective.* Parties have longer-term as well as short-term goals, and sometimes these will conflict. In such situations, the resulting behavior may not be myopically rational.
5. The main longer-term consideration of party leaders is a concern about future elections. These is frequently a trade-off between a party's short-term office (and policy) objectives and its longer-term electoral incentives.

Combined with more traditional assumptions in coalition theory, these suppositions enable us to make sense of the formation of minority cabinets. Let us give them a closer look and spell out the argument in greater detail.

Majority size and winning

The notion of winning is crucial to analyses of political competition
and especially to coalition theory. If the size principle is to have any
explanatory or predictive power, we must at least be able to stipulate
the meaning of winning and plausibly be able to assume that the
players (parties) seek to do so. In empirical applications to government formations the meaning of winning has been linked to the effective decision point in the legislature, the proportion of votes
needed to pass legislation. This has generally been taken to require
an absolute majority. Any winning government must therefore control an absolute majority of the legislative seats.

There are several reasons to question this assumption. We know
that many legislative decisions do not require absolute majorities,
but rather qualified majorities (as in the case of two-thirds requirements in constitutional matters in many countries) or simple majorities or even just pluralities. The latter cases become important when
governments can benefit from abstentions or divided oppositions (see
Laver, 1986). We also know from previous studies that minority
cabinets are in fact quite common. Chapter 3 will present further
evidence to this effect. If "winning" governments are not the only
feasible solutions, then there is also no compelling reason to assume
that party leaders favor only such governments. The remainder of
this chapter specifies the conditions under which they may not.

Party objectives

Political parties are commonly defined as organizations that contest
political elections and seek governmental office (see Epstein, 1967;
Sartori, 1976). If these definitions characterize party objectives, we
should expect parties to maximize either votes (Downs, 1957) or
power (Riker, 1962). But it is unnecessary and clearly unrealistic to
make such rigid assumptions. Parties evidently have goals beyond
those implied by the minimal definition, partly because of their organizational complexity (Wilson, 1973). Parties need members and
activists as well as voters, and these cannot all be compensated
through the present or expected spoils of office (see Schlesinger,
1984). In fact, many voters and activists are motivated largely by

public policy concerns. Given the ease of voice and exit in competitive parties (Hirschman, 1970), party leaders have to be responsive to the policy concerns of their followers (Robertson, 1976).

Moreover, party leaders are normally selected on the basis of long and loyal service to the party. That is to say, they have previously been among the rank-and-file members and then gradually climbed the organizational ladder. It is reasonable to expect that their commitment to the party at lower rungs was motivated at least partly by policy concerns, or at least that they have internalized some policy norms along the way. Therefore, although party leaders may have a strong personal stake in their party's power ambitions, they can hardly be oblivious to its stated and perceived policy objectives.

We should therefore expect party behavior in government formations to be influenced by policy as well as power motivations. The balance between these motivations will vary from polity to polity, from party to party, and from time to time. It will depend partly on the nature of political institutions and political culture, and partly on organizational characteristics. Policy objectives are least likely to matter if parties are internally extremely hierarchical and undemocratic, interparty competitiveness low, and political corruption endemic. However, these features do not generally characterize the set of political systems we shall investigate. The precise determinants of the relative strength of power and policy orientations are beyond the scope of this analysis. The issue is further complicated by the fact that office seeking may be instrumental toward policy pursuits, and vice versa (see Budge and Laver, 1986). For present purposes I merely assume policy influence to be a significant motivation in the game of government formation.

The utility of government participation

Coalition theorists who assume power motivations commonly conceive of payoffs in terms of government portfolios. This conception has the advantages of compatibility with constant-sum assumptions and tractability in empirical analysis. Once policy motivation is introduced, however, the picture becomes more complicated. If parties are policy motivated, the government formation game is not necessarily constant sum. Moreover, it is no longer reasonable to posit the attainment of cabinet portfolios as a necessary condition for payoff. In other words, it may not be necessary to hold government office in order to benefit from public policies. Opposition parties may attain policy objectives in two different ways. First, their policy objectives may fortuitously be served by the governing parties, without any effort by the opposition to bring about this outcome. Second, the opposition parties may be able to exert deliberate policy influence, particularly through efforts in the legislative arena. The second possibility is the more intriguing one, the more predictable one, and the one we shall pursue here.

If parties seek policy objectives, they must strive to effect parliamentary legislation. It is true that in some political systems, many important decisions are made outside the party–parliamentary channel of representation, for example, in corporatist networks of labor unions, employers' associations, and bureaucrats (see, e.g., Berger, 1981; Schmitter and Lehmbruch, 1979). However, the importance of the corporatist challenge to parliamentary politics is limited by four important factors: (1) Corporatism is not ubiquitous. Essentially, strong corporatist institutions and practices exist mainly in smaller Northern European democracies (Katzenstein, 1985). Incidentally, these are also polities with strong political parties. Thus, corporatist representation has not displaced party representation even where the former has been most highly developed. (2) Corporatism does not encompass all or even most policy areas. Since the key players in corporatist representation are economic interest groups, many policy areas fall beyond the scope of these networks. Typically, corporatism mainly affects policy areas such as incomes policies, industrial relations, and sometimes fiscal policies. (3) Even in strongly corporatist nations, political parties and parliamentary institutions generally maintain the power to dismantle corporatist institutions and withdraw authority. Such reassertion of party–parliamentary power has indeed been common in recent years, particularly under conditions of austerity and social conflict (see Katzenstein, 1985; Regini, 1984). (4) Moreover, even where strong corporatist institutions do exist, many political parties do not enjoy access, either in their own right or by interest group proxy. For these parties, parliamentary influence is the only game in town.

Let us then take a closer look at the legislative arena and the opportunities for policy influence it offers to the various parties. Obviously these opportunities are greater for governing parties than for those in opposition. But even opposition parties can enjoy some policy influence in most parliamentary democracies. Thus, the role of the opposition is not simply to criticize and present an alternative government, functions that have been emphasized in descriptions of the Westminster model of government. Continental European oppositions are not nearly as impotent as this model would have us believe, and even its applicability to British politics is increasingly questionable (Norton, 1981; Schwarz, 1980). Studies of, among others, the Italian (Di Palma, 1977), Norwegian (Olsen, 1983), and Fourth Republic French (Williams, 1964) legislatures have demonstrated that very significant policy influence can be enjoyed by parties outside the cabinet.

We should therefore think of the policy influence of the various parties in and out of government as a matter of degree. And the relative policy influence advantage of governing over nongoverning parties varies from polity to polity. We can conceive of this systemic variable as a *policy influence differential*. The higher the policy influence differential, the greater the power of the government vis-à-vis the opposition. The smaller the differential, the less of an advantage it is to be in office. The notion of a single system-specific measure of policy influence differential is of course a simplification of reality. In the real world, some political parties in opposition can exert greater influence than others. Likewise, some parties can be more influential than others in office. And obviously, the opportunities for policy influence will depend heavily on the characteristics of the government formed. But we should think of the systemic policy influential differential as a summary measure of the expected marginal increase in policy influence potential of the typical party facing a decision whether or not to participate in government.

Note that the policy influence differential thus refers to a *potential* and not to the actual power exercised by parties in government or opposition. Even in systems where the opposition enjoys relatively generous opportunities for policy influence, some parties may deliberately or through incompetence fail to exploit them. Note also that in a strict sense the policy influence differential gives us an expression of the potential influence of the opposition only as compared with the governing parties in the same country, and not in comparison with oppositions elsewhere. In other words, a low differential may obtain either because both government and opposition are powerful, or because both are impotent.

How, then, can we identify the policy influence differential in a given political system? Note first that although in principle the differential depends as much on the strength of the government as on the opposition, reality is a little different. Oppositional strength varies more cross-nationally than governmental strength, for fairly obvious reasons. Political systems are rather free to develop powerless oppositions, but not to have powerless governments. Hence, a low policy influence differential is likely to reflect a strong opposition rather than a weak government.

The policy influence differential is low in polities with strongly deliberative legislatures. In the literature on comparative legislatures, such assemblies have been referred to as transformative (Polsby, 1975), active (Mezey, 1979), or as exhibiting a high degree of viscosity (Blondel, 1973). The deliberative powers of legislatures are closely related to the strength of their committee systems. The more institutionalized, the more autonomous, and the more specialized the legislative committees, the greater the deliberative strength of the assembly at large (Blondel, 1973; Lees and Shaw, 1979; Loewenberg and Patterson, 1979). Although there is no perfect correlation between committee strength and deliberative powers, a decentralized and autonomous committee structure appears to be at least a necessary condition for a strong legislature (Polsby, 1975: 278). It is interesting to note that stronger committees have been a prominent feature in prescriptions for a strengthening of the British House of Commons (King, 1981).

While strong committees benefit legislatures generally, they favor the opposition especially. Under parliamentary democracy, the commanding heights of the legislature are normally controlled by the same parties that hold governmental office. And plenary sessions are ill designed for exercises of oppositional influence. Parties in opposition have to do their work away from the centers of public attention, because opportunities are more available and compromises less embarrassing to the government. Hence, I shall in later chapters measure the policy influence differential by the strength and decentralization of the legislative committee system. The stronger and more decentralized the committees, the lower the policy influence differential.

The policy influence differential in turn affects the calculus of government participation. The lower the differential, the lesser the incentives for policy-motivated parties to hold office, and the more likely that opportunities for expansion of the governing coalition will be passed up. Hence, the greater the probability of minority government formation. However, the policy influence differential will always be positive, since it is difficult to imagine a political system in which the opposition would be systematically more powerful than the government. Consequently, on these grounds alone it will never be rational to abstain from governmental power. The policy influence differential remains a measure of the relative *benefits* of governing, and the full explanation requires that we investigate the *costs* of holding office as well.

The temporal horizon

Politicians are creatures of memory and anticipation; that is to say, they have a temporal perspective on their activities. In particular, parties and candidates are oriented toward the relatively foreseeable future. An incumbent who harbored no concern about his political future would be unlikely to live to see one, at least under competitive circumstances. If elections are competitive, parties need to concern themselves with their performance in future contests for the support of the electorate. This concern has typically been neglected in theories of government formation.

Of course, the recognition of the importance of future elections is not absent from the literature on political parties. In the Downsian model, parties are indeed expected vote maximizers. But there has been a curious gulf between Downsian theory and coalition theory in the importance accorded to electoral motivations (see, however, Austen-Smith and Banks, 1988; Laver, 1988). I do not argue for the wholesale adoption of the Downsian assumption. The argument here continues to be that party leaders pursue some mixture of power and policy objectives. The pursuit of electoral

support is only a means toward those ends, but it is a most important means. Votes are the currency of democratic politics; they
can be used to purchase power as well as policy influence. Parties
therefore engage in instrumental vote seeking in order subsequently to realize their more fundamental objectives. The "shadow
of the future" thus looms in the cabinet formation game in the
form of concern about upcoming elections (Axelrod, 1984). Thus,
parties may let their decisions about cabinet participation in the
short run be influenced by their expectations regarding the future
electoral consequences of their behavior.

The electoral trade-off

The very notion of costs associated with government participation is
a rare one in the literature on cabinet formation, and it can only be
understood against a temporal dimension. In the short run, it is always
better for political parties to be in office than in opposition, regardless
of their mix of office and policy objectives. It is only when the future
is systematically taken into account that the costs of governing become
clear.

The typical trade-off parties face is between power (and policy
influence) now and electoral success in the future. Since future
electoral success is instrumentally valued for power or policy reasons, the trade-off ultimately breaks down to a choice between
gratification (in the form of office or policy) now or later. The
reason this temporal trade-off exists is that government incumbency typically represents an electoral disadvantage, which we can
call the *incumbency effect*.

There are several reasons why incumbency should be an electoral
liability, all of them relying on some assumption of retrospective
voting (see Fiorina, 1981). Opposition parties are not saddled with
the same responsibilities and can more freely choose their campaign
issues and strategies. Moreover, incumbents have their reliability and
responsibility more severely tested (Downs, 1957: 104–5). That is to
say, governing parties can more easily lose the confidence of the
electorate because of failure to act consistently with their promises
or previous records. Governing parties may also make themselves
unpopular by antagonizing special interest groups, by arrogance or

abuse of the privileges of office, or simply as a consequence of media scrutiny and persecution (Rose and Mackie, 1983). The consequence of a negative incumbency effect is to lower the incentives for immediate government participation.

Several empirical studies have shown that governing parties do in fact tend to lose votes in subsequent elections. In a study of 15 countries and about 100 elections, Powell has found a clear tendency for incumbent parties to suffer at the polls. Incumbents tended to lose in two-thirds of all elections, and their net losses averaged about 2% of the total vote (Powell, 1981). In a more extensive study of the electoral effects of incumbency, Rose and Mackie have obtained virtually identical results. These authors have found incumbency to be a liability in 65% of more than 300 elections, and the tendency is quite consistent across three broad "culture areas" (Rose and Mackie, 1983). Empirically, incumbents appear particularly vulnerable during periods of economic hardship, such as when unemployment and inflation rates rise (Eulau and Lewis-Beck, 1985; Lipset, 1982; Strom and Lipset, 1984).

We need not reach a definitive conclusion as to precisely why incumbency is an electoral liability. Suffice it to say that there is such a tendency and that it has several plausible explanations. What matters to my argument is that parties recognize this fact and incorporate it in their decision calculi.

Everything else being equal, rational actors always prefer to have their reward now rather than in the future. Hence, the costs of holding office must be fairly large and obvious before they produce a change in party behavior. This in turn means that the expected *competitiveness* and *decisiveness* of the upcoming elections must be substantial. We can think of electoral competitiveness as the sensitivity of a party's electoral result to its previous behavior. The more competitive the election, the more it matters whether or not the party has been in office. But strict electoral competitiveness is not the whole story. In calculating the costs and benefits of taking office, a party leader will consider not only the votes he or she is likely to lose as an incumbent, but also the consequences of this loss for future attainment of office and policy influence goals. These consequences are determined by the decisiveness of electoral outcomes for coalitional bargaining power after the election.

The more bargaining power the party stands to gain or lose at the margin, the more decisive the election.

The electoral calculus

The projected costs of governing are thus a product of several factors. Operationally, even the distinction between competitiveness and decisiveness must be broken down further. Four distinct factors affect the costs of holding office and thereby the disincentives to government participation:

1. *Identifiability of governmental alternatives.* If elections are to be decisive settings for government formation, voters must be presented with clear governmental options prior to the election. For elections to be vehicles of governmental choice, the electorate must have some way to sort out possible coalitional configurations among the set of competing parties (see Powell, 1981b). For this purpose, voters typically rely on commitments made by the parties during the campaign or at other times prior to the election. Once such commitments are made, they commit and constrain parties in subsequent negotiations. The degree to which pre-electoral coalitional commitments are made by the relevant parties thus becomes a key component of electoral decisiveness.

2. *Electoral competitiveness (volatility).* Competition is a major concern in political science. Our concern here is with interparty electoral competitiveness. I have previously defined this as the sensitivity of electoral results to party behavior. One obvious prerequisite for such sensitivity is that voters are willing to change parties, that their party differentials are relatively low. Although the potential for such voter movements is very difficult to measure, we *do* have reliable accounts of actual voter shifts between parties from one election to the next. Electoral volatility is such an aggregate measure of the net shifts between all parties (see Pedersen, 1979; Przeworski, 1975). The greater the level of electoral volatility, the more party leaders have to worry about possible repercussions in future elections.

3. *Electoral responsiveness of government formations.* Even the conjunction of pre-electoral identifiability and volatility does not ensure that the costs of governing will be a significant motive in party

calculations. Consider the following perverse example: In election after election, the task of forming a government is always offered to the parties that have just lost ground. Under these circumstances, parties are quite unlikely to be deterred by the possibility of suffering electoral losses while in office. Hence, a nonperverse responsiveness of government formations to electoral verdicts is clearly a prerequisite for the costs of incumbency to obtain. In other words, winners must not only emerge through the electoral process, they must also be subsequently rewarded.

4. *Electoral proximity*. The last requisite of electoral decisiveness is that there be some measure of temporal coincidence between elections and government formations. If the process of government formation typically were totally decoupled from the electoral cycle, we would not say that the latter determined the former. More important, there would be much less reason to believe that parties could be deterred from government participation by the prospects of elections to come. If elections had no impact on government formation, or if that impact was very much delayed and indirect, the electoral stakes obviously would be much lower than if the linkage was more direct and immediate. For future elections to enter into the calculations of party leaders in a significant way, the expectation must be that these elections will be proximate in time to the formation of future governments.

We are now ready to put the pieces together and explain the formation of minority governments. Recall that minority governments are solutions that occur when the process of adding members to a protocoalition stops before the majority threshold is reached. This "premature" halt is caused by rational decisions by party leaders involved in the negotiations. These leaders have concluded either that they do not wish their coalition to become larger, or that they prefer opposition to the coalition option with which they have been presented. In either case, their decision is based on the assumption that the net benefits of participating in this potential government are lower than those of at least one alternative (opposition or a smaller government).

The net benefits of participating in a given government, of course, are equal to the difference between the expected benefits of holding office and its expected costs. When parties are policy motivated, the policy influence differential is a major determinant of the benefits of governing. The greater the differential, the greater the benefits. The costs of governing, on the other hand, are decided by the anticipated competitiveness and decisiveness of future elections. Minority governments should be most likely to form when the benefits are low and the costs great, that is, when the policy influence differential is small and elections competitive and decisive for bargaining power.

Some objections

This is the core of the thesis that will be tested in the following chapters. Before proceeding to the empirical tests, however, let us consider some objections that may be raised against this argument. As these issues are addressed, the thrust of my argument should become clearer.

First, one might question the assumption that some of the "core" parties would be willing to participate in a minority government, but not in one with majority support. If a party is willing to bear the costs of incumbency, why not seek a more viable coalition? The answer to this query is really rather straightforward. Each party's decision whether or not to participate in government is based on a calculation of the costs and benefits of governing. As the coalition is enlarged, some benefits clearly diminish. Each party gets a smaller share of the cabinet portfolios, and more policy compromises have to be made.

This, of course, is precisely Riker's argument, except that he tends to consider minority solutions as ineligible. We have seen that they need not be, and there is no reason that Riker's logic should not apply below the majority threshold. Quite plausibly, parties may attach a certain value to majority status per se, but this "majority bonus" need not outweigh the disadvantages resulting from a larger coalition. On the other side of the balance sheet, the costs of governing are likely to increase as the government gets larger. Each party must make more compromises, and the likelihood of intracoalitional rifts increases. These problems are especially visible as one moves from a single-party to a two-party government. They could quite plausibly translate into greater electoral costs, and in Chapter 4 I present evidence that they actually do.

A second possible objection takes the following form: If one argues that parties may willingly decline to govern now, why assume that they are motivated by a desire for office in the future? In a nutshell, why govern tomorrow if you do not want to do so today? Again, we have to return to the calculus of the costs and benefits of governing. It is not that political parties in principle are uninterested in governing, but that the projected costs may exceed the benefits for the particular coalition they are offered. After the next election, the same parties may hope to be offered a more desirable opportunity, due to greater bargaining power. Perhaps one or several parties figure they have a realistic probability of gaining a parliamentary majority, which of course would give them total bargaining power. Parties close to the majority threshold should value the marginal vote particularly highly and should therefore especially eschew participation in coalition governments. The steadfast refusal of coalitions by the Irish Fianna Fáil and the Norwegian Labor party is in fact strikingly consistent with this argument.[9] In individual cases it may also be that the costs of governing are likely to decline in the future because of better economic times or a more favorable issue agenda. Or it may be that the preferred coalition partner is unavailable today, but likely to be amenable to future cooperation.

A third possible objection takes the argument concerning the costs of governing to an extreme. If this is true, one might argue, would there not be circumstances under which the costs of governing would exceed the benefits for all relevant parties, so that no party would wish to hold office? If so, what explains the fact that governments nevertheless invariably form? If we grant the assumption that the calculus of governing may be negative for all parties and all options, we are left with a collective action problem (see Olson, 1971). Presumably, all parties (or at least the great majority) are committed to the maintenance of parliamentary institutions and therefore to the provision of some government. Needless to say, without a government these institutions, and perhaps the entire political system, may break down.[10] It is reasonable to expect party leaders to recognize this

---

[9] The case of the Norwegian Labor party is discussed in Chapter 6.

[10] It is possible that the occasional occurrence of nonpartisan caretaker governments does in fact reflect situations in which no party can be persuaded to take the reins of government. See Chapter 3 for empirical details.

danger, and it is quite likely that a government would be provided as a public good. The circumstances for such a public goods provision are very favorable: The number of players is small; they are highly visible and in close interaction; and the public good is highly valued by all or most of them. But situations where no party would want to govern under any circumstances are improbable. As potential coalitions are whittled down, the costs of governing decline and benefits may well increase for the core parties. At some point, and particularly if a single-party government is offered, government participation will have a higher expected utility than any alternative for at least one party. Hence, single-party minority governments should be attractive even in situations where the costs of forming larger coalitions are prohibitive.

Two final points must be clarified before we proceed. One concerns coalition membership. I have argued that marginal parties fail to be added to the coalition because of either *exclusion* (involuntary) or *voluntary abstention*. Sometimes marginal parties are not allowed to join; at other times they choose not to. Although this distinction is intuitive, it is not crucial to the argument, and perhaps not very consequential in practice. In many cabinet formation situations, core and marginal parties will be in agreement whether to expand the coalition. If two parties are far apart in their policy positions, cooperation and compromises will look unattractive to both. Also, it is always uncomfortable to join a club where one is not welcomed by some of the existing members. This is particularly true of cabinet-level politics, which requires fine orchestration and at least a modicum of good faith. Hence, parties should tend to converge in their evaluation of the desirability of any potential coalition.

Finally, we need to return briefly to the time horizons of the main players, the leaders of political parties. I have argued that these actors are not strictly myopic, that they have a time horizon that enables them to take future elections and governments into account. I have also indicated that the value of these future events is discounted as compared to the present. However, I have made no specific assumption about the extension of the time horizon or the magnitude of the discount rate for future events. To put it baldly: Party leaders have fairly limited time horizons and steep discount rates. In practical terms, they are unlikely to look more than one electoral period ahead.

There are three good reasons for this relative short-sightedness: (1) Elections are in the long run quite unpredictable, the anticipated adverse incumbency effect notwithstanding. (2) Party leaders have limited professional lives. Their success in their respective parties and their personal gratification depend on getting the spoils of government once in a while. Hence, government participation cannot be deferred indefinitely. (3) Many political decisions are unique and irreversible. To the extent that a party is committed to certain policy initiatives, it simply cannot afford to wait for more favorable opportunities.

The scope of the explanation

I have argued that minority governments form when the incremental process of adding members to a protocoalition stops before majority status has been reached. This happens because core members of the coalition want no further expansion, because marginal parties do not want to join, or both. Such decisions are made when the expected costs of governing exceed the benefits for the relevant parties, that is to say, when the net benefits of governing are negative. The net benefits of governing are positively related to the policy influence differential between government and opposition, and negatively to electoral decisiveness and competitiveness. Hence, minority government formation should be positively correlated with electoral decisiveness (including competitiveness) and negatively with the magnitude of the policy influence differential.

The theory I have developed is intended as a general, although probabilistic, explanation of minority government formation in parliamentary democracies. However, the explanation may not be equally applicable to all polities and all government formations. While any explanation of this sort must necessarily involve abstraction and simplification, verisimilitude remains a virtue. Where the explicit and implicit assumptions that have been made are not plausible, the hypotheses should be treated with a great deal of caution. The scope of the empirical test will accordingly be restricted to political systems with the following characteristics:

1. Stable political institutions;
2. Liberal treatment of oppositions and political adversaries; and
3. Well-organized and resourceful political parties.

It is perhaps most important that the political system be stable, in the sense that party leaders can confidently predict that in the foreseeable future elections will be held and governments formed according to the same rules as today. Also, these decision makers should expect to encounter roughly the same competitors and coalition partners. The significance of these conditions should be evident. If the future is perceived as uncertain, unpredictable, and uncontrollable, it makes little sense to defer the gratification of holding office. Also, a certain "shadow of the future" is very useful in eliciting cooperative behavior (Axelrod, 1984).

The explanation also presupposes parliamentary systems that are liberal in Dahl's (1966, 1971) sense of tolerating oppositions and permitting free public contestation for office. If party leaders expect to be persecuted or harassed in opposition, we would hardly see them opt for abstention from power. Thus, the formation of minority governments requires trust on the part of the prospective opposition as well as the government.

Finally, the explanation I have proposed assumes party leaders able to forgo short-term benefits for longer-term ones. Such leaders are likely to emerge only if their parties possess the necessary organizational discipline and resources to wait. If party leadership turnover is rapid or unpredictable, then those in charge will have few incentives to take the longer-term view. If the party rank and file will not support unpopular decisions, leaders may not want to defer the gratification of holding office. If the party depends crucially on the spoils of government to reward its activists, then the decision to forgo these benefits becomes a very painful one. Thus, not all parties can afford to act strategically out of long-range considerations.

The three scope conditions that have been discussed are critical to any assessment of the adequacy of the explanation that has been offered. They will guide the empirical analysis in the following chapters.

Research design

The next chapters will test the explanation offered earlier against competing accounts of minority government formation and performance. My aim will be to evaluate the merits of the various explanations comparatively. Note, however, that the different hypotheses are not necessarily incompatible.

My explanation of minority government formation contains two theoretical variables: electoral decisiveness (including competitiveness) and the potential policy influence of the parliamentary opposition (as a proxy for the policy influence differential). Chapter 3 will discuss the operationalization of these variables. We shall see that it is possible to develop good quantitative indicators, which in many cases meet interval-level requirements. Since we shall also consider large numbers (several hundred) of government formations, we shall be well positioned for statistical data analysis. Such tests will be performed in Chapters 3 and 4.[11] Chapter 4 will also have the special task of examining whether my assumptions concerning party expectations can be verified. If this is so, my explanation gains credibility as a *rational-expectations* argument.

The extensiveness of the cross-national design is a liability as well as an asset. While an explanation that holds up across a large number of political systems must be considered robust, there is always a possibility that the scope conditions are violated and the assumptions unrealistic for some of the polities and parties included. The internal logic of the argument cannot well be traced across a large number of cases and contexts. It will be easy to lose sight of country-specific factors that affect government formation. For these reasons, I shall supplement the cross-national analysis with case studies of cabinet formation and performance in two selected polities.

These case studies, which will be presented in Chapters 5 and 6, serve several different functions. *Within-case* explanation of each case, however, will be just as important as *cross-case* comparisons (George, 1982). Within-case explorations will take two different forms: a *congruence* and a *process-tracing* procedure (see Eckstein, 1975). In other words, we shall consider whether the value of the dependent variable (government formation and performance) is consistent with the implications of the independent variables, as well as

---

[11] Since the statistical techniques employed here will be fairly conventional and commonly used, no special effort will be made to discuss their mathematical foundations or relevance to the study of politics. The statistical models require no assumptions that are not commonly made in cross-national studies of this nature. Where there is reason to believe that the assumptions of the models are seriously violated, these problems will be discussed.

whether the causal links implied by the theory can be substantiated. Congruence testing is not unique to case studies, but these will be of value in controlling for violations of empirical assumptions and ascertaining the robustness of the theoretical explanation (see Smelser, 1973). Process tracing, on the other hand, can be pursued only in the case studies and not in the aggregate cross-national analysis. This task is of particular importance in a rational-choice analysis, where causal relationships are commonly specified at high levels of abstraction and without much empirical substantiation.

For these purposes, I have chosen to take a closer look at two political systems, Italy and Norway, within a twofold research strategy. Among the relevant nations, few could differ more in terms of contextual factors that might influence government formation and performance. Yet the two countries have in common a high frequency of minority cabinets (Norway higher than Italy), and we shall investigate the extent to which the same variables can be employed to explain similar outcomes. If a common explanation fits both Italy and Norway, then it is bound to be a highly robust one.

In short, the research design is twofold, where the most rigorous and extensive hypothesis testing takes place in the two chapters devoted to cross-national aggregate data analysis. However, this analysis will be scrutinized and complemented by the country studies in Chapters 5 and 6. This combination of extensive and intensive research strategies should help us to solve the puzzle of minority governments.

3. Forming minority governments

Let us briefly recapitulate the argument thus far. My objective is to explain the formation of minority governments, as well as their performance in office. In Chapter 1, I reviewed and critiqued existing explanations of minority cabinets. Chapter 2 presented an alternative explanation of minority government formation. I argued that minority governments may emerge as equilibrium solutions reached by rational actors under specific structural conditions. To the extent that political parties value policy influence and electoral success, government participation need not be their best strategy. Rather, different institutional and electoral conditions generate different incentives for government participation and thus, inversely, for minority governments.

In this chapter, these competing explanations of minority government formation are tested against cross-national data. As a first step, I put the conventional explanations of minority government formation to the test. Subsequently, I operationalize and test the explanation developed in Chapter 2. Finally, the explanatory power of the competing hypotheses is compared.

The incidence of minority governments

In order to subject minority governments to closer scrutiny, we shall examine every postwar government in all parliamentary democracies with a significant record of minority governments. More specifically, this sample includes all advanced Western parliamentary democracies with a history of at least two minority cabinets since 1945. For each country, the data include all governments formed from May 1945 through 1987.

I have adopted this time frame to control for the effects of severe political crises and discontinuities. World War II represented a fundamental break with traditional patterns of political competition and cabinet formation even in countries that were not directly involved (e.g., Sweden). And, of course, in a large number of nations, the war resulted in a complete change of regime. Many nations experienced all-party governments during and immediately after the war. Such governments are not included in this analysis, even in cases where they were formed after the war. Instead, each country's record begins with the first partisan cabinet formed after the cessation of hostilities in Europe. For all intents and purposes, this sample includes the entire universe of post-1945 minority governments.[1]

In counting governments I have followed each particular country's conventions,[2] except that any of the following has been considered a sufficient condition for a change of government:

1. Any change of prime minister;
2. Any change of parties represented in the cabinet;
3. Any general election; or
4. Any by-election resulting in a change in the government's parliamentary basis from majority to minority status, or vice versa.[3]

My counting rules yield a somewhat larger number of governments than the official record in many countries.

The choice of these criteria deserves a few words of explanation. Criteria 2, 3, and 4 are necessary to ensure that majority and minority governments are mutually exclusive categories. In addition, these criteria minimize *intracabinet* variation in parliamentary support and partisan composition, both critical properties in our analysis. And although changes of prime ministers are often attributed to such

---

[1] In Europe, the only minority cabinet excluded is the Austrian Kreisky government of 1970–1. Obviously, not all 15 nations have had continuous histories of parliamentary democracy since 1945. In such cases, the time span covered is shorter. Thus, our Israeli record begins in 1949, and the French ends with the demise of the Fourth Republic in 1958. The first Portuguese government included is the first Gonçalves cabinet of 1975, and the first Spanish government the one formed by Suárez in July 1977.

[2] One problem with respect to counting rules involves governments, particularly in France and Italy, that fail their vote of investiture. The most common practice is to include such cases, and this has also been my choice here.

[3] These criteria correspond to one of five measures of cabinet durability identified by Arend Lijphart (1984b).

Table 3.1. *Governments by country and type, 1945–87*

Country	Majority	Minority N	Minority %[a]	Nonpartisan	Total	Mean parliamentary basis
Belgium	27	4	13	0	31	61.4
Canada	9	8	47	0	17	54.3
Denmark	3	22	88	0	25	40.2
Finland	21	11	28	7	39	55.2
France (IVth Rep.)	18	12	40	0	30	51.0
Iceland	15	4	21	0	19	52.7
Ireland	10	7	41	0	17	50.3
Israel	26	3	10	0	29	63.5
Italy	28	20	42	0	48	51.7
Netherlands	16	3	16	0	19	61.2
Norway	9	12	57	0	21	47.5
Portugal	11	2	12	4	17	61.8
Spain	2	3	60	0	5	50.6
Sweden	9	12	57	0	21	47.1
United Kingdom	16	2	11	0	18	53.4
Total	220	125	35.1	11	356	53.6

[a] Minority governments as a percentage of all governments.
Sources: Keesing's *Contemporary Archives*; Mackie and Rose (1982).

nonpolitical factors as death and failing health, such occasions at least present an opportunity for renegotiation of government and legislative coalitions (see Blondel, 1968).

Within the parameters I have mentioned, the data include a total of 356 governments in the following 15 countries: Belgium, Canada, Denmark, Finland, France, Iceland, the Republic of Ireland, Israel, Italy, The Netherlands, Norway, Portugal, Spain, Sweden, and the United Kingdom. With the exceptions of Canada and Israel, all of these countries are Western European. Stable parliamentary democracies are rare outside of Western Europe and the Commonwealth, and so, predictably, are minority governments. In short, my data cover nearly half of the world's stable democracies, more than half of all parliamentary regimes, and a large majority of those with multiparty systems. Let us begin by breaking the sample down by country and cabinet type, as shown in Table 3.1.

Frequency

The overall frequency of minority governments in these 15 democracies is as high as 125 of 356, or 35.1%. This corresponds to an average of more than eight minority cabinets per country, or about two per decade. This record can only be described as very substantial, whether in absolute or relative terms. In Denmark, Spain, Norway, and Sweden, more than half of all governments have been undersized. The most extreme case is Denmark, where only 3 of 25 governments have *not* been minority cabinets. And in Canada, Italy, Ireland, and France, minority cabinets have accounted for at least 40% of all governments. Clearly, minority governments are a very common phenomenon across a variety of polities. Their normalcy becomes even more evident if we exclude nonpartisan solutions and majority party governments from the analysis. The latter type of government almost invariably forms whenever possible, that is, in any *majority situation*. In minority situations, on the other hand, majority coalitions and minority administrations are the natural alternatives. And under these circumstances, minority solutions have been chosen 42.8% of the time.

The frequency of minority governments has increased over time. In the 1940s, they accounted for less than 25% of all governments in these 15 countries. The comparable figure for the 1970s was more than 40%. During the latter decade, only 45 of 88 governments formed were of majority status.[4] Although the incidence of minority cabinets has receded somewhat in the 1980s, it remains at a higher level than in the early postwar years.

The high number of minority governments could be a misleading indicator of their commonness if such cabinets tended to be of very short duration. Measured as a proportion of cabinet duration, minority governments do account for a somewhat smaller share (28.2%), yet their total tenure of more than 140 cabinet years is very substantial. In minority situations, minority governments represent 36.6% of total tenure. Thus, minority governments represent a substantial

---

[4] In addition, a modest number of nonpartisan governments formed during the 1970s, most notably in Portugal. Hence, the percentage of minority governments plus the percentage of majority governments do not add up to 100.

share of all governments in minority situations, whether as a proportion of the number of governments formed or of tenure in office.

Parliamentary basis

The distinction between majority and minority governments dicho-
tomizes the continuous variable of parliamentary basis (support).
Finer distinctions might reveal interesting patterns within each class
and help us understand how minority governments function. For
example, Herman and Pope (1973) have argued that minority governments tend to be so close to majority size as to be functional
equivalents. In fact, the dispersion of the legislative support enjoyed
by minority governments is far greater than an "almost-winning-size"
explanation would lead us to expect. No fewer than 24 governments
have had a parliamentary basis of less than 35%, and approximately
60% of all minority governments have enjoyed less than 45% support
in parliament.[5]

Very large coalitions are even more numerous, as approximately
one-third of all majority coalitions have relied on 65% or larger
majorities. Their mean parliamentary basis is as high as 62.6%. Only
in the Anglo-American democracies (including Ireland) do governments tend to converge around the majority threshold. Paradoxically,
coalition governments are rare in these nations, so the clustering of
governments around the 50% level is attributable more to electoral
results than to the designs of coalition makers. The data do not permit
a rigorous test of coalition theories based on the size principle (Dodd,
1976; Riker, 1962), but the high incidence of undersized as well as
very large governments suggests that such theories would have only
modest predictive (or postdictive) power in this context.

Party composition

The composition of the governments in our sample deserves closer
scrutiny. Table 3.2 presents a breakdown of the number of parties

[5] Parliamentary basis is the proportion (here reported in percentage terms) of legislative seats held by the parties represented in the cabinet. External support parties are
not counted unless so specified. For bicameral legislatures the figures represent party
strengths in the lower chamber. See the discussion of this variable in Chapter 1.

Table 3.2. *Government composition by numerical status*

Composition	Majority	Minority	Total
Single-party	48	79	127
Coalition	172	46	218
Total	220	125	345

Note: Nonpartisan governments excluded.

in government by numerical status (majority vs. minority). There is a strong and intuitive relationship between numerical status and composition. On the one hand, most coalition governments are majority governments, and almost 80% of all majority cabinets in these 15 countries are coalitions. On the other hand, almost two-thirds of all minority governments consist of only one party. Note that *minority cabinets are typically not coalitions* but are structurally more similar to majority party governments. Thus, their parliamentary basis typically reflects the size of a single governing party (often the largest). The fact that minority cabinets tend to consist of only one party is consistent with the explanation in Chapter 2, since participation in single-party governments should be less of an electoral liability.

External support

Appearances might yet deceive us about the incidence of minority governments. These are often explained as majority governments in disguise: governments with an equally secure, but less visible, basis in the assembly (Daalder, 1971; De Swaan, 1973). In a weak sense, this is a trivial proposition. To the extent that minority cabinets produce legislative majorities, it is quite to be expected that the necessary outside support comes more frequently from some opposition parties than from others.

However, if the commitment of these external supporters is just as strong as that of parties inside the government, then there would be no reason to expect minority governments to perform differently from majority coalitions. I have sought to identify externally supported administrations in this stricter and more interesting sense.

Thus, any government is classified as externally supported that enjoys the parliamentary support of any party not represented in the cabinet if its support: (1) was negotiated prior to the formation of the government, and (2) takes the form of an explicit, comprehensive, and more than short-term commitment to the policies as well as the survival of the government.

By these criteria, 37 of the governments in our material are externally supported. However, some of the externally supported cabinets were of majority size to begin with, and in other cases the additional support was not sufficient to give the cabinet a majority. For only 14 governments does external support make the difference between minority and majority status. Let us call these *formal minority governments*. The remaining 111 minority cabinets will be referred to as *substantive minority governments*. The parliamentary basis of substantive minority governments is on average only slightly above 40%. Formal minority governments are only marginally larger, but approach 60% when external support is included. They thus tend to be considerably larger than majority party governments and almost as large as majority coalitions. We shall return to the issues of external support agreements and formal minority cabinets in Chapter 4.

Explaining minority governments

Chapter 1 reviewed the received wisdom on minority governments. Although this literature is meager, I have previously identified various accounts of the attributes of such governments and the circumstances under which they form. These explanations, which collectively I have referred to as the conventional explanation of minority governments, will now be put to the test successively.

Crisis and instability

One of these propositions within the conventional view is that minority governments are symptoms of some sort of political crisis or instability (Friesenhahn, 1971; Taylor and Herman, 1971; von Beyme, 1970). According to this view, minority solutions should covary negatively with the stability of the political system. It is not altogether clear what type and magnitude of instability or crisis should be as-

sociated with minority governments. However, no plausible interpretation stands up against the empirical evidence. No association of
minority governments with severe systemic crises could be defended
in view of the high incidence of such cabinets across a wide range of
highly respectable democracies. There simply has not been enough
serious instability in polities like Sweden, Canada, and Norway to
explain their multitude of minority governments.

A more probabilistic interpretation would predict a positive correlation between the incidence of minority governments and levels
of systemic instability. Again, even a cursory reading of the data is
enough to reject this proposition. When these 15 polities are ranked
according to the relative incidence of minority governments, Denmark, Norway, Sweden, and Canada are at the top of the list, and
Portugal, the United Kingdom, and Israel are at the bottom. This
ranking is hardly positively correlated with systemic instability.

A third and even more permissive interpretation would link governmental minoritarianism to *cabinet* instability (Dodd, 1976: 133–
9). The higher the number of governments per country over a given
period of time, the more common minority solutions should be.
Again, this hypothesis finds no empirical support. With the exception
of Denmark, the 15 countries in the sample break down naturally
into one group of low cabinet stability (Belgium, Finland, France,
Israel, Italy, and Portugal) and one high-stability group (the remaining 8 countries). Minority governments constitute 26.8% of all governments in the unstable countries and 37.2% in the stable polities.
Thus, minority governments are associated with *high*, rather than
low, cabinet stability. Furthermore, when only minority situations
are considered, minority governments account for 28.1% of the governments in the countries with low cabinet stability and a whopping
54.8% in the more stable polities. Even if Denmark is counted among
the unstable countries, the relationship between cabinet stability and
minority governments remains strong and contrary to expectations.
Hence, we can safely reject the hypothesis that minority governments
are symptoms of political instability.

Political culture

A second explanation links minority governments to historical
heritage and political culture (Daalder, 1971; Lijphart, 1977, 1984a;

Luebbert, 1986; Powell, 1982a). Such explanations tend to be more plausible than testable. As one would expect, none of the four European nations characterized by Lijphart as consociational (Austria, Belgium, the Netherlands, and Switzerland) have had frequent minority governments, but this tendency need not be a function of their consociational practices per se. More generally, explanations that focus on durable or historically distant factors are difficult to reconcile with the substantial variations in the incidence of minority governments in the same countries over time. Chapter 5 will illustrate such temporal variations in the case of Italy.

Fractionalization

Conventionally, minority governments are also associated with political fragmentation and party system fractionalization (Budge and Herman, 1978; Dodd, 1976; Sartori, 1976). Fractionalization measures the extent to which the legislature is composed of many and small, rather than few and large, parties. Arguably, the more fractionalized the parliamentary party system, the more difficult the formation of a winning coalition and the greater the likelihood of an undersized solution.

This hypothesis has been tested against available data on Rae's index of fractionalization for legislative seats (Rae, 1971).[6] Table 3.3 demonstrates that the average fractionalization scores for the legislature in which substantive (and even formal) minority governments form are lower than for majority coalitions. Although the difference in mean fractionalization scores is not dramatic, it is directly contrary to the hypothesis. At the very least, this result clearly does not support the conventional view of minority governments. As one would expect, majority party governments form in radically less fractionalized systems than any of the other types.

---

[6] Rae's F measures the probability that two randomly selected legislators would belong to different parties. Thus, Rae's F ranges from zero (where only one party is represented) to 1 (in a perfectly atomized legislature). If there is no majority party, the score is always higher than 0.5. While a wide array of fractionalization measures exists, Rae's index remains the most common.

Table 3.3. *Fractionalization and polarization by cabinet type*

Cabinet type	Fractionalization	Polarization	(N)
Majority party	.571 (.072)	.016 (.026)	(48)
Majority coalition	.754 (.060)	.185 (.111)	(172)
Minority formal	.749 (.058)	.219 (.132)	(14)
Minority substantive	.723 (.069)	.152 (.134)	(111)
Nonpartisan	.765 (.057)	.213 (.051)	(11)
All governments	.720 (.088)	.152 (.125)	(356)

Note: Mean values, standard deviations parenthesized. Fractionalization = Rae's F for seats; polarization = aggregate legislative representation of extremist parties as proportion of all seats.
Sources: Keesing's Contemporary Archives; Mackie and Rose (1982); Powell (1982a).

Cleavage conflict and polarization

Political polarization and cleavage conflict constitute another explanation of minority government formation, sometimes in combination with other explanatory factors. According to Dodd, polarized parliaments should experience frequent minority governments, particularly under conditions of fractionalization and instability (1976: 57–70; also Powell, 1982a; Sartori, 1976). However, the meaning of polarization in these analyses is neither consistent nor unambiguous. In Sartori's terminology, polarization refers to the overall ideological distance within the party system, whereas in other usages the concept denotes bipolar distributions of the electorate on various conflict dimensions, the cumulations of such cleavages, or the resultant social tensions and hostilities (Putnam, Leonardi, and Nanetti, 1981).

I have chosen to measure polarization as the proportion of all parliamentary seats held by extremist parties. Extremist parties (whether serious "contenders" or "protest parties") are parties that exhibit any of the following characteristics:

1. A well-developed nondemocratic ideology;
2. A proposal to break up or fundamentally alter the boundaries of the state; or
3. diffuse protest, alienation, and distrust of the existing political system.

This measure of party system extremism has been developed and employed by Powell (1982a), whose operationalization and classifications I have adopted virtually unchanged.[7] Although Dodd's operationalization of polarization is different, the essence of his argument should be well captured, since he uses polarization as an indicator of the general a priori willingness to bargain for cabinet participation (Dodd, 1976: 61). Extremist parties are precisely the kind of parties that are unlikely to be willing to enter such negotiations.

Table 3.3 reveals that polarization is related to cabinet type in a pattern almost identical to fractionalization. Majority party governments form in radically less polarized systems than any other cabinet type. Nonpartisan administrations form in the most polarized, as well as the most fractionalized, systems.[8] But there is no tendency for minority governments to form in more polarized environments than majority coalitions. On the contrary, substantive minority governments are associated with markedly lower levels of polarization than majority coalitions. The small number of formal minority governments in our sample, however, have formed under highly polarized conditions.

Proximate conditions

What cabinets are formed is affected not only by the political macrostructure but also by properties of the formation process itself, the *proximate conditions* of government formation. Conventional wisdom has it that minority governments form only when all other options have been exhausted, or when no other options exist. Minority governments should accordingly be associated with particularly long cabinet crises and numerous formation attempts. I have tested these

[7] See Powell (1982a: 92–6, 233–4). My only modification of Powell's indicator is that I have measured extremism on the basis of proportions of *parliamentary seats* rather than popular votes. This adaptation follows from my primary interest in legislative rather than electoral processes. In my classification of individual parties, I have deviated from Powell in only one case: the Justice party (Retsforbundet) in Denmark. The Justice party actually participated organically in two centrist governments from 1957 to 1960 and only ceased to do so when it lost all parliamentary representation in the 1960 elections.

[8] These systems, of course, are Finland and Portugal, where both fractionalization and polarization levels have been high.

Table 3.4. *Proximate conditions of cabinet formation*

Cabinet type	Formation attempts	Crisis duration	(N)
Majority party	1.04 (.29)	8.4 (22.9)	(48)
Majority coalition	2.01 (1.51)	31.3 (42.6)	(166)
Minority formal	2.07 (1.49)	36.7 (46.1)	(14)
Minority substantive	2.00 (1.38)	13.5 (18.4)	(109)
Nonpartisan	2.27 (1.56)	27.5 (25.1)	(11)
All governments	1.89 (1.40)	22.7 (35.3)	(348)

Note: Mean values, standard deviations in parentheses. Crisis duration in days.

hypotheses against two aspects of the formation process of every government: (1) the total number of formation attempts during the cabinet crisis,[9] and (2) the duration of the cabinet crisis in days.

Table 3.4 reports the average number of formation attempts by cabinet type. There is a moderate tendency (not reported) for minority governments to follow a larger number of formation attempts than those of majority size (2.02 vs. 1.79 attempts). However, the further breakdown in Table 3.4 reveals that majority party governments hardly ever require more than a single formation attempt. When substantive minority governments are compared directly with majority coalitions, the difference washes out entirely, as the former cabinet type averages 2.00 formation attempts, versus 2.01 for majority coalitions.

These findings are corroborated by data on the duration of cabinet crises. Here, the counterintuitive result is that while the average crisis preceding a majority government formation lasts 26.2 days, the comparable figure for minority governments is only 16.1, or almost 40% *less*. There is a dramatic difference in crisis longevity between ma-

[9] Formation attempts have been counted by premier-designate (formateur) as well as by the set of parties involved in the attempt. Thus, a new attempt is counted with every change of formateur, and also with every change in intended party composition. The greatest measurement problem relates to the sometimes ambiguous distinction between formateurs and informateurs. As the name implies, politicians in the latter category are entrusted with fact-finding missions for the head of state, and they are not necessarily expected to be involved in the ensuing cabinet formation. In practice, however, serious candidates for the premiership are at times designated as informateurs in order to keep options open and save the designated person the embarrassment of possible failure. I have sought to discount genuine informateur missions.

jority party governments (8.4 days) and majority coalitions (31.3 days). Substantive minority governments (13.5 days) are closer to the former than to the latter.

The critical determinant of crisis duration may simply be the number of parties involved in the formation process. The more parties, the longer the crisis. Since minority governments tend to consist of only one party, few parties are likely to be involved in the preceding negotiations. This may be the reason that their cabinet crises are nearly as short as those of majority party governments.

A simple breakdown of crisis duration by the number of parties in the subsequent government (not reported in the tables) substantiates that the critical difference is between single-party governments and all others. As the number of governing parties increases from one to two, the average cabinet crisis goes from 11.8 to 29.2 days. There is no consistent tendency, however, for crisis duration to go up further as the number of governing parties increases beyond two. These results clearly suggest that minority governments are not typically the outcome of unsuccessful bargaining among a large number of parties.

The rational-choice explanation of minority government formation

There is evidently minimal support for any of the conventional explanations of minority governments. Nor do these accounts commend themselves in terms of clarity, generality, or parsimony. Hence, the need for a more satisfactory explanation seems more acute than ever. The following section outlines the alternative theory developed in Chapter 2 and proceeds to operationalize and test this explanation. My fundamental assumption is that minority government formation can be understood as a result of *rational decisions* made by political parties, or more specifically, by the parliamentary leaders of these organizations. A proper understanding of the rationality of party behavior in the process of cabinet formation requires a challenge to some common assumptions in applications of coalition theory to government formation. These assumptions represent implausible stipulations about political parties and their institutional environment. Briefly, my alternative assumptions are as follows:

1. Majority size is not necessarily the *effective decision point* in the sense that all cabinets must meet this requirement to survive or function legislatively. Legislative coalitions may differ from executive coalitions in membership.
2. Political parties seek *policy influence* and *electoral advantage* in addition to office benefits.
3. If parties are policy seekers, government participation may not be a *necessary condition for payoff*.
4. Party leaders are not concerned strictly with immediate gratification. Rather, party behavior must be understood in a *temporal* perspective, where short-term portfolio gains may be sacrificed for longer-term electoral advantage.
5. Critical decisions affecting cabinet formation often take precisely this form of a trade-off between power and electoral prospects.

How do these considerations help us make sense of minority governments? The critical difference between minority governments and majority coalitions is that certain marginal parties do not enter the government. When minority governments form, it is because a larger coalition is not desired by these marginal parties, the existing members of the protocoalition, or both. To put it differently, minority governments form when the benefits of office holding are outweighed by the costs for a majority segment of the party system.

The costs of governing can be counted in votes and indirectly in policy influence. Government incumbency tends to result in subsequent electoral losses, and coalition governments lose more than others (Rose and Mackie, 1983; Strom, 1985). Moreover, coalitions typically involve policy compromises as well as projected electoral misfortunes. With these costs in mind, potential governmental parties may forgo the immediate gratification of holding office if doing so promises future benefits. Future coalitional bargaining power figures prominently among such anticipated benefits. A decision to remain in opposition temporarily implies no lack of interest in governing in the long run, but rather a willingness to wait for more favorable circumstances.

The conditions most favorable for abstention from power are where (1) policy can be influenced even from opposition status, and (2) future elections are likely to be competitive and decisive for bargaining power. In two-party systems, elections monopolize bargaining power and thereby normally directly determine cabinet composition. In multiparty systems, however, this is not necessarily so. In minority situations, interparty negotiations may or may not be tightly constrained by electoral results. We can conceive of multiparty systems as located along a continuum of electoral decisiveness. In systems of high decisiveness (e.g., Germany), government selection is almost as direct as in two-party systems, whereas in low-decisiveness contexts (e.g., Belgium), elections have little direct impact on coalitional bargaining power.

Thus, my explanatory variables are:

1. The potential influence of the parliamentary opposition; and
2. The decisiveness of elections for coalitional bargaining power.

With increases in electoral decisiveness and oppositional influence, I expect the parliamentary bases of governments, everything else being equal, to diminish, and minority governments to be more common. Theoretically these conditions should favor narrowly based governments generally, but in this context they account specifically for minority government formation. The following section will operationalize and test these hypotheses.

Oppositional influence

This variable, which measures the benefits of governing (or, more precisely, the policy costs of being in opposition), represents the opportunities for legislative influence open to parliamentary oppositions. The predicament of opposition depends on a number of factors. Among these are the internal structure and procedures of the legislature, as well as its role in the larger political system. Internally, a strong and decentralized committee structure offers much better prospects for oppositional influence than the more centralized and less deliberative mode of decision making traditionally found in such parliaments as the British House of Commons.

The greater the potential influence of the opposition, then, the lower the relative benefits of governing, and the higher the probability of minority governments. In view of the critical role of committees in legislative deliberations, I have constructed a five-point index of the potential for oppositional influence based on the properties of parliamenatry committees. This index aggregates the following five indicators, each of which has been dichotomized:

1. *The number of standing committees.* Committee specialization is a precondition for effective decision making. And specialization is difficult to attain without differentiation of the committee structure. In other words, a minimum number of standing committees is necessary for effective deliberation and hence for influential oppositions. Operationally, I have counted more than 10 standing committees as necessary for high oppositional influence.

2. The rationale behind the next two indicators is similar to the foregoing argument. Effective decision making further depends on whether or not these standing committees have *fixed areas of specialization.* Committees with fixed jurisdictions are indicative of more deliberative legislatures and thus higher levels of oppositional influence.

3. I next consider whether such jurisdictions correspond to *ministerial departments.* If so, the standing committees are likely to exercise more effective oversight. Hence, the opposition can also play a more significant role.

4. A fourth indicator is whether there are any restrictions on the *number of committee assignments* per legislator. If such restrictions exist, individual legislators are more likely to be specialists in the areas in which they serve. This enhances the status of the opposition by providing it with a countervailing basis of expertise. Moreover, restrictions on committee assignments make it more difficult for the government to manipulate membership allocations to its advantage.

5. Finally, oppositional influence is affected by whether committee chairs are *proportionately distributed* among the parliamentary parties. The alternative to proportionality is normally that the government controls all chairs, which, of course, is less desirable from the point of view of the opposition.

Fixed jurisdictions coinciding with ministerial departments, restrictions on committee assignments, and proportional distribution of committee chairs are interpreted as high scores. As all the features captured by the resultant measure of oppositional influence are stable institutional properties, the scores on this variable vary *between*, but not *within*, political systems.[10] Each government's score is simply the sum of positive values; thus the hypothetical range is from 0 to 5. The observed distribution, however, ranges from 1 to 5.

Note that I am concerned with the structural opportunities for oppositional influence, and not with the actual power enjoyed by parties out of office. This distinction is important for the direction of the causal relationship. If oppositional influence were measured as actually exercised power, the direction of the causal relationship I have identified could arguably be reversed. Although influential oppositions may facilitate the formation of minority governments, it is also possible that minority governments *cause* oppositions to be more influential. This reverse relationship is much less plausible when oppositional influence is defined in terms of institutional constraints. The incidence of minority cabinets is unlikely to alter the basic structure of the national assembly, as measured here. Historically we find strong continuities in the legislative institutions of the countries and time periods under investigation. Thus, if patterns of government formation have an impact on legislative institutions, it could only be evident in the very long run. Table 3.5 presents a survey of oppositional influence by country.[11]

The decisiveness of elections

The second variable is the decisiveness of elections for government formation, which taps costs of governing in future elections. This variable has four components operationalized as follows:

1. *The identifiability of viable government alternatives.* Unless the voters are presented with clear governmental options prior to the election, we can hardly call these elections decisive. How-

---

[10] This is not to deny that legislative structure occasionally changes in significant ways. The classifications here, however, represent the institutional structure in the mid-1970s (Herman, 1976).

[11] The data that are presented in summary form in Table 3.5 have been borrowed from Herman (1976). Herman's data have been supplemented by the following sources: Ameller (1966); Williams (1964); Pondaven (1973) (the latter two on the Fourth Republic); Nordal and Kristinsson (1975) (on Iceland); and *Quien es quien en las Cortes Generales, 1979–1983* (1980) (on Spain). Data on Portugal were graciously supplied by the Portuguese Embassy to the United States.

Table 3.5. *Oppositional influence by country*

Country	No. of committees	Speciali- zation	Corres- pondence	Member- ship	Chairs	Overall value
Belgium	+	+	+	−	+	4
Canada	+	+	+	−	−	3
Denmark	+	+	+	−	−	3
Finland	+	+	−	−	+	3
France	+	+	+	+	−	4
Iceland	+	+	+	+	−	4
Ireland	−	−	−	−	+	1
Israel	−	+	−	−	+	2
Italy	+	+	+	+	−	4
Netherlands	+	−	+	−	−	2
Norway	+	+	+	+	+	5
Portugal	+	+	+	−	+	4
Spain	+	+	+	−	−	3
Sweden	+	+	+	−	+	4
United Kingdom	−	+	−	−	−	1

Note: See text for operationalization of indicators.
Sources: Herman (1976) and others (see text).

ever, political systems vary widely in the extent to which such governmental options are presented to the electorate (Powell, 1982a). I have scored the identifiability of pre-electoral governmental options in each polity impressionistically as low (0), medium (.5), or high (1) on a decade-to-decade basis.

2. *Electoral competitiveness or volatility.* Decisive elections require significant fluctuations in the distribution of seats between the various parties from election to election. I call this electoral competitiveness and measure it as the electoral volatility (for seats) between successive elections (Pedersen, 1979).

3. *Electoral responsiveness.* A third requirement is that governments be formed by parties that have gained rather than lost seats in the election. In other words, the relationship between electoral success and government participation must be non-perverse. Thus, every government has been scored according to the proportion of electoral gainers among its constituent parties.[12]

[12] Parties that retained their proportion of seats have been excluded from the com-

4. *Proximity*. Finally, electoral decisiveness requires that governments be formed in close proximity to general elections. The
proximity score for each political system is simply the proportion
of government formations that have taken place immediately
following a general election, again measured on a decade-to-
decade basis.

Political parties presumably react to electoral decisiveness through
some incremental process of learning. Party decisions are therefore
likely to reflect historically prevailing levels of electoral decisiveness
in each country more than short-term fluctuations. This assumption
is reflected in our measures, which have been averaged over the
decade in which the government formed. All four component variables are bounded by the values 0 and 1. Table 3.6 presents a summary
of electoral decisiveness scores by country. Factor analysis of the four
components of electoral decisiveness revealed that governmental
identifiability and electoral proximity load strongly on the same factor, whereas competitiveness and responsiveness do not. Evidently,
electoral decisiveness is a multidimensional phenomenon, but identifiability and proximity seem to capture the same dimension. I have
therefore combined the latter two indicators into a measure of *electoral salience*.[13]

Testing the rational-choice explanation

My hypotheses predict that as electoral decisiveness and oppositional
influence increase, the parliamentary bases of the governments
formed should diminish, and the likelihood of minority government
formation increase. We shall test these hypotheses through linear
regression models where the parliamentary basis of each government
is the dependent variable. Only minority situations with partisan outcomes are included, which is to say that majority party and nonpartisan governments are excluded. Majority situations are excluded
because minority governments are not a feasible option, nonpartisan

putations, except when they formed single-party governments. Any party gaining an
absolute parliamentary majority has been counted as a winner.

[13] The variable electoral salience has been constructed by standardizing the identifiability and proximity measures, and then for each government adding up the two
standardized scores.

Table 3.6. *Electoral decisiveness by country*

Country	Identifiability	Volatility	Responsiveness	Proximity
Belgium	.10	.08	.58	.48
Canada	1.00	.20	.76	.82
Denmark	.76	.12	.63	.65
Finland	.00	.08	.54	.37
France	.00	.18	.47	.14
Iceland	.59	.10	.51	.69
Ireland	.87	.08	.86	.77
Israel	.14	.14	.44	.38
Italy	.12	.09	.47	.23
Netherlands	.00	.08	.47	.68
Norway	.83	.10	.69	.52
Portugal	.50	.16	.56	.41
Spain	.50	.21	.80	.80
Sweden	1.00	.06	.45	.62
United Kingdom	1.00	.07	.94	.75
All countries	.39	.11	.58	.49

Note: Mean values. See text for operationalization of variables.

administrations because they can be assigned no value for parliamentary basis.

In interpreting these models I shall primarily focus on the parameter estimates rather than the overall fit of the model (see King, 1986). There are several reasons not to expect large coefficients of determination (R squareds). One theoretical reason is that the explanation I have offered is by design partial. The incidence of minority governments depends on the relative value of office holding to all relevant parties. This value depends partly, but only partly, on the macrostructural conditions identified by the variables developed earlier. But the relative value of office holding will also vary according to a host of situational and organizational factors that are not captured by this analysis. As discussed in Chapter 2, this explanation should thus capture only some of the structural factors that induce parties to make the calculi that ultimately result in minority governments. We should therefore expect these structural preconditions to be systematically related to minority government formation, but not to tell us the whole story.

Second, the linear regression design assumes that the outcome (parliamentary basis) is continuous and that all values are feasible. In reality, parliamentary basis is a much more discrete variable, especially in party systems of low fractionalization. In a three-party system, for example (such as Canada or Ireland), there are only seven possible government solutions and at most seven values parliamentary basis could take. Moreover, some of these solutions may be highly implausible, such as the grand coalition or a government of the smallest party alone. Hence, the "lumpiness" of the dependent variable is likely to limit the fit of the regression model.

We begin the analysis by estimating a model including only the four predictors from the rational-choice explanation: opposition influence, electoral salience, volatility (competitiveness), and responsiveness. The results are presented as model 1.1 in Table 3.7. Since all of these variables should be positively correlated with minority governments, I expect negative coefficients throughout this model. Indeed, all four variables exhibit negative relationships, three of the four with highly significant t-values. Volatility shows the weakest relationship, which is marginally significant by conventional standards. The coefficient of determination (R squared) is not impressive, as the model explains just over 10% of the variance in parliamentary basis. Keep in mind, however, that we should not expect large R squareds. Also, the model as a whole is clearly significant and there are no implausible fitted values. The predictions fall in the relative narrow range from 38% to 63%.[14]

The coefficient for opposition influence is the easiest to interpret. A one-point increase on this scale (which corresponds to 93% of one standard deviation) reduces predicted parliamentary basis by 3.3% of all seats. Similarly, the reduction produced by an increase of one standard deviation in responsiveness is about 3%, for volatility approximately 1.5%, and for electoral salience just over 3%. These results give strong and consistent support to the explanation of minority governments I advanced in Chapter 2.

Model 1.2 raises the stakes by including a number of alternative

[14] The other models in Table 3.7 produce a somewhat greater range of fitted values. However, none yields predictions close to zero or 1 (the hypothetical bounds). The very narrow Scandinavian governments (Ullsten, Hartling, etc.) and the very oversized Israeli governments of national unity in the 1960s are responsible for very large residuals in all models.

Table 3.7. *Linear regression models of government formation*

Variables	Model 1.1 Coef.	t-value	Model 1.2 Coef.	t-value	Model 1.3 Coef.	t-value	Model 1.4 Coef.	t-value
Constant	.806	17.16	.834	4.83	.855	17.91	.975	5.48
Opposition influence	−.033	3.75	−.015	1.52	−.036	4.03	−.021	2.09
Electoral salience	−.017	3.36	−.041	4.71	−.021	4.15	−.047	5.47
Volatility	−.002	1.71	−.002	1.44	−.003	2.42	−.003	2.01
Responsiveness	−.129	2.92	−.117	2.58	−.142	3.22	−.126	2.77
Crisis duration			$4.3 \cdot 10^{-4}$	1.83			$4.4 \cdot 10^{-4}$	1.84
Formation attempts			−.011	1.87			−.012	1.90
Fractionalization			$8.8 \cdot 10^{-3}$	.05			−.035	.20
Polarization			−.474	4.35			−.490	4.32
Government extremism			.104	1.84			.047	.73
Investiture			.027	1.31			.023	1.05
Number of cases	292		285		273		253	
R^2	.115		.207		.157		.267	
Adjusted R^2	.103		.178		.144		.237	
F	9.33		7.13		12.47		8.82	

Note: The dependent variable is the proportion of legislative seats held by the parties represented in the cabinet. All models exclude majority situations and nonpartisan governments. Model 1.3 excludes caretaker governments. Model 1.4 excludes caretaker and formal minority governments.

explanatory variables. Four such variables have already been discussed in this chapter, namely, fractionalization (Rae's F for seats), polarization, crisis duration, and the number of formation attempts. Model 1.2 also includes two additional variables that have not figured prominently in conventional explanations: government extremism and constitutional investiture requirements. Nor are these variables derived from the explanation in Chapter 2, although they are in no way inconsistent with my rational-choice argument.

Government extremism

This variable is based on the assumption that coalitional bargaining power depends on position in the policy space. Parties with a centrist location have much greater bargaining power than parties at the extremes, particularly in low-dimensionality spaces. It is natural to assume that this bargaining advantage makes it easier for centrist parties to form minority governments than it would be for extremist parties. In one-dimensional space, minority cabinets should therefore tend to be governments of the political center, with bipolar oppositions. From their strategic location in the political center (perhaps the core), such cabinets should be able to divide and rule the opposition. The variable *government extremism* measures the proportional distribution of the opposition along the left–right dimension. For example, a government whose entire opposition was positioned to its right would have a score of 1. On the other hand, a centrist government with the opposition evenly divided between rightists and leftists would have a score of .5.[15] Government extremism should be positively related to parliamentary basis.

Investiture

Finally, I have included a dummy variable for constitutional requirements of parliamentary investiture at the time of government for-

---

[15] This variable (government extremism) presupposes a meaningful ordering of all parliamentary parties in all countries on a left–right dimension. This is obviously a strong assumption. However, fortunately many empirical efforts to construct such rankings have been made. In constructing my own variable I have sought to maximize consistency with previous authoritative rankings.

mation. Six countries have such constitutional provisions: Belgium, France, Ireland, Israel, Italy, and Spain. The reasoning here is that minority governments are more difficult to form if a new government needs an immediate vote of confidence in its first encounter with the national assembly. The countries with investiture requirements have a score of 1, the others zero, and we expect a positive correlation with parliamentary basis.

This more fully specified model is estimated as model 1.2 in Table 3.7. The introduction of six additional variables does not affect the signs of any of the variables contained within the explanation I have advanced. However, it does change the relative strength of the various relationships. Note that the coefficient for opposition influence falls to about half its previous magnitude and slightly below conventional significance levels. The estimates for volatility and responsiveness are affected only marginally. On the other hand, electoral salience is the most powerful predictor of minority government formation in this model, with a very impressive t-value. As electoral salience increases by one standard deviation, parliamentary basis declines by no less than 7.3% in this model.

Polarization turns out to be the second strongest predictor in this model. Recall that the bivariate relationship between polarization and parliamentary basis is positive, although hardly significant, and thus contrary to conventional expectations. In model 1.2 we find that when we control for other variables, high polarization is in fact related to narrow parliamentary support. The arguments of Dodd and Powell are thus supported here, once we have taken account of the effects of elections, legislative institutions, and other factors in model 1.2. However, this result also dovetails nicely with the rational choice explanation. High levels of polarization indicate that for large segments of the party system the government participation calculus always yields negative results. Polarization also means that the policy distance between parties is high and compromises accordingly costly.

The number of formation attempts and crisis duration are significantly related to parliamentary basis in model 1.2. However, although many formation attempts increase the likelihood of undersized governments, long cabinet crises actually *diminish* the probability of minority cabinets. Party system fractionalization, on the other hand, shows no significant relationship to the incidence of minority governments. Government extremism is as expected associated with large governments, and an investiture requirement boosts parliamentary basis by an average of 2.7%. These two relationships are therefore consistent with expectations, but relatively weak. The overall explanatory power of the model increases significantly from model 1.1, and model 1.2 can account for about one-fifth of the variance in parliamentary basis.

However, we should not expect the models to predict all minority governments equally well. There are circumstances under which the relevant party leaders may not seek a durable and effective government, but simply a stopgap administration. In such cases, government formations may be based on much less elaborate calculations. *Caretaker* governments, then, may not be particularly predictable from a rational calculus. I have sought to identify caretaker administrations on the basis of programmatic statements made at the time of investiture. Governments that professed no legislative ambitions beyond routine administration have been classified as caretakers. Caretaker administrations tend to be *interim* governments, that is, governments designed to be dismissed after a short and normally well-defined tenure. Such governments are not numerous.[16] Model 1.3 reestimates model 1.1 excluding caretaker cabinets. This only reduces the number of cases from 292 to 273.

Note that the overall fit of the model improves appreciably with the exclusion of only these 19 cases. All four predictors now perform markedly better. But note that the improvements for volatility and electoral salience are larger than for the two other coefficients, and that electoral salience rather than opposition influence has the largest *t*-value in this model. Explained variance increases by about 40%. In short, the exclusion of a small number of caretaker governments improves our ability to predict minority governments and significantly improves the fit of the rational-choice explanation. Model 1.4 reestimates the expanded model 1.2 with the exclusion of caretaker governments. In addition, model 1.4 also excludes formal minority governments. Model 1.4 offers substantially better fit than model 1.2, explaining about one-quarter of the total variance in parliamentary

---

[16] Note that my definition of caretaker governments is a strict one, which does not include unambitious cabinets unless they expressly designate themselves as confined to routine administration.

basis. All of this improvement can be accounted for by the four variables associated with my rational-choice explanation. All four coefficients are markedly larger than in the previous model, but electoral salience is by far the strongest predictor in the model. A change of one standard deviation produces an 8.4% drop-off in parliamentary basis, as compared to a change of 6.4% due to an equivalent change in polarization, the second strongest predictor in the model.The coefficient estimates for the remaining variables in the model are on the whole very similar to those for model 1.2.[17] The counterintuitive tendency for long cabinet crises to inhibit minority government formation is confirmed. Note, however, that the effect of government extremism is reduced to less than half when caretaker and formal minority governments are excluded. Apparently, minority cabinets of these types are especially likely to benefit from a favorable centrist bargaining position.

The four models presented in Table 3.7 consistently support the hypotheses developed in Chapter 2. Of a total of 16 coefficient estimates for the four explanatory variables, all have the expected signs, and only 2 fail to meet a one-tailed significance test at the.05 level. The relationships hold up well in the 10-variable models, and the estimates improve measurably when caretaker and formal minority governments are excluded. Overall, electoral decisiveness is a far stronger predictor than oppositional influence. And among the three dimensions of electoral decisiveness, electoral salience is clearly the most consequential. But even competitiveness and responsiveness are highly significant predictors of minority government formation in most of these models.

The relatively lesser impact of oppositional influence is entirely to be expected for two reasons: (1) The anticipation of upcoming elections may *in itself* be sufficient to induce parties to abstain from power. Parties may be deterred from coalitions by the fear of losing bargaining power irrespective of policy prospects. However, the opportunities for oppositional influence would never in isolation from other considerations produce the same result. Parties would always prefer to be in government to opposition, as long as everything else is equal.

[17] It should be added that the exclusion of caretaker and formal minority governments should not be expected to improve the fit of most conventional explanations, since many of these portray minority governments in precisely these terms.

(2) Besides, oppositional influence is a much cruder ordinal-level measure and is therefore likely to be afflicted with a higher degree of measurement error.

Logistic regression models

I have mentioned some of the limitations of linear regression models for investigating minority government formation. For one thing, these models assume the outcome (parliamentary basis) is a continuous variable. We have noted that the outcome is in fact much more discrete and also naturally bounded by the values zero and 1 (or 100 in percentage terms). Besides, the models in Table 3.7 do not recognize the qualitative difference between 49% and 51% legislative support that is at the very heart of this analysis.

We shall therefore turn to a set of logistic regression (logit) models as a supplement to the estimates in Table 3.7. Instead of predicting the precise parliamentary basis of government solutions the logit models estimate the probability of majority versus minority outcomes. The logit models in Table 3.8 otherwise replicate the design in Table 3.7. The dependent variable is dichotomous, with the value 1 representing majority coalitions and zero minority governments. Note that the expected signs in Table 3.8 are the same as those in the previous table. And indeed the parameter estimates are highly consistent with those of the linear regression models. Observe that the four explanatory variables in model 2.1 are all related to minority government formation in the expected direction and at high levels of significance. Again, electoral salience is by far the strongest predictor. This basic four-variable model correctly predicts almost 70% of the cases, an improvement of 27% over predictions of the modal category (majority coalitions). Contrary to the linear regressions, however, this simplest model is also the most successful one.

The 10-variable model (2.2) is considerably less efficient in its predictions. In this case, the explanatory power of responsiveness and especially opposition influence drop substantially when the 6 additional variables are introduced. However, electoral salience and volatility remain significant, and all signs remain consistent with expectations. Several of the 6 variables added exhibit strong relationships. Polarization again favors minority governments, and this

Table 3.8. *Logistic regression models of government formation*

Variables	Model 2.1 Coef.	Model 2.1 t-value	Model 2.2 Coef.	Model 2.2 t-value	Model 2.3 Coef.	Model 2.3 t-value	Model 2.4 Coef.	Model 2.4 t-value
Constant	4.075	5.28	-4.023	1.28	4.825	5.73	-1.609	.45
Opposition influence	-.340	2.45	-.074	.44	-.339	2.32	-.161	.87
Electoral salience	-.343	4.37	-.454	3.06	-.423	5.05	-.549	3.38
Volatility	-.044	1.99	-.059	2.30	-.068	2.90	-.074	2.61
Responsiveness	-1.494	2.22	-.934	1.25	-1.605	2.28	-1.292	1.58
Crisis duration			.015	2.62			.027	3.28
Formation attempts			-.135	1.68			-.187	2.09
Fractionalization			8.777	2.64			7.936	2.08
Polarization			-6.072	3.16			-6.197	2.67
Government extremism			2.110	2.19			1.339	1.15
Investiture			.814	2.14			.963	2.19
Number of cases	292		292		273		260	
Correct predictions (%)	69.2		64.4		67.8		68.9	
Reduction in error (%)	27.4		16.1		21.4		18.2	

Note: The dependent variable is *numerical status* (0 = minority government; 1 = majority government). All models exclude majority situations and nonpartisan governments. Model 2.3 excludes caretaker governments. Model 2.4 excludes caretaker and formal minority governments.

estimate has the highest *t*-value in this model. As in the linear models, crisis duration is negatively and formation attempts positively related to minority government formation. Contrary to the previous models and to expectations, however, fractionalization produces majority governments. The same effects are produced by government extremism and investiture requirements, both with solid *t*-values in this model.

The exclusion of caretaker and formal minority governments in models 2.3 and 2.4 boosts the explanatory power of electoral salience and volatility and reduces that of polarization. The tendency for protracted cabinet crises to inaugurate majority governments is also even stronger when these cases are removed from the analysis. Much as in the linear regression model, the effect of government extremism is much reduced from model 2.2 to model 2.4. However, the exclusion of caretakers and formal minority governments has little influence on the overall predictive accuracy of the models.

Note the high level of consistency between the two versions of the dependent variables. As in the linear models, all 16 parameter estimates involving the four original variables carry the expected signs. And again, electoral salience is the single strongest predictor in three of four models. The six additional variables behave much as in the linear regressions, although their overall effects are somewhat more significant.

The number of government parties

The models we have estimated so far have relied on two different dependent variables to capture the distinction between majority and minority cabinets. The explanation of such outcomes is, of course, the principal objective of this study. However, the hypotheses developed in Chapter 2 have broader applicability. If this rational-choice argument is correct, then electoral decisiveness and oppositional influence should enable us to predict not only parliamentary basis, but also, and perhaps more directly, the *number of parties* accepting cabinet responsibility.

As a final step in this part of the analysis, we shall therefore consider two models where the number of parties in government is the dependent variable. The explanatory variables are the same sets of 4

Table 3.9. *Linear regression models of the number of governing parties*

Variables	Model 3.1		Model 3.2	
	Coef.	*t*-value	Coef.	*t*-value
Constant	6.304	15.09	−3.811	2.67
Opposition influence	−.417	5.28	−.183	2.27
Electoral salience	−.466	10.28	−.430	5.96
Volatility	.049	3.85	.025	2.06
Responsiveness	−1.454	3.70	−.667	1.78
Crisis duration			$7.9 \cdot 10^{-4}$	.41
Formation attempts			−.106	2.14
Fractionalization			11.047	7.63
Polarization			−3.735	4.15
Government extremism			1.754	3.76
Investiture			.687	3.98
Number of cases	292		285	
R^2	.379		.514	
Adjusted R^2	.370		.496	
F	43.78		28.97	

Note: The dependent variable is the number of parties represented in the cabinet. Both models exclude majority situations and nonpartisan governments.

and 10 that we have investigated in Tables 3.7 and 3.8. Again, only minority situations with partisan outcomes will be considered. Models 3.1 and 3.2 in Table 3.9 are thus identical to models 1.1 and 1.2 except for the dependent variable. Again, a linear regression is not fully appropriate, since the observed outcome is discrete and necessarily equal to or greater than 1. Since the models will predict fractions of parties in government, overall model fit necessarily suffers.[18]

Given these limitations, the explanatory power of models 3.1 and 3.2 is quite impressive. Note that all four parameter estimates in model 3.1 have very high *t*-values, and collectively these four variables explain well over a third of the variance. Unexpectedly, volatility is positively correlated with the number of parties in government, but the other signs are all in the expected directions. The effect of elec-

[18] Predictions of fewer than one party in government are of course particurlarly implausible. However, models 3.1 and 3.2 make relatively few such predictions (model 3.1 only four), and there are no negative fitted values in either model.

toral salience is especially impressive. An increase of one standard deviation in this variable corresponds to a drop-off of .83 parties in government. Note that this parameter estimate is almost unchanged in the 10-variable model (3.2).

However, in this expanded model, fractionalization carries the largest *t*-value. Its parameter estimate tells us that when fractionalization goes up one standard deviation (.09), the number of governing parties increases by almost exactly one. We should hardly be surprised to find a strong positive relationship between fractionalization and the number of parties in government. Simply put, one could hardly find five-party coalitions in three-party systems. Fractionalization is therefore best thought of as a control variable that captures the increased *availability* of parties in fragmented systems.

Note also that polarization significantly reduces the number of parties in government, whereas government extremism and investiture requirements have the opposite effect. Both of the latter relationships are strong and in the expected directions. The estimates for the two variables measuring properties of the cabinet crisis are consistent with previous models, but their effects are comparatively modest. Observe finally the impressive overall fit of model 3.2, which accounts for about half the variance in the number of governing parties. In sum, the analysis presented in Tables 3.7, 3.8, and 3.9 offers substantial support for the rational-choice explanation of minority government formation. It also indicates that electoral decisiveness is a more important explanatory factor than oppositional influence. It may be that to parties considering government participation future electoral success is a more important consideration than immediate access to policymaking. The average party may be more of a vote seeker than a policy seeker. If this is correct, then it would certainly have profound implications for coalition theory, which has tended to ignore vote-seeking behavior altogether.

Residual analysis by country

Before we leave the analysis of minority government formation, let us examine a couple of the aforementioned models a little more closely. Table 3.10 presents a country-by-country analysis of the predictions and residuals of models 1.4 and 2.4. For each model, the second column in Table 3.10 reports the proportion of correct predictions (majority vs. minority) per country. For model 1.4, the mean residual is also reported, as well as the mean *absolute* value of the residuals. The third column thus tells us whether the model has any systematic *bias* toward over- or underprediction of parliamentary basis in each country. The fourth column reflects the overall *efficiency* of the estimates for each country. The relationship between mean residuals and mean absolute residuals can also give us an indication of how much the "lumpiness" of parliamentary basis detracts from the fit of the overall model. If mean residuals are close to zero, but mean absolute residuals are large, particularly in party systems of low fractionalization (e.g., Canada and Ireland), then we can infer that much of the unexplained variance is due to the lumpiness of the dependent variable. If, on the other hand, mean residuals are almost as large as mean absolute residuals, then there are likely to be unmodeled explanatory factors that vary systematically between countries.

The results in Table 3.10 do not suggest that the discreteness of parliamentary basis is a major problem in the analysis. On the contrary, the residuals for "few-party systems" such as Canada, Ireland, and the United Kingdom are very modest. One clear tendency is for model 1.4 (and probably others) to overpredict parliamentary basis in the Scandinavian countries (Denmark, Norway, and Sweden), as well as in Ireland. Some systematic factor may thus account for the tendency for governments in the Scandinavian countries to be even smaller than the model predicts. Two possibilities exist that would be consistent with the rational-choice explanation. First, Scandinavian parties may be particularly willing to trade office for electoral advantage, a possibility that seems quite plausible in view of the close electoral balance between socialists and nonsocialists (especially in Norway and Sweden) and the virtual absence of clientelistic office seeking. Second, due to the network of consultative institutions, the policy influence differential between government and opposition may be even smaller than my legislative committee variable indicates. Chapter 6 will allow us to examine one of the Scandinavian cases more closely.

Iceland and Portugal, on the other hand, have tended to have much broader governments than the model would predict. Clearly these are also the two countries most poorly predicted by the model. The

Table 3.10. *Residual analysis by country*

Country	Model 1.4				Model 2.4	
	(N)	Correct predictions[a]	Mean residual[b]	Mean absolute residual[b]	(N)	Correct predictions[a]
Belgium	(25)	88	4.8	10.6	(25)	88
Canada	(8)	100	2.5	3.5	(8)	100
Denmark	(23)	78	−6.0	8.0	(23)	78
Finland	(28)	75	0.6	14.3	(28)	75
France	(27)	74	−0.6	10.4	(27)	67
Iceland	(18)	28	7.2	17.2	(19)	53
Ireland	(9)	44	−4.1	4.1	(10)	70
Israel	(22)	100	0.0	9.9	(24)	96
Italy	(31)	71	−1.7	5.9	(33)	76
Netherlands	(15)	93	1.9	11.0	(16)	94
Norway	(15)	60	−4.0	4.5	(15)	67
Portugal	(10)	50	9.8	16.8	(11)	55
Spain	(3)	100	4.0	4.0	(3)	100
Sweden	(17)	47	−5.5	8.0	(17)	53
United Kingdom	(2)	50	−1.5	1.5	(2)	100

[a]In percentages of cases.
[b]In percentages of legislative seats.

Portuguese deviations are quite understandable within the explanation I have advanced. Recall from Chapter 2 that this theory presupposes stable political institutions and the expectation of fair treatment of the opposition. These assumptions are clearly less applicable to Portugal in the 1970s than to just about any other country or government under scrutiny here. The political instability of the 1970s presumably made the relevant parties much more reluctant to let go of power than my explanation assumes. In the aftermath of the revolution, deferring gratification was just too risky.

Finally, the difficulty of predicting Finnish governments is demonstrated by the large absolute residuals. However, this is not due to any systematic bias toward over- or underprediction. Rather, the range of government solutions in Finland has been unusually large, with abrupt shifts between very undersized and very oversized governments.

Conclusions

In this chapter we have surveyed the universe of minority governments and analyzed the conditions under which they form. In looking for causes of minority government formation, we have examined macrostructural characteristics of political systems as well as the immediate properties of cabinet crises. Throughout the analysis, competing explanations have been tested against the data at our disposal. Conventional explanations associate minority cabinets with political instability, fractionalization, polarization, and long and difficult formation processes. My results offer little support for these propositions. In fact, in some cases the data show the exact opposite to be true. My alternative explanation sees minority governments as consequences of rational party behavior under conditions of competition rather than conflict. On the whole, the data have given considerable support to this theory.

The conventional view may not be unreasonable as a historically bounded proposition. It is not difficult to see how events in major European countries in the interwar period could give rise to negative perceptions of minority governments. Unquestionably, fear of minority governments is a result of the historical lessons of the interwar

Table 3.11. *Patterns of government formation: a typology*

		Electoral decisiveness	
		High	Low
	High	Inclusionary (Norway)	Captive government (Italy)
Influence of opposition	Low	Adversarial (United Kingdom)	Captive opposition (Netherlands)

period and particularly of the experiences of the Weimar Republic. These lessons were reinforced by many other governments of the same era and subsequently by the fate of the Fourth Republic. However, they do not represent today's realities.

Minority governments are still frequently associated with turbulent Southern European politics. They are in fact more common in the Scandinavian countries and the Anglo-American world (including Ireland). In fact, the countries most influenced by the Westminster model of democracy seem inclined to turn to minority governments rather than majority coalitions when their two-party systems fragment. Traditionally, minority governments have been portrayed as defective coalition governments. Our results suggest that at least *substantive* minority governments may share more characteristics with majority party governments than with majority coalitions. The functional role of the typical substantive minority government is that of an *imperfect majority party government*. Its formation reflects the jockeying for electoral advantage typical of systems where the majority prize is a realistic expectation for at least one party.

Let us now simplify the analysis somewhat to get a more configurative understanding of government formation. If we dichotomize each of the two basic explanatory variables, we can construct a four-cell typology of patterns of government formation. Table 3.11 presents the typology with examples of the political systems represented by each cell.

In *inclusionary* political systems (notably the Scandinavian countries), elections are competitive and parliamentary oppositions influential. These are perfect conditions for minority governments, which have been very prevalent in these countries. Between 1973 and 1982 (inclusive), no fewer than 19 of 21 Scandinavian governments were undersized. With respect to government participation at any given time, inclusionary systems are the very opposite of what the term would seem to imply. However, policy making is inclusionary, and so is office holding *over time*.

The *adversarial* cell is basically occupied by polities patterned after the Westminster model of democracy.[19] In these systems, elections are at least as decisive and competitive as in the inclusionary type, but the legislative costs of being in opposition are greater. Since majority situations are more common in Britain, Canada, and Ireland than in the inclusionary systems, the overall frequency of minority governments is lower. Even in adversarial systems, however, minority governments outnumber majority *coalitions* by a considerable margin.

The *captive government* type is probably the closest approximation to the traditional image of political systems conducive to minority governments. Italy is a good example of this configuration. Opposition status entails no great loss of policy-making power, but also no great prospects for a better tomorrow. Government parties tend to suffer electorally, but not to the benefit of the loyal opposition. Minority governments are fairly common in captive government systems, although not as common as majority coalitions. Contrary to the two previous types, undersized cabinets in captive government systems are not associated with alternation in office. Rather, this cabinet solution represents a breathing spell for marginal government parties, which for electoral or other reasons prefer not to shoulder the burden of incumbency.

The incentives for minority government formation are least in *captive opposition* systems, such as the Netherlands. Here, parliamentary oppositions (as distinct from extraparliamentary elites and subcultures) are relatively powerless and their electoral prospects dim. Under these circumstances, there are few incentives to abstain from power, and accordingly such captive opposition systems as the Netherlands and Israel tend to have the most oversized coalitions and the lowest incidence of minority governments.

---

[19] This term has been adopted from Finer (1975).

This typology helps us identify different dynamics of minority government formation. In inclusionary and adversarial systems, minority governments are vehicles of alternation in office, whereas in captive government systems they may not be. In Chapters 5 and 6 we shall flesh out examples of one captive government and one inclusionary system, respectively. But let us first consider more generally what happens *after* minority governments have taken office.

4. Minority governments in office

The previous chapter identified the conditions under which minority governments are most likely to form. In this chapter, we shall take a closer look at the performance of minority (and other) governments once they are in office. Two puzzles will be at the center of our attention: (1) How do minority governments manage to build legislative majorities for their policy programs, and (2) how well do they do in office compared to alternative cabinet types? Thus, the first question will ask *how* minority cabinets perform, the second *how well*.

There are somewhat different reasons why we should be interested in these two issues. The first question, how minority cabinets manage to build legislative majorities, is simply a puzzle that cabinet studies have not adequately solved. The second query, concerning minority cabinet performance in office, has been answered more often, but not much better. Chapter 1 presented an overview of this literature on minority government performance. Minority cabinets, we have learned, are commonly portrayed as lacking viability as well as effectiveness compared to majority governments. The mere absence of a government majority is in itself commonly taken as an indication of cabinet ineffectiveness.

But my objective here is not simply to contest the conventional wisdom, or even to add to our knowledge of minority cabinets. The theoretical explanation of minority cabinet formation I have developed in the preceding chapters ultimately rests on a number of assumptions concerning cabinet performance. I have argued that political parties under certain conditions tend to prefer to participation in a majority coalition either (1) being in office alone (or with a small number of partners) in a minority government, or (2) opposition. In either case, and particularly for parties opting for opposition, expectations of future electoral advantage must be a powerful motivation. For parties choosing to form a government alone, their monopoly on office benefits may also help offset the anticipated policy compromises caused by their lack of a legislative majority.

Minority governments and majority building

For participants in minority governments, the problem of constructing legislative majorities begins long before the government actually takes office. Expectations of how this legislative support could come about have presumably entered into the calculations of all the parties faced with the choice between participation in this form of government and one with majority support. This is not to say that the information upon which parties make such decisions is good. There may in fact be a great deal of uncertainty concerning the legislative course of a prospective minority cabinet.

Formal minority governments

In some cases, however, this uncertainty is virtually nil. Or rather, the government's legislative support is just as firmly committed as if it had been a majority government. Of course I am speaking here of *formal* minority governments. Recall that externally supported governments are administrations whose legislative support is negotiated prior to government formation through explicit, comprehensive, and more than short-term contracts. Some externally supported cabinets are formal minority governments. Such cabinets control less than a majority of all legislative seats unless their support parties are counted, but have parliamentary majorities when the latter are included. If such cabinets were the predominant type of minority cabinet, our inquiry into the legislative majority building could stop right here. As Chapter 3 demonstrated, however, formal minority governments are *not* a very large proportion of all minority governments.

Let us begin our discussion of majority-building strategies by considering the incidence of formal minority governments in some-

Table 4.1. *Varieties of external support*

Country	External support		Formal minority cabinets	
	Number	Percentage of all governments	Number	Percentage of all minority cabinets
Belgium	0	0	0	0
Canada	0	0	0	0
Denmark	4	16	2	9
Finland	3	9	3	27
France	5	17	2	17
Iceland	0	0	0	0
Ireland	1	6	0	0
Israel	11	38	3	100
Italy	12	25	4	20
Netherlands	1	5	0	0
Norway	0	0	0	0
Portugal	0	0	0	0
Spain	0	0	0	0
Sweden	0	0	0	0
United Kingdom	0	0	0	0
Total	37	11	14	11

what greater detail. Recall that the number of support agreements may exceed the number of formal minority cabinets for two different reasons: First, each government may have support agreements with more than one party, and second, some minority governments may remain undersized (and hence substantive) even after their support parties have been counted. Table 4.1 breaks external support agreements and formal minority cabinets down by country. The first column simply counts the number of governments *with at least one support agreement.*[1] Note that although a total of 37 governments have some form of external support, only 14 are formal minority cabinets.

Coincidentally, the ratio of formal minority cabinets to all undersized governments is precisely the same as that of externally supported governments to all governments (one in nine). Thus external support is no more common in situations where it would give the govern-

[1] Therefore, Table 4.1 does not tell us the total number of support agreements in each case of external support. Such a report would, however, be of modest theoretical interest.

ment a majority than otherwise. Or, in other words, pivotal parties are no more likely to enter formal support agreements than any others. This is a surprising result, since one might assume that in the market for support agreements pivotal parties would be in special demand. Perhaps pivotal parties fully exploit that bargaining advantage. Alternatively, we may overestimate the disadvantages of operating without a prenegotiated legislative coalition.

This brief survey of external support agreements clearly demonstrates that they are much more common in some polities than in others. Israel and Italy collectively account for half of all formal minority governments and over 60% of all externally supported cabinets. All 3 minority cabinets in Israel have relied on external support, as have eight other governments with majority support to begin with.[2] Italy has seen 12 externally supported governments, 4 of which have been formal minority cabinets. On the other hand, 8 of 15 democracies have never experienced a single case of external support, and the 14 formal minority cabinets are distributed among no more than five different political systems.

Clearly, support agreements are not randomly distributed across countries. Besides Israel and Italy, only Denmark, Finland, and France (Fourth Republic) have any record of formal minority governments. Only polities with some frequency of support agreements have also experienced formal minority cabinets. On the other hand, it is *not* generally the case that political systems with a high number of *substantive* minority governments also account for a large number of *formal* ones. No formal minority governments have formed in Canada or Ireland, which collectively have produced 15 substantive minority cabinets. And of 46 minority governments in the three Scandinavian countries (Denmark, Norway, and Sweden), only 2 (both Danish) have been formal.

Formal support agreements cannot be explained in isolation from alternative legislative strategies. Before we can explain the frequency of support agreements in Israel and Italy, or their absence in Scandinavia and the Anglo-American world, we therefore need to consider the choice of legislative strategy more broadly.

---

[2] Many of these Israeli cases of external support to majority coalitions are accounted for by the Paoli Agudat Israel, a party that particularly in the 1960s frequently found cabinet participation incompatible with its religious commitments.

Strategies of majority building

Formal minority governments are the tip of the iceberg. They illustrate how a small proportion of undersized governments solve the problem of building legislative majorities. And they suggest that related to them is a vast array of other majority-building strategies that are less visible to the casual observer. These strategies can be ordered along two dimensions: (1) the consistency of the membership of the government's legislative coalition, and (2) the policy content of government concessions to support parties. We shall discuss these dimensions successively and then look at some actual practices in different countries.

Membership consistency

Recall that I made three definitional requirements of external support agreements. Such "contracts" had to be (1) formalized (explicit), (2) comprehensive in policy terms, and (3) more than short-term in duration. In addressing majority-building strategies in general, we can consider these three requirements to represent an extreme degree of *membership consistency*. Governments with external support agreements have legislative coalitions consisting of the same parties across policy dimensions and over time. However, minority governments can seek legislative coalitions that are much less consistent in membership. That is to say, legislative support agreements may cover a narrower range of issues, a shorter time frame, and/or be less binding than what we require of external support agreements that qualify for formal minority status.

At the opposite extreme from formal minority governments would be administrations content (or forced) to build their legislative majorities from issue to issue with whatever party would demand the fewest concessions. I shall refer to such practices as ad hoc coalitions or *shifting majorities*. While such a strategy leaves the government with maximum flexibility to exploit favorable issue opportunities, it also renders it maximally susceptible to defeat. Between this extreme and that of formal minority governments, there is a wide variety of "bundling" strategies open to minority cabinets. Thus, undersized governments could cement support from a specific set of parties in a narrow issue area for a long period of time, or on a broad range of issues for a short period of time. Either sort of agreement could be highly formalized and public, or implicit and secret.

Minority governments thus face choices along different dimensions of aggregation. However, these choices are not mutually independent. Such governments may, for example, find it difficult to form long-term membership-consistent legislative coalitions that are *not* formalized. Yet there is considerable variation in the legislative majority-building strategies that have actually been pursued by different minority cabinets. Some of this variation may occur between different governments in the same political system. However, a large part of these differences is driven by variation in the institutional environment and therefore varies more *between* countries than *within* them. We shall discuss examples from three different polities a little later.

General policy content of government concessions

In building legislative coalitions at whatever level of aggregation, minority governments have to be willing to offer concessions to the parties they court. Such concessions may take a variety of forms, depending on what the government has to offer and what the support parties want. By definition, cabinet portfolios are not one of the government's concessions in cases of substantive minority governments. However, the government may seek to secure legislative support by offering subcabinet offices in any number of government agencies and enterprises.

Alternatively, the governing parties may hold out offers of policy concessions. Such concessions may involve compromises on the issues under consideration, but it is also entirely possible for governments and support parties to engage in logrolling, whereby the government buys legislative support on one issue for concessions in a totally different issue area. A party representing a linguistic minority may, for example, be brought to support the government's foreign policy position in exchange for concessions on education policy. A further possibility is for the government to offer narrow and particularistic policy concessions in exchange for support on much broader issues.

Such particularistic concessions may, for example, target specific local or demographic clienteles of support parties.

We shall distinguish different majority-building strategies according to their *general policy content*. The more minority governments (or protocoalitions behaving as prospective minority cabinets) compromise on the major policy decisions facing the legislature (whether issue-to-issue or by logrolling), the higher the general policy content of their concessions. At the low end of this dimension, then, we find governments that rely on subcabinet offices and/or particularistic policy concessions (e.g., constituency services) for their legislative majorities.

By assumption minority governments minimize the office and policy concessions they make in order to gain the requisite legislative support. However, they may face difficult choices in determining which mix of policy and office benefits to offer. As I shall argue, their decision as to this trade-off will reflect both supply and demand conditions. For now, let us simply think of these choices as located along a continuum of general policy content.

Cross-national variations in majority building

Let us consider some cases of typical patterns of majority building in different political systems. Before any attempt can be made to explain these differences, I shall describe them and point out some representative cases. Figure 4.1 illustrates the two main strategy dimensions just described: coalition membership consistency and the general policy content of government concessions.

Figure 4.1 also contains the names of five polities that exemplify different types of majority-building strategies: Israel for high levels of both issue aggregation and policy content, Italy for similarly high aggregation but somewhat lower policy content, Denmark for high policy content but intermediate levels of aggregation, Norway for high policy content and low aggregation, and finally Ireland for low policy content and moderate aggregation. Since it is next to impossible to "measure" these variables, these various characterizations are meant only to be approximate and comparative. Although cases differ more cross-nationally than intertemporally, we also have to recognize

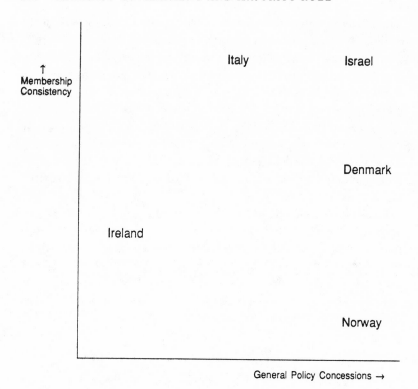

Figure 4.1. Coalition-building strategies with illustrative cases.

some variation from government to government in each country. I shall flesh out an example of majority building in each case to deepen our understanding of the variety of strategies for the formation of legislative coalitions. However, since Italy and Norway are discussed in separate chapters in this book, only Israel, Denmark, and Ireland will be discussed here.

Israel: consistent memberships and policy concessions

Since its founding in 1949, Israel has hardly been typified by minority governments. Only 3 of 29 governments over these four decades have been undersized, and all of these have in fact been formal minority cabinets. Moreover, oversized coalitions are more characteristic of

Israel than of any other country in this study. Mean parliamentary basis is 63.5%, higher than that of any other country. No fewer than 9 governments have had a parliamentary basis exceeding 70%, not counting external support. Thus Israel accounts for about one-fifth of all governments with such broad support.

As mentioned, the three Israeli minority governments (Begin I, Begin III, and Shamir I) have all been externally supported, and all have held close to a majority of the seats in the 120-member Knesset even without this support. Let us look at Begin III (1981–3), the longest-lived of these three cabinets, as an example of majority building in the Israeli context.

Menachem Begin was the incumbent prime minister as the Israelis went to the polls in 1981. In the election, Begin's Likud front eked out a narrow one-seat plurality over its main competitor, the Labor Alignment. Although both Likud and Labor claimed electoral victory, on July 15 President Navon formally entrusted Begin with the task of forming a new government. Three weeks later Begin succeeded in concluding an agreement with the National Religious party and Tami, both of which joined his coalition government. The coalition agreement also included the ultra-orthodox Agudat Israel, which, however, received no representation in the cabinet. The parties in Begin III collectively controlled 57 of the 120 seats in the Knesset, or 61 if Agudat Israel's external support is included. The new cabinet was thus a formal minority government.

The nature of the coalition agreement between the Agudat Israel and the other ruling parties illustrates the comprehensiveness and formalization of such legislative coalitions in Israel. The four parties issued a joint policy declaration containing a total of 83 clauses. The first of these confirmed the continuing validity of the policy program of the previous government, which had largely consisted of the same parties. Of the remaining clauses, more than half pertained to various religious practices and observances, mostly reflecting the concerns of the Agudat Israel. Among these issues were more liberal military service exemptions for *yeshiva* (seminary) students and tighter restrictions on the sale of pork in Jewish-populated areas. They were referred to by the Labor opposition as a "new peak of religious coercion."

Thus, the new government came to power on the basis of a very detailed and comprehensive policy program, and the Agudat Israel was an integral part of the legislative coalition behind this program. The party's decision not to accept any ministerial portfolios was religiously based and signified no lack of commitment to the government's policies. This commitment persisted throughout the 25 months Begin III remained in power. The precarious nature of Begin's legislative majority nonetheless caused the government some narrow escapes, especially after two Likud deputies defected to the opposition in May 1982. Two months later, however, the right-wing Tehiya party, which had three deputies, voted to join the ruling coalition (*Keesing's Contemporary Archives,* pp. 31120, 32159–60).

The Israeli proclivity toward membership-consistent and formalized legislative coalitions is at least partly due to some of its constitutional features. The constitution (the Basic Law of Government of 1968) requires that incoming governments present a program and receive an investiture vote in the Knesset (Seliktar, 1982). Governments that lose votes of confidence are also required to step down (Laver and Schofield, in press), and parliamentary defeats by the government are considered serious. These are obstacles to a more ad hoc majority-building practice.

Policy negotiations also get interwoven with the intense bargaining over portfolios that characterizes Israeli cabinet crises. The constitution limits the negotiation process to four months, and many Israeli cabinet crises have in fact been protracted. These detailed bargains are in part due to the great constitutional power of the prime minister to reshuffle personnel and to shift jurisdiction within the government (Seliktar, 1982). Parties not receiving the prime ministership therefore seek to extract very specific concessions and guarantees from the party so favored. The existence of religious parties with intense policy preferences and low interest in spoils makes it possible for the larger parties to purchase legislative support at a low cost in office benefits. The existence of these parties with a low demand for office facilitates the Israeli pattern of highly aggregated agreements with minimal office concessions.

Ireland: modest consistency and particularistic concessions

The Irish Republic has a governmental record very different from that of Israel. No postwar Irish government has ever been oversized, and the largest share of legislative seats held by the government is 57%. Of 17 postwar governments, 7 have been undersized. Like several other countries with high frequencies of minority cabinets, Ireland is basically an imperfect two-bloc system. Since the 1950s, single-party governments of the Fianna Fáil have alternated with coalitions of the two other major parties, the Fine Gael and the Irish Labour party. Fianna Fáil has historically found it difficult to gain an outright majority in the Dáil, and five of Ireland's seven minority governments have been single-party administrations of the Fianna Fáil.

Contrary to most other Western European polities, Ireland has retained a small number of independent members of the Dáil. To a large extent the survival of these independents is a function of the Irish single transferable vote (STV) electoral system, which has reinforced the localism of Irish party politics (Carty, 1981; but see also Mair, 1987). Traditionally, independent deputies were often nonpartisan local patrons or notables, but in recent years a larger proportion have been defectors from one of the major parties. In the postwar period the number of independents elected has varied from 1 in 1969 to 14 in 1951. Independents have frequently collectively been pivotal when minority governments have been in office, and it is with these TDs (*Teachta Dála*, members of Parliament) that governments have preferred to negotiate.

Ireland offers a clear contrast to Israel in the majority-building strategies most commonly employed by minority governments. Support agreements have rarely been publicized, and legislative coalitions have tended not to be very consistent in membership. Irish governing parties have been much more content to seek particularistic alliances and ad hoc support. Concessions offered to supporters have typically been in the form of policy of purely local interest.

This pattern was evident in the first two postwar Fianna Fáil minority cabinets, de Valera II (1951–4) and Lemass II (1961–5). Lemass was elected Taoiseach (prime minister) with the support of two independents (TDs Carroll and Sherwin), and there were unsubstantiated rumors that the support of these independents had been secured by promises of political favors (Farrell, 1987: 140).[3] Farrell goes on to make this description of the support relationship:

---

[3] Farrell (1987) places little trust in these rumors, arguing that the fear of an early dissolution sufficed to keep the independents voting for the government.

Certainly, independent deputies supporting this latter government [Lemass II] had considerable ease of access to ministers and, it can be assumed, had a more privileged status than party backbenchers. While these independents benefited in terms of ensuring enhanced capacity to satisfy their own constituents, there is no evidence to suggest that they had any influence either on the general direction of government policy or on the control of parliamentary dissolution. (1987: 140)

The cost of legislative support went up in the early 1980s when two consecutive elections within a year failed to produce decisive results – a situation in which either Fianna Fáil or the coalition of Fine Gael and Labour had a majority. In 1981 a minority coalition of the latter two parties under Garret Fitzgerald came to power with the critical support of one of six independent deputies, Jim Kemmy. Fitzgerald apparently tried to build ad hoc majorities without any concessions of either office benefits or policy. Kemmy attempted to negotiate budgetary policy concessions in the areas of taxation, welfare services, and consumer subsidies. When these appeals to the government were unsuccessful, he voted against its budget and helped to bring it down.

The elections that followed produced a minor swing toward the Fianna Fáil, which nevertheless managed to win only 81 of the 166 seats in the Dáil. Three Sinn Féin and four independent deputies were elected. As the Sinn Féin deputies refused to commit themselves to any government, the Fianna Fáil leader, Charles Haughey, had to seek the support of at least two independents. In the end Haughey was elected Taoiseach with the support of independents Neil Blaney (Independent Fianna Fáil) and Tony Gregory, a former member of Sinn Féin. Gregory's support was particularly costly. In a written agreement, which was subsequently published by Gregory, Haughey had to agree to new welfare and nationalization schemes, plus a variety of pork barrel projects for Gregory's Dublin constituency. Despite these concessions, Gregory refused to recognize any binding commitment to the government, which was defeated after only eight months in office on a vote of confidence, in which Gregory abstained and Sinn Féin voted against (Farrell, 1987; *Keesing's Contemporary Archives,* pp. 31042 31042–3, 31445–8, 32022).

Even in the Gregory case the government's concessions had a large particularistic (pork barrel) content, and the agreement failed to cement a legislative coalition over very many issues. In other cases, the Irish proclivity toward office benefit concessions and disaggregated legislative coalition building has been even more obvious. There are several institutional reasons for this tendency. The Irish constitution requires the Taoiseach to be elected by the Dáil, but not on the basis of any specific legislative program. This practice, which contrasts with, among others, Israel and Italy, clearly facilitates ad hoc legislative coalition building.

The demands of the potentially pivotal members of parliament are also quite different from the Israeli case considered earlier. Whereas Israeli minority governments typically are faced with intensely ideological parties elected in a single national constituency, Irish governments commonly confront a collection of independent deputies, who for electoral reasons have very strong incentives to secure benefits for their constituencies. Hence the Irish predilection for particularistic government concessions.

Denmark: issue-specific coalitions and policy concessions

A third and final example will reveal yet another pattern of legislative coalition building. Denmark is, as Chapter 3 has shown, the epitome of a political system given to minority governments. Of 25 postwar governments, only 3 have *not* been undersized. Hence, legislative majority-building practices have of necessity been developed. Danish legislative coalitions are, like the Israeli cases, largely built on policy concessions. However, especially since 1973 they tend to "bundle" issues much less than Israeli governments, although perhaps more than their opposite numbers in Ireland. And although Denmark resembles Norway and Sweden in the extent to which government concessions are policy based, it differs somewhat from the extreme disaggregation, or ad hoc majority building, of these two neighboring countries.

The bifurcation of the party system into a socialist and a nonsocialist bloc is somewhat less pronounced in Denmark than in the other Scandinavian countries (Fitzmaurice, 1983: 258; Särlvik, 1983: 138). Yet only in the years from 1957 to 1964 and again from 1978 to 1979 has the country been governed by coalition cabinets that have bridged this divide. Legislative coalitions between socialists and nonsocialists have been much more common, especially in the 1940s and 1950s and after 1973. Clearly, electoral considerations have been an important deterrent to formalized cooperation between socialists and nonsocialists (Fitzmaurice, 1986; Särlvik, 1983; Strom, 1986).

Given the multitude of Danish minority governments, it is no wonder that a variety of legislative coalitions have been tried. Some Social Democratic governments (notably Krag III and IV) have relied heavily on the "captive" support of the Socialist People's party (SF). Other Social Democratic governments (e.g., Hansen I, Jørgensen II) have preferred to seek cooperation from the centrist "bourgeois" parties. Governments led by Liberals (V) (Kristensen, Eriksen I and II, and Hartling) have cooperated closely with the Radicals (RV) and the Conservatives (KF). And some governments have preferred shifting ad hoc legislative coalitions.

Yet the most salient feature of Danish coalition politics, especially in recent years, is the formation of relatively formalized legislative accommodations (*forlig*), which have tended to be fairly durable but sharply bounded in policy space. In other words, Danish minority governments have bundled issues temporally but not across all policy dimensions. Therefore, different coalitions have often been built in different policy areas. Thus, governments may rely on one policy coalition for their budgetary policies, but have a different majority (or no majority, as the case may be) for their foreign policies. Commonly, such agreements have been negotiated bilaterally and often with a coalition larger than minimum winning size (see Särlvik, 1983: 121–2; Thomas, 1982). The concessions offered by Danish governments have been almost exclusively policy based, if for no other reason than because spoils in Danish politics are so restricted.

The four-party nonsocialist governments under Poul Schlüter (since 1982) offer examples of such majority-building strategies. The four parties participating in Schlüter's three cabinets (the Conservatives, the Liberals, the Center Democrats, and the Christian People's party) have never been close to a parliamentary majority in their own right. Schlüter's first "four-leaf-clover" government relied heavily on the Radicals for legislative support. However, the Radicals refused to support the government on defense and environmental issues. Hence, the government regularly lost votes on defense issues in its first three years and in 1984 had to reach an accommodation with the Social Democrats on the defense budget. Previously, Schlüter had lost votes on the NATO medium-range missile deployment issue, but survived a no confidence motion on this issue in June 1983, when the libertarian Progress party supported the government. In addition, Schlüter has faced a Folketing (Parliament) much less enamored with the European Community than his governments have been.

The Radicals also have balked at some of Schlüter's austerity budgets. Thus, in 1983 the support of the Radicals and the Progress party arrived only at a late stage of deliberation, and in 1984 the government's budget was defeated, leading to premature parliamentary dissolution. (The election returned the government with an improved parliamentary basis.) However, on economic policies Schlüter has often been able to forge alliances with the right-wing Progress party. Hence, his governments have in general achieved greater success in domestic policy areas than in foreign and security policy.

The patchwork of legislative coalitions that has characterized Danish politics has been a matter of necessity rather than choice. Danish cabinets have frequently found themselves in the unenviable position of needing the legislative support of *several* opposition parties. The willingness of opposition parties to commit themselves to wholesale legislative support has at least since 1973 been severely circumscribed by two distinctive features of Danish party politics in this era: *intense electoral competition* and *policy dispersion* along multiple dimensions. Since the early 1970s Denmark has experienced one of the highest rates of electoral volatility in the Western world (Pedersen, 1983, 1987). And the familiar left–right dimension characteristic of Scandinavian politics has been replaced by at least two issue dimensions of competition (Holmstedt and Schou, 1987; Pedersen, 1987). These conditions have promoted cabinet instability and made opposition parties shy even of the compromises implicit in legislative coalitions.

The ability of minority governments to form and survive in spite of these obstacles is clearly aided by institutional arrangements. The Danish constitution has little to say about the process of government formation, and the confidence requirement is purely negatively formulated: "A Minister shall not remain in office after the Folketing has passed a vote of no confidence in him" (Article 15; quoted in Pesonen and Thomas, 1983: 83). According to Pesonen and Thomas,

The negative formulation, which contrasts with the Swedish practice, . . . has permitted the relatively frequent minority governments which Denmark has experienced, often as the only feasible solution to a fragmented political system, and allows governments to seek their support from different quarters for different issues. (1983: 83)

Danish minority governments have not only survived. They have often shown "a remarkable ability to deliver the goods" (Elder, 1975), as when the economic achievements of Schlüter's first government were described by the *Financial Times* as "spectacular" (*Keesing's Contemporary Archives*, 1984: 32686).

Explaining legislative strategies

The examples of Israel, Ireland, and Denmark illustrate the great diversity of legislative strategies employed by minority governments. After juxtaposing three such different cases, one might be tempted simply to note their uniqueness or to revert to purely historical explanations. It is possible, however, to explain the differences between these three political systems in a fairly simple manner without going deep into their histories. In discussing these cases, I have offered some preliminary explanations of their differences. It is now time to tie these explanatory efforts together in a coherent framework.

As I have already argued, legislative strategies differ in terms of both coalition membership and the general policy content of the governments' concessions. We need to look at different factors to explain variation along each of these two dimensions. Differences in membership consistency are largely a function of two factors: the government's *bargaining power* and its *agenda control.*

Minority governments without a comprehensive support agreement constantly need to build legislative majorities. For this end, they can offer a variety of office and policy inducements to members of the opposition. The government's objecive is to purchase support for the best possible legislative program at the lowest possible cost. Everything else being equal, minority governments would prefer purely ad hoc coalitions. By negotiating each issue separately and on an ad hoc basis, the typical minority government can in each case pick the least "expensive" coalition partner available. This is especially profitable if there are many feasible coalition partners, if different policy dimensions have different salience for the various opposition parties, and if their trade-off functions between office and policy differ.

Formal external support agreements, therefore, are the *least* attractive legislative strategy for minority governments that want to maximize their policy influence. However, support agreements may offer some additional viability. And we shall see that such agreements may enhance cabinet durability under some circumstances. Formal minority solutions should therefore be the recourse of risk-averse parties preoccupied with their viability in office. Parties that are more willing to trade off durability for policy influence should prefer shifting majorities. Governments that expect to be stable should be least concerned about marginal gains in durability and most inclined to ad hoc majority building. The stronger the government, therefore, the greater the tendency toward shifting coalitions. The "strength" of the government in turn depends largely on its bargaining power and the degree to which it enjoys agenda control.

Bargaining power

Social scientists have made several notable attempts to formalize and measure bargaining power (e.g., Banzhaf, 1965; Holler, 1982; Shapley and Shubik, 1954). Valuable as they are, the power indexes that have been developed are of limited utility for our purposes. The most serious restriction is that they treat all "winning" coalitions as equiprobable, an assumption that is patently implausible to the extent that parties are policy seekers, or even vote seekers. For minority governments seeking legislative coalitions, bargaining power is maximized when (1) a large number of possible coalitions that satisfy their legislative demands exists, (2) membership in these coalitions is dispersed across a large number of opposition parties, and (3) these parties are close to the government in policy space. The greater the number of coalitions that would do, the lesser the dependence on any small set of partners. The more policy compatible these partners are, the better off the government is, and the greater the probability that it will build shifting majorities.

Advantages in bargaining power have facilitated the frequent and durable minority governments formed by Social Democrats in Norway and Sweden. These governments have generally only had to secure the support of either the respective party to their left, or *any one* of the bourgeois parties to their right. Besides, the Social Democrats have frequently been fortunate enough to control the median legislator along the dominant left–right axis, which makes them very difficult to dislodge. Similarly, several Irish Fianna Fáil cabinets have had the good fortune of needing only a small number of votes from a pool of independent deputies. Israeli minority cabinets have also faced a choice among a number of small parties but have been constrained by the extreme policy positions taken by many of these parties. Danish and Italian minority cabinets, on the other hand, have suffered from the need for *multiple* partners and the relative lack of such parties in their policy neighborhood.

Agenda control

The second factor that affects the degree of the consistency of coalition membership is the government's agenda control. To the extent that the government can choose the timing, framing, and coupling of issues before the legislature, it is better positioned to select its preferred level of issue aggregation. Since unconstrained governments generally prefer a disaggregated agenda, a high degree of agenda control favors an ad hoc issue-by-issue legislative strategy.

Two institutional features that affect the government's control of the agenda have already been discussed in the analysis of government formation, namely, *investiture requirements* and *legislative committee structure*. Lax investiture requirements and a decentralized committee structure are factors that promote minority government formation in the first place. The same features promote ad hoc (shifting) legislative coalitions once the government is in office. If a government does not have to seek parliamentary approval for a comprehensive legislative program before assuming office, it is obviously much better positioned to pursue ad hoc majorities. And if issues in different areas can be dealt with independently in separate and mutually insulated committees, the government has similar opportunities. If such committees hold closed meetings and enjoy deference on the floor, so much the better.

Agenda control is the key to understanding formal support agreements. Curiously, the property that best seems to predict the presence of such agreements and formal minority governments is a republican form of government. Of the 345 partisan governments in the sample, 188 represent republican regimes and 157 monarchies. However, 32 of 37 support agreements and 12 of 14 formal minority governments are found in the former regime type. This seemingly peculiar correlation is neither a pure coincidence nor a consequence of republicanism per se. Rather, republicanism tends to coincide with modern constitutions and legislatures, where investiture and confidence procedures tend to be highly formalized and explicitly regulated. On the other hand, countries that have retained a monarchical form of government typically have informal and ambiguous rules based on tradition and interpretation. This constitutional flexibility allows incoming governments to take more risks in building legislative coalitions. Monarchies thus afford their governments much more agenda control, especially in their investiture regulations. As noted by Pesonen and Thomas (1983), the laxity of Scandinavian investiture requirements has greatly facilitated the shifting legislative coalitions that characterize these countries. These practices have been further promoted by the decentralization and intimacy of committee deliberations in these countries (Arter, 1984). The more rigid republican constitutions, on the other hand, predispose governments toward external support agreements.

Despite the fact that the country has a republican constitution, Irish minority cabinets have profited from the fact that the incoming Taoiseach need not present a comprehensive policy declaration. The British parliamentary legacy may also facilitate informal and shifting legislative coalitions. On the other hand, Italian and Israeli governments have much less control of the agenda at investiture. In the Italian case, this is partly offset by the extensive delegation of legislative powers to the parliamentary committees. Yet a higher level of issue aggregation is in these countries coupled with a lower degree of agenda control.

Government concessions

The policy content of government concessions is shaped by three general factors: (1) the relative availability of different forms of benefits, such as policy influence, constituency services, and office benefits; (2) the relative value placed on these various benefits by the governing parties; and (3) the relative demand for different benefits by the parties whose support is sought. In other words, policy content is affected by supply as well as demand conditions.

Political systems differ greatly in the extent to which they offer government incumbents office spoils and opportunities to render services to constituents. Italy, with its plethora of public agencies and enterprises, offers governing parties a vast array of rewards. The Scandinavian nations, on the other hand, place rather severe restrictions on the availability of public offices and monies. Likewise, the demand of opposition parties for office and policy goods varies greatly between and within political systems. At one extreme, minor Israeli religious parties such as the Agudat Israel and the Paoli Agudat Israel have been motivated almost exclusively by intense policy preferences. At the other extreme, independent Irish deputies in the Dáil have often been driven by a strong concern for services for their constituents, sometimes coupled with a desire for office benefits for themselves.

Such differences in demand are in turn driven partly by organizational features of political parties and partly by institutional characteristics of the political system. Clientelistic parties and parties of notables will tend toward particularistic demands with a low policy content. Internally democratic mass parties will tend toward the other extreme. And electoral systems will induce particularistic demands to the extent that they promote constituency ties over party cohesion.

Finally, the policy content of the government's concessions to the opposition depends on how highly the governing parties themselves value the various goods at their disposal. If the marginal value to the governing parties of the policy compromises that must be made in order to build a legislative majority is lower than the alternative cost in particularistic benefits and services, then policy concessions will be made. Of course, the utility of different benefits to governing parties depends on the same factors that affect the preferences of opposition parties. However, since preferences may vary within countries, governing parties may seek legislative coalition partners with complementary preferences (see Luebbert, 1986, for a related argument). Thus, office seekers in the Likud may prefer to build alliances with the intense policy seekers in the smaller religious parties.

In sum, similar patterns of policy content can be driven by different supply and demand conditions. Whereas in Israel the high level of policy content is driven mainly by the strong demand of the religious parties, in Scandinavia a similar level of policy content appears to be a function more of the limited institutional supply of office benefits. The particularism of Irish concessions seems primarily caused by the demands of the pivotal players in that legislature. Italy presents a more complex picture that falls between these extremes in policy content. The Italian case will be described in greater detail in Chapter 5.

Performance in office

Let us now turn our attention to the *quality* of minority government performance in office. Measuring the performance of parliamentary governments is no easy task. Harry Eckstein (1971) has pointed out some general problems of studying political performance, which apply in full force to the issue of government performance. Performance measures easily become too vague and general (e.g., "system maintenance"), or they are defined in excessively narrow and arbitrary terms, which may even be politically controversial (e.g., allocations of government expenditure).

Although few students of political performance claim to have developed an exhaustive account of requisite functions, many have adopted an essentially functionalist approach (Eckstein, 1971; Powell, 1982a). Some notion of politically central and necessary activities can serve as a reasonable guide to political performance. Studies of *government* performance have not often been derived explicitly from such conceptions, but functionalist thinking again underlies much of this work (see Almond and Powell, 1978; Blondel, 1968; Di Palma, 1977; Finer, 1975; Spiro, 1959). Two sorts of government performance measures have dominated the literature: government duration (stability) and quantitative measures of parliamentary legislation. Both are comfortably derived from a systemic functionalist perspective, in the sense that legislative activity certainly is a crucial activity in modern democracies and that a minimum of government stability appears to be a requisite for decisional efficacy.

So far we have adopted not only a functionalist, but also a systemic, perspective on government performance. However, functions and the performance relevant to them may well be identified on a subsystemic rather than systemic level. That is to say, we may try to identify the critical activities of *cabinets* more narrowly defined without direct regard for their consequences for the polity as a whole. This shift in focus does not necessarily alter the operational variables involved in analyzing cabinet performance, since legislative productivity and stability can be construed as subsystemic as well as systemic requisites.

There is, however, a fundamentally different approach to the study of government performance. Instead of asking the functional question, we could derive cabinet performance measures from the objectives (utility functions) of the political parties that form them. Rather than asking whether the activities of a particular government serve the needs of the political system or its legislative subsystem, we could seek to determine whether they further the objectives of the participating parties. If, for example, we take political parties to be office seekers, we could ask to what extent a specific cabinet fulfilled the office objectives of the parties of which it was composed. To the extent, then, that parties are office seekers, policy seekers, and vote seekers, we can use these utility stipulations to derive measures of government performance.

This is what the remainder of this chapter will do. I shall first discuss a very conventional measure of office-seeking performance, namely, *cabinet duration*. Next I shall consider two more indirect measures of policy-seeking performance: the *cause* and *mode* of the government's *resignation*. These measures will in Chapters 5 and 6 be supplemented with more contextually sensitive measures of policy-seeking cabinet performance in Italy and Norway. Finally, I introduce two measures of vote-seeking cabinet performance: *electoral success* and *alternation*.[4]

---

[4] Clearly the treatment of policy objectives in this chapter is a formal one, which does not address such substantive concerns as, e.g., the government's contribution to economic growth. This research strategy is partly due to the technical difficulty of identifying such policy consequences. More basically, however, my overriding concern is to enhance the validity of these performance measures across all countries and parties. Whereas different parties may vary in their primary economic objectives, it seems safe to assume that they all want their governments to be durable, electorally successful, and internally consensual.

This derivation of performance measures from the objectives of the participating political parties does not preclude assessments of systemic or subsystemic performance. Many of the empirical measures we shall consider could well be incorporated into a functional analysis of government performance. We shall consider these issues at the end of the chapter.

Office performance

Just as the assumption of office pursuit is the most common one in coalition theory, so also are office-related measures the most common in studies of cabinet performance. Specifically, government performance is often measured as *cabinet duration,* in the number of days, weeks, months, or years different governments remain in office after inauguration (Blondel, 1980; Browne, Frendreis, and Gleiber, 1986; Dodd, 1976; Lijphart, 1984b; Sanders and Herman, 1977; Warwick, 1979). The longer this duration, the more successful the government. We assume, then, that once in office, incumbents will seek to perpetuate the coalitional arrangements that brought them these benefits.[5]

We may wish to distinguish between government *durability* (as a theoretical expectation) and actual duration (as an observed value) (see Browne, Frendreis, and Gleiber, 1984), although these terms are used interchangeably and loosely in much of the literature. My measure here is strictly one of duration, measured in whole months from the date of the formal investiture. Any discussion of durability is therefore strictly shorthand for these observations. Termination dates are a little more difficult to establish than formation dates. In cases where the administration continued in office through general elections, the date of the election is used as a termination point. Otherwise, the termination point is the date the prime minister submitted the government's resignation.[6] Duration figures have been rounded off to the nearest whole number of months. Changes of government are defined as previously.

---

[5] The underlying assumption may be that any cabinet that forms is likely to be and remain in Nash equilibrium, which means that no party can improve its payoff by any unilateral action, such as defection from the government.

[6] Resignations that were subsequently withdrawn or refused have been discounted.

Table 4.2. *Duration by cabinet type (in months)*

Cabinet type	Mean	Standard deviation	(N)
Majority party	30.0	16.9	(44)
Majority coalition	17.7	14.6	(166)
Minority formal	13.2	9.3	(14)
Minority substantive	14.1	12.9	(107)
Nonpartisan	4.1	2.7	(11)
All governments	17.5	15.0	(342)

The conventional wisdom suggests that minority governments are less durable than those with a majority. We also expect to find that coalitions are shorter lived than single-party governments. However, Dodd (1976) argues against the latter expectation, stressing the critical effect of minimum winning size. The results presented in Table 4.2 are consistent with the prevailing expectations. Both types of majority governments have on average been longer lived than either type of minority government, whereas the latter have tended to last much longer than nonpartisan administrations. Among majority governments, single-party cabinets have been much more durable than coalitions.

It is not difficult to see that coalitional status (coalition vs. single party) is much more strongly correlated with duration than numerical status (majority vs. minority). On average, majority coalitions have lasted 25% longer than substantive minority governments. However, majority party cabinets have been more than twice as durable as substantive minority governments and about 70% longer lived than majority coalitions. In other words, whereas the average duration difference between substantive minority and majority coalition governments is about 3.5 months, a majority party government tends to outlast either of these cabinet types by more than a year.

The durability advantage of single-party governments over coalitions is well supported for minority as well as majority governments. The average duration of single-party governments, regardless of numerical status, exceeds that of coalition governments by almost 40% (21.8 vs. 15.8 months). Interestingly, the liability in longevity for coalition governments is most pronounced for substantive minority governments. Whereas such coalitions last on average only 7.8 months, substantive minority cabinets consisting of only one party are only insignificantly shorter lived than majority coalitions (17.2 vs. 17.7 months).

These figures reflect the fact that many majority party governments last an entire regular legislative term, whereas only a small proportion of other cabinets do. These differences will be illuminated in the next section. But note also that neither minority cabinets nor majority coalitions are anywhere near as transitory as nonpartisan governments. In fact, even formal minority cabinets are three to four times as durable as administrations without a partisan basis. Hence, it would certainly be incorrect to think of either minority or coalition governments as purely transitional. Some such governments may indeed be no more ambitious than caretaker administrations, but the generalization would be invalid.

Except for majority party cabinets, the duration figures are on the whole rather unimpressive and much lower than those reported in many other studies (e.g., Dodd, 1976). These low figures are in large part an artifact of restrictive counting rules, which yield a larger number of shorter-lived governments than many alternative conventions (see Lijphart, 1984b). For example, my 21 Swedish postwar governments would be reduced to 8 if only changes in partisan composition counted as changes of government. Also, the fact that governments rather than countries are the units of analysis in effect skews the sample toward the low end of the duration range. The less durable governments in a given country are, the more heavily that country is weighted in this sample of governments.[7] The justification for the counting rules I have adopted is spelled out in Chapter 3. The point here is simply that duration figures are especially sensitive to these choices and should be interpreted accordingly.

Policy performance

Cabinet duration is of course no guarantee of legislative effectiveness. Sometimes the opposite may be the case, as when governments are

---

[7] However, my restrictive counting rules, in which each general election automatically constitutes a change of government, actually counteracts some of the overrepresentation of polities with low-duration governments.

tolerated precisely because they are inoffensive and do not "rock the boat." Obviously, then, duration figures cannot tell us much about the relative policy performance of different cabinet types. Unfortunately, there are few alternative sources of cross-nationally comparable data. Policy effectiveness is greatly constrained by a whole host of institutional factors, for which it is next to impossible to control across 15 countries. Chapters 5 and 6 will introduce a variety of country-specific data on legislative performance in Italy and Norway. These analyses make use of the best data available in each case and are therefore not strictly comparable. To replicate these analyses for each of 15 countries would clearly be beyond this volume.

Since direct and comparable measures of policy effectiveness are difficult to come by, I shall employ two variables that more indirectly tap this performance dimension. These measures are the *cause* and *mode* of the government's resignation. I assume that the circumstances surrounding a government's demise reflect its policy effectiveness. Most particularly, these circumstances are likely to reflect the degree of cohesion within a government, which must be at least a necessary condition for policy effectiveness.

Causes of government resignation have been divided into six categories:

1. Government disunity (inter- or intraparty);
2. Parliamentary defeats on votes of confidence;
3. Parliamentary defeats on other bills;
4. Elections, whether regularly scheduled or premature;
5. Systemic, as when a government is driven to resign because of war, an international crisis, civil unrest, or other critical events outside the legislative or electoral arena; and
6. Personal or constitutional factors, such as the death, ill health, or voluntary retirement of the prime minister, scandals of various sorts, or, in some countries, the election of a new president.

These categories have in practice proved to be sufficiently exhaustive and mutually exclusive to present few ambiguities. One proof of the fit lies in the fact that the broadest and least well defined category (systemic causes) accounts for the smallest proportion of cases (3%).[8] A breakdown of causes of resignation by cabinet type is presented in Table 4.3. My assumption is that certain causes of resignation reflect a more troubled life than others. In particular, resignations out of internal disunity or parliamentary defeat indicate a lesser degree of policy cohesion and effectiveness than others. Electoral resignations, especially if they are in fact constitutionally mandated, are an especially benign way to go. Personal and constitutional resignations are in large part equally innocuous, as when Urho Kekkonen resigned the Finnish premiership in 1956 after he had been elected president, or when Winston Churchill retired from the British prime ministership in 1955. However, in some cases personally caused resignations reflect profound individual or institutional failures, as in the Italian case of Arnaldo Forlani's resignation in 1981 in the wake of the P–2 Masonic conspiracy scandal, which involved a large number of prominent Italians and shook the state and the Christian Democratic party in their foundations.

Table 4.3 reveals large and systematic differences in causes of resignation between cabinet types. Since there have been so few formal minority or nonpartisan governments, it makes little sense to analyze these figures in detail. The most striking difference in resignations is between majority party governments and all others. Majority party governments exhibit by far the most "benign" pattern. More than two-thirds of these resignations have been due to elections, and many of the remainder have been caused by retirements or other simple changes of personnel within the governing party.

The most interesting difference for present purposes is between substantive minority and majority coalition cabinets. Note that almost half of all majority coalitions have suffered the trauma of internal disunity, a fate shared by only just over one-fifth of all substantive minority cabinets. On the other hand, minority governments are the

---

[8] One apparent problem with these categories is that government disunity might be a cause of a subsequent parliamentary defeat on a confidence motion or other bill. Such cases have been coded as parliamentary defeats. They are, however, less common than one might believe. The prevalent doctrine of collective cabinet responsibility makes government disunity on a confidence motion a very unlikely event in most political systems. Even the anticipation of defeat on some other important bill is most often enough to send the government packing before any actual vote is taken. Presumably, the electoral and legislative ramifications of such defeats weigh heavily on the minds of party leaders.

Table 4.3. Cause of resignation by cabinet type (percentages by cabinet type)

Cabinet type	Government disunity	Parliamentary confidence	Parliamentary-policy defeat	Electoral	Systemic	Personal/constitutional	(N)
Majority party	5	0	0	68	0	27	(44)
Majority coalition	47	4	6	31	4	8	(166)
Minority formal	36	14	0	29	0	21	(14)
Minority substantive	21	22	10	35	4	8	(106)
Nonpartisan	27	9	18	36	9	0	(11)
All governments	32	9	7	37	3	11	(341)

only cabinet type commonly defeated on votes of confidence. This is hardly surprising, since majority governments can lose confidence votes only if some of their own supporters break ranks on these most important of votes. On the other hand, substantive minority governments in turn have a slight "edge" over majority coalitions in electoral resignations.

All in all, substantive minority governments have done no worse, and arguably a bit better, than majority coalitions in causes of government resignations. If substantive minority governments are broken down into single-party and coalition cabinets, interesting distinctions again appear. Single-party minority governments resign more often due to electoral, systemic, or personal or constitutional causes, and less often because of internal disarray or legislative defeats. Thus, the most prevalent subtype of minority governments has even greater advantages over majority coalitions than the class of substantive minority governments as a whole.

The cause of resignation, as defined earlier, informs us of the institutional setting in which each government has met its fate. However, this classification scheme cannot serve as a fully reliable guide to the trauma of resignation. To be sure, defeats on confidence motions are hardly trivial and do not often befall legislatively successful cabinets. However, even such resignations can be engineered by the government itself, as in 1972, 1979, and 1987, when Italian minority governments led by Giulio Andreotti (1972 and 1979) and Amintore Fanfani (1987) deliberately lost votes of confidence in order to clear the way for parliamentary dissolution.

To complement the picture of government resignation and clear up some of the ambiguities, let us therefore consider also the *mode* of resignation, which I have classified in terms of these three categories:

1. *Defeat* or *crisis*, when the government is forced to resign or does so under adversity;
2. *Voluntary* resignations, when the government is under no strong pressure to resign, but does so in order to reshuffle personnel, broaden its parliamentary base, and so on;
3. *Technical* resignations, when the resignation is neither voluntary nor due to any defeat or crisis. Technical resignations tend to

Table 4.4. *Mode of resignation by cabinet type (percentages by cabinet type)*

Cabinet type	Crisis/defeat	Voluntary	Technical	(N)
Majority party	45	20	34	(44)
Majority coalition	84	5	11	(165)
Minority formal	57	43	0	(14)
Minority substantive	66	18	16	(107)
Nonpartisan	82	18	0	(11)
All governments	72	13	15	(341)

be artifacts of my rules for counting governments, as when the prime minister dies or the government goes through a general election without any change in premiership, partisanship, or numerical status.[9]

These modes of resignation fall into a clear hierarchy of severity, with defeat/crisis signifying the greatest and technical resignations the least amount of trauma. Voluntary resignations form the intermediate category, mostly because of the heterogeneity of this category. Voluntary resignations may be prompted by some crowning legislative success, as when Danish premier Jens Otto Krag retired after successfully leading his country into the European Community. On the other hand, Giovanni Leone's voluntary resignation in 1969 was by his own admission precipitated by his government's inability to bring to an end a general strike by government employees or to win support for its legislative agenda.

Table 4.4 presents a breakdown of modes of resignation by cabinet type. The results are quite compatible with those in Table 4.3. Again majority party governments exhibit the most favorable pattern of resignations, with technical resignation accounting for a third and crises and defeats for less than half. As in many other respects, nonpartisan governments have the least benign record, but in this case majority coalitions run a close second. Five of six majority coalition resignations have been due to crises or defeat, as compared

[9] For a general election to count as a technical resignation, there must have been no change of premiership, partisanship, or numerical status. In all other cases, general elections have been assigned to the category *defeat or crisis*.

to two-thirds of the resignations of substantive minority cabinets. The latter cabinet type also has the second highest proportion of technical resignations.

As far as resignations can tell us a story about policy performance, therefore, substantive minority cabinets have a clear advantage over majority coalitions. As in the previous analysis, single-party undersized governments have a somewhat more favorable profile than minority governments consisting of several parties. The face validity of these results is enhanced by the fact that the superiority of single-party cabinets in general and majority party cabinets in particular is so consistent with the other measures of government performance. Even readers who would prefer more direct measures of policy performance (and who would not?) should find that these results supplement and reinforce the data on office and electoral performance.

Electoral performance

The final performance category pertains to the success of various cabinets in subsequent elections. To the extent that parties are vote seekers, this must be a critical part of their own balance sheet for government participation. As I argued earlier, the expectation of a thumbs down from the electorate is precisely the most likely reason that a party may decline an opportunity to participate in government. And the tendency for incumbents, and especially coalition governments, to lose support is an important element in the calculus I have sketched out.

As in the case of policy performance, I shall present two complementary measures of electoral performance, namely, *electoral success* and *subsequent alternation*. Electoral success is simply the governing parties' aggregate gain or loss in percentage points of total popular vote in the next general election. Thus, the unit of analysis is the set of governing parties collectively. The results for the various cabinet types are reported in Table 4.5. Note that the electoral incumbency cost is shared by all cabinet types.[10] Overall, the mean loss of vote

---

[10] Note that no figures are calculable for nonpartisan governments, for the obvious reason that they are not composed of identifiable parties that contest elections. The same exclusion applies to the analysis of alternation (later in this chapter).

Table 4.5. *Subsequent electoral success by cabinet type (in percentage points of total popular vote)*

Cabinet type	All governments			Pre-electoral governments only		
	Mean	Standard deviation	(N)	Mean	Standard deviation	(N)
Majority party	−3.04	5.09	(44)	−2.73	5.32	(30)
Majority coalition	−4.54	6.44	(164)	−4.26	6.39	(52)
Minority formal	−0.97	3.65	(14)	−2.10	3.54	(4)
Minority substantive	−1.30	6.57	(105)	−1.24	6.27	(37)
All governments	−3.15	6.39	(327)	−2.91	6.11	(123)

share amounts to more than 3%, which is sufficient to support my theoretical argument and consistent with previous findings.

These incumbency costs, however, are far from equally shared by all cabinet types. Minority governments have on average lost less than half as much as majority party governments and not much more than one-fourth as much as majority coalitions. These very heavy casualties (4.5%) suffered by majority coalitions could indeed be an effective deterrent to the formation of such governments. Relative to existing vote shares the differential between majority coalition and minority governments is somewhat less dramatic, since majority coalitions obviously have more votes to lose. However, their average losses are still twice as large as those of substantive minority cabinets.

Electoral gains or losses can most meaningfully be attributed to governments holding office at the time of elections. In some of the cases we have considered, however, three or four governments may have intervened between the resignation of the government in question and the next general election. The right-hand side of Table 4.5 excludes such cases and limits the analysis to governments in office at the time of elections. This exclusion does not change the results in any meaningful way, except that cabinets in office at election time systematically perform a little better than the others, regardless of type.[11] Since the incentives for vote seeking are also greater for gov-

---

[11] The only exception to the electoral advantage of governments in office at election

ernments facing elections, the results are consistent with the thrust of my theoretical argument as well as with the previous results. The results are also consistent if we use parties, rather than governments, as the unit of analysis. The only notable difference is that majority party governments do somewhat better. Parties in substantive minority governments have the highest likelihood of electoral gain, followed by majority party cabinets. Parties in majority coalitions face the dimmest prospects.[12]

We can gain a richer understanding of the electoral fortunes of various cabinet types by considering a second measure of electoral performance: subsequent alternation. Alternation measures the degree of turnover in office from one government to the next. Obviously, the greater the turnover, the worse the performance of the first government. Thus, alternation allows us to consider how electoral results play themselves out at the next stage of interparty deliberation. In other words, this variable gives us an indication of the consequences of electoral results for the bargaining power of the parties in office.

Operationally, I measure alternation as the aggregate proportion of legislative seats held by parties changing status between government and opposition in the change of government in question.[13] Since this is an unconventional variable, a hypothetical example may clarify. Let party A in a given legislature have 45% of the seats, party B, 35%, and party C, 20%.[14] Party A rules alone in government 1. If government 2 consists of parties B and C, all parties will have changed status between governments 1 and 2, and the alternation score of government 1 will be .45 + .35 + .20 = 1. If, on the other hand, government 2 was a coalition of parties A and C, then only C would have changed status (by entering government), and the alternation score for government 1 would be .2.

Table 4.6 shows the actual alternation scores of the various cabinet

---

time concerns formal minority governments. Given the small number of such governments, this exception is hardly meaningful.

[12] These results are available from the author upon request.

[13] Where general elections intervene between two governments, alternation scores reflect the shares of seats held by the various parties *after* the election. For technical reasons the maximum alternation score is .98.

[14] Readers who like empirical examples may think of this party system as the Irish Republic and the parties as Fianna Fáil, Fine Gael, and the Irish Labour party, respectively.

Table 4.6. *Subsequent alternation by cabinet type*

Cabinet type	All governments			Nontechnical resignations only		
	Mean	Standard deviation	(*N*)	Mean	Standard deviation	(*N*)
Majority party	.216	.404	(44)	.328	.461	(29)
Majority coalition	.190	.246	(158)	.212	.252	(139)
Minority formal	.124	.167	(14)	.124	.167	(14)
Minority substantive	.297	.353	(105)	.340	.359	(88)
All governments	.226	.310	(321)	.262	.320	(270)

Note: Alternation scores represent the proportion of legislative seats held by parties changing governmental status.

types. Note the discrepancy between these results and the figures for electoral success. Substantive minority governments have been subject to the greatest amount of subsequent turnover, and majority party cabinets have experienced greater losses than majority coalitions. Thus, the governments that experience the greatest electoral damage seem to suffer the least loss of bargaining power, and the most electorally successful governments are most apt to be replaced.

Note also the large standard deviation for majority party governments compared to majority coalitions. These results indicate that the typical pattern of turnover varies fundamentally between these two cabinet types. Majority party cabinets typically form in two-party or near two-party (Westminster) systems (Lijphart, 1984a), where a change of government means either a full rotation in office or no partisan change at all. Majority coalitions form in more fragmented party systems where intermediate degrees of turnover are much more feasible and common. The right-hand side of Table 4.6 presents the results when technical resignations, as discussed earlier, are excluded from the analysis. In this subset, the average alternation scores of substantive minority and especially majority party governments rise substantially.

Overall, the most interesting result in Table 4.6 is that *substantive minority governments resemble majority party governments rather than majority coalitions.* We have seen several signs of familiarity between these two cabinet types. These similarities suggest that although substantive minority governments are alternatives to majority coalitions, they reflect payoff structures and party expectations that have more in common with majority party governments. With the help of the more intensive analyses in Chapters 5 and 6, we shall return to these issues in the concluding chapter.

Country-by-country analysis

So far we have not attempted to disaggregate the performance results by country or any other background variable. As the final part of the performance analysis, Table 4.7 breaks the results down by country for four variables: duration, mode of resignation,[15] electoral success, and alternation. I shall extract only a few points from the wealth of information presented in this table.

Note first that in the few countries where formal minority cabinets form, they have tended to be more durable than substantive minority cabinets and almost as durable as majority coalitions. In most countries where minority cabinets have attained some longevity, however, they have typically not been externally supported. These results underscore the *defensive* nature of external support agreements and the fact that they are promoted by specific institutional arrangements that limit the government's agenda control and hinder minority government formation in the first place.

Whereas the results for government resignations exhibit a great deal of cross-national variation, the figures for electoral success are impressively uniform across countries. Note that majority coalition governments have suffered a mean loss in *every* country where such cabinets have formed. Even the other cabinet types have tended to fall "in the red," but less consistently so. Note, however, that of the countries that have experienced both majority coalitions and substantive minority cabinets, the undersized governments have had the electoral advantage in 10. The exception is the Netherlands, which has had only three minority governments. The results also show that

---

[15] The results presented for mode of resignation are the percentage of cases falling in the crisis/defeat category.

Table 4.7. Performance by cabinet type and country

Country	Duration[a]				Crisis resignation (mode)[b]				Electoral success[a]				Alternation[a]			
	FM	SM	MC	MP	FM	SM	MC	MP	FM	SM	MC	MP	FM	SM	MC	MP
Belgium	—	1.8	17.8	15.3	—	50	96	100	—	0.3	-3.7	-6.6	—	.25	.21	.32
Canada	—	18.6	—	40.0	—	50	—	63	—	3.7	—	-7.4	—	.22	—	.34
Denmark	23.5	19.2	28.7	—	50	68	67	—	-0.7	-0.7	-4.1	—	.03	.28	.30	—
Finland	13.7	6.3	17.2	—	67	38	85	—	-0.1	-1.8	-3.6	—	.19	.30	.22	—
France	4.5	3.7	5.2	—	100	90	94	—	5.1	-4.2	-11.6	—	.10	.22	.17	—
Iceland	—	5.3	32.4	—	—	75	64	—	—	-2.5	-4.0	—	—	.35	.37	—
Ireland	—	22.3	44.7	28.1	—	83	67	57	—	-3.6	-6.8	-3.2	—	.77	.63	.28
Israel	12.7	—	15.4	—	33	—	71	—	-5.8	—	-5.6	—	.21	—	.11	—
Italy	12.5	5.4	11.5	—	50	81	100	—	-1.2	0.6	-2.1	—	.07	.08	.07	—
Netherlands	—	3.3	28.7	—	—	100	93	—	—	-4.9	-1.9	—	—	.35	.22	—
Norway	—	18.4	31.0	31.7	—	73	67	33	—	-1.7	-2.7	1.4	—	.57	.33	.00
Portugal	—	17.0	8.3	—	—	100	60	—	—	6.4	-6.5	—	—	.48	.15	—
Spain	—	21.7	—	43.0	—	33	—	0	—	-16.7	—	-4.4	—	.20	—	.00
Sweden	—	28.1	23.2	15.0	—	36	60	50	—	-0.6	-1.0	-3.1	—	.20	.14	.00
United Kingdom	—	18.5	—	31.0	—	50	—	27	—	-0.6	—	-1.7	—	.48	—	.26
All countries	13.2	14.1	17.7	30.0	57	66	84	45	-1.0	-1.3	-4.5	-2.8	.12	.30	.19	.22

Abbreviations
FM   Formal minority
SM   Substantive minority
MC   Majority coalition
MP   Majority party
[a]Means
[b]Percentages

the favorable electoral performance of formal minority governments is in large part due to the two French cases.

Note finally that in general minority cabinets seem to perform best where they are most common. Consider Canada and Denmark, where substantive minority governments exceed the cross-national mean on all four performance indicators. It is evidently no accident that such cabinets get formed time and again in these countries, and this regularity supports the argument that rational anticipation is likely to produce minority cabinets in these polities.

Minority governments in office: a summary

This chapter has examined the record of minority governments once in office. I have asked two basic questions: How do minority cabinets build legislative majorities, and how well do minority governments serve the objectives of the parties that form them? In the first part of the chapter, I sketched out different majority-building strategies, gave examples, and analyzed the conditions most conducive to each. In the second part of the chapter, I have considered minority government performance relative to three stipulated objectives of political parties: office, policy, and votes.

The analysis of minority government performance leaves us with a surprisingly favorable impression of these cabinets. To be sure, undersized governments tend to be somewhat less durable than majority coalitions, and the participating parties are more likely to be replaced in subsequent cabinet transitions. On the other hand, minority governments enjoy substantial advantages in electoral success and are less likely to resign under traumatic circumstances. Clearly, minority governments are in most respects inferior to *single-party* majority cabinets. However, these two cabinet types are not alternatives to each other.

It would be reasonable to ask whether the observed differences between minority governments and majority coalitions are in reality spurious and caused by structural factors that predispose parties toward one cabinet solution or another. In a previous analysis I have addressed this issue by controlling for the set of determinants of government formation examined in Chapter 3. Although some of these factors did in fact interact with numerical status, none of the relationships we have found changed in any fundamental way when this set of controls was introduced. Interested readers can consult the published results (Strom, 1985).

Given the performance trade-offs between minority governments and majority coalitions, what choices should we expect rational parties to make? The most basic answer is that we certainly cannot rule out minority cabinets on performance grounds. To the extent that party leaders can accurately anticipate the performance differentials we have observed, there is no reason to expect them always to favor majority coalitions. On the contrary, *majority coalitions should be preferred only by parties that are strongly office motivated.* Policy-seeking and especially vote-seeking parties might well find minority governments to be a more attractive option. The more government stability a potential governing party is willing to trade off for policy effectiveness and electoral advantage, the more inclined it will be to opt for a minority cabinet. This is entirely consistent with the theoretical argument I developed in Chapter 2. To make sense of minority governments, we must assume that political parties (or their leaders) are future oriented (vote seekers), policy motivated, or preferably both. The empirical analysis shows that party leaders with such utility functions might indeed find minority governments especially attractive on the basis of their record in office.

The advantages of minority governments for such party leaders is of course no reason for the disinterested observer to take a benign view of this cabinet type. And we may ultimately want to determine what consequences minority government formation has for the political system as a whole, rather than just for the parties in government. This is too broad a question to answer in a general way here. However, the performance data we have examined may give us some leverage. Although these data were derived from a rational actor perspective on political parties, they may illuminate a functional question as well. In other words, if we knew the social value of different levels of alternation, government duration, electoral success, and circumstances of resignation, we might weigh the social costs and benefits of each cabinet type, just as I suggested in the calculus for each particular party.

There is no question that such a social calculus is much more complicated and controversial. It is difficult to say what optimal levels of alternation and electoral success might be, and whether minority governments or majority coalitions would be closer to these values. Alternation is commonly considered a key to accountability, and on this score minority cabinets have a clear advantage. However, a scenario in which the electorate invariably soured on the incumbents hardly suggests the ultimate political harmony. The societal value of office performance is a little less difficult to establish. Frequent changes of government between elections are rarely desirable. Neither are traumatic government resignations. On these grounds, however, the choice between majority coalitions and minority governments again becomes a trade-off.

This is as far as the data allow us to go in resolving this issue. In sum, minority governments have certain performance advantages and certain liabilities when compared to alternative cabinet solutions. At the very least, it is not clear that the bottom line is negative, either for parties considering participation in such cabinets or for the political system as a whole. In the concluding chapter, we shall consider these results in a broader context and examine their consequences for our theories of democratic party systems.

5. Italy: the politics of co-optation and defection

Chapter 2 argued the need to supplement the quantitative cross-national approach in the previous chapters with a small number of critical case studies. This chapter focuses on the Italian case. Beyond its value in the pairing with Norway, the Italian experience is singularly relevant to any effort to understand contemporary minority governments. One reason is simply the high overall number of minority cabinets, which at 20 is surpassed only by Denmark. The *proportion* of undersized cabinets is not equally high in cross-national terms, but at 42% Italy is well above the mean for the 15 nations in this study.

Italy also represents a geographic region replete with minority governments. However, the country is alone among the Southern European nations in having a continuous history of parliamentary democracy since World War II. Whether or not this longevity reflects political stability need not be addressed here (on this topic see, inter alia, Arian and Barnes, 1974; Di Palma, 1977; La Palombara 1987; Sartori, 1982; Tarrow, 1980). At any rate, historical continuity makes Italy a richer lode than France, Portugal, or Spain for present purposes. Besides, students of Italian politics have demonstrated a strong interest in government formation, and a multitude of scholars interested in party systems, coalitions, and parliamentary democracy have showered their attentions on Italy.

In sum, Italy represents a theoretically and numerically important case, as well as a polity in which government formations are widely perceived to be important phenomena. This chapter will present an evaluation and reinterpretation of the role of minority governments in Italian politics. With the possible exception of the French Fourth Republic, the feebleness and malaise associated with minority governments appear nowhere better demonstrated than in the history of

post-Fascist Italy. My task will be to present a more generous interpretation of these governments.

Italian parties and elections after fascism

The rebirth of Italian democracy after fascism was a slow and tortuous
process, beginning with the fall of Mussolini in 1943 and failing to
reach its completion until well after the election of the first legislature
in 1948. This prolonged gestation was clearly due to the delicate
nature of the project, given the diversity of the participants and the
lack of a strong tradition of mass democracy. Moreover, the major
protagonists, the Christian Democrats and the Communists, had virtually no prior experience in parliamentary government. As a consequence of this lack of tradition and experience, the postwar "rules
of the game" of Italian politics came to owe much to the process by
which the regime was founded.

In the words of Giorgo Galli (1972: 259) the Italian political system
is considerably more expressive than instrumental (see Gordon and
Babchuk, 1959). Processes of interest articulation are better institutionalized than policy making and implementation. Institutionally
this bias toward articulation has gone hand in hand with a virtual
monopolization of political power in the party system. Party government, or *partitocrazia,* is a crucial aspect of Italian politics, and the
extraordinary importance of political parties is due at least partly to
specific circumstances surrounding the birth of the post-Fascist political order. Between 1947 and 1949 the hammering out of a new
constitution coincided with the consolidation of the party system
(Galli, 1983).

The prominence of party government in Italy highlights the importance of political parties in cabinet formation and maintenance.
This is not to downgrade the importance of the political institution
in which the parties operate. Parliamentary parties are not uniformly
dominated by their respective extraparliamentary organizations, and
there is a measure of respect for parliamentary independence. This
autonomy of parliamentary parties varies from party to party. It has
tended to be stronger among the Christian Democrats (DC) than in
the Socialist party (PSI), and stronger again in the latter than in the

Communist party (PCI) or the Italian Social Movement (MSI) (Cotta, 1979; Manzella, 1977: 40–2). The parliamentary reform of February 1971 may have contributed to a general "parliamentarization" of the political parties, as a consequence of the enhancement of Parliament as a decision-making institution (Leonardi, Nanetti, and Pasquino, 1978).

In policy space the Italian parties can be meaningfully ordered along a left–right dimension.[1] Given the incidence of party births, deaths, mergers, and policy shifts, ordinal party placements along this dimension have varied over time (see Marradi, 1982: 49). However, the conception of one dominant spatial dimension is a useful device in the study of Italian politics. The parties themselves seek to project their images in these terms and have succeeded in transmitting their ideological images to a large segment of the electorate, which is quite adept at placing them accordingly. Almost 80% of Italian survey respondents have been able to place the two major parties correctly on the left–right dimension (Barnes, 1977: 97). A conventional ordering of the larger parliamentary parties, applicable to the greater part of the postwar period, puts the Communist party (PCI) at the far left, followed by the Socialists (PSI), the Social Democrats (PSLI/PSDI), the Republicans (PRI), the Christian Democrats (DC), the Liberals (PLI), the now-defunct Monarchists (PNM/PDIUM), and the neo-Fascist Italian Social Movement (MSI) at the extreme right. A recent content analysis of postwar Italian party programs confirms the primacy of the left–right dimension and the relative positions of the major parties (Mastropaolo and Slater, 1987).

Postwar elections

Italy has a bicameral legislature consisting of the Chamber of Deputies (Camera dei Deputati) with 630 deputies, and the Senate (Se-

---

[1] The Italian policy space is not unidimensional. Traditionally, the left–right dimension has been crosscut by a clerical–anticlerical axis, which separates the DC from the other parties of the political center. Second, some observers have argued that the left–right dimension may not be continuous. Terms like *arco costituzionale* (constitutional arch) and *area democratica* (democratic area), which have served to exclude the MSI (in both cases) and the PCI (in the latter case), attest to such discontinuities toward the extremes of the left–right dimension. These qualifications notwithstanding, the left–right dimension remains by far the most important ordering device for the Italian party system.

nato) with half as many members. Governments are responsible to both chambers equally. Although different versions of proportional representation are used in elections to the two chambers, the relative strength of the various parties has deviated little from one chamber to the other. The only noteworthy difference is that the small parties have found it somewhat more difficult to gain representation in the upper chamber (the Senate). The electoral system is on the whole rather free from distortion, except that the volatility of the minor parties is somewhat exacerbated (Seton-Watson, 1983; Wertman, 1977). Given the negligible differences in party representation between the two chambers, the electoral results in Table 5.1 pertain to the composition of the Chamber of Deputies only. Two tendencies stand out. One is the remarkable stability of DC representation over time, the other the comparative instability of some of the smaller parties (PLI, PRI, PNM). The parties at the extremes of the left–right dimension (the PCI and the MSI) gained steadily from the early 1950s to the mid-1970s, while the smaller parties of the so-called mezze ali ("half-wings") lost ground.

Table 5.2, which reports the distribution of votes (in percentage points) among the three blocs (left, center, and right) for postwar elections to the Chamber of Deputies, again illustrates the fundamental electoral stability of the Italian party system. In every election between 1953 and 1979 the center bloc hovered within three percentage points of half the total vote, and the DC and the PLI have until recently competed for a rather constant 45% of the electorate (Parisi and Pasquino, 1980). The strength of the center bloc is a crucial property of the type of party system Sartori has described as "polarized pluralism," and for which Italy is an obvious model (1976: 134ff).

Within this overall pattern of electoral stability, there has been a clear secular trend toward gains for the political left (in effect, the PCI) at the expense of the right and the minor parties of the center. The lay centrist parties (PSI, PSDI, PRI, PLI), which collectively controlled 181 seats in the Constituent Assembly of 1946 (32.6%), had by 1976 been reduced to 91 seats in the Chamber (or 14.4%). By 1987 they had rebounded enough to gain 143 seats (22.7%). The gradual decimation of the political right has been another crucial development in postwar Italy. The Italian Social Movement (MSI)

Table 5.1. *Composition of the Camera dei Deputati, 1946–87*

Party	1946	1948	1953	1958	1963	1968	1972	1976	1979	1983	1987
DP/PDUP	0	0	0	0	0	0	0	6	6	7	8
PR	0	0	0	0	0	0	0	4	18	11	13
Other leftist	11	1	0	1	1	23	1	1	1	0	0
PCI	104	133	143	140	166	177	179	227	201	198	177
PSI		50	75	84	87		61	57	62	73	94
PSU/PSIUP	115					91					
PSLI/PSDI		33	19	23	33		29	15	21	23	17
PRI	25	9	5	6	6	9	15	14	15	29	21
Other centrist	2	3	3	3	3	3	3	3	5	6	7
DC	207	307	263	273	260	266	266	262	261	225	234
PLI	41	18	13	17	39	31	20	5	9	16	11
PNM/rightist	51	14	40	25	8	6	0	0	0	0	0
MSI	0	6	29	24	27	24	56	36	31	42	35
LV	0	0	0	0	0	0	0	0	0	0	13
Total	556	574	590	596	630	630	630	630	630	630	630

Abbreviations

DP   Democrazia Proletaria (Proletarian Democracy)
PR   Partito Radicale (Radical party)
PCI   Partito Comunista Italiano (Communist party)
PSI   Partito Socialista Italiano (Socialist prty)
PSU   Partiti Socialista Unificati (United Socialist party)
PSDI Partito Socialista Democratico Italiano (Social Democratic party)
PRI   Partito Repubblicano Italiano (Republican party)
DC   Democrazia Cristiana (Christian Democrats)
PLI   Partito Liberale Italiano (Liberal party)
PNM   Partito Nazionale Monarchico (Monarchist party)
MSI   Movimento Sociale Italiano (Italian Social Movement)
LV   Lista Verde (Green List).

Note that several of these parties have contested one or more elections under names and labels that differ from those listed here.
Sources: Adapted from Mackie and Rose (1982); Marradi (1982: 40–1); *European Journal of Political Research*, various issues.

Table 5.2. *Voting blocs in Italian elections, 1946–87 (percentages of popular vote for the Camera dei Deputati)*

Bloc	1946	1948	1953	1958	1963	1968	1972	1976	1979	1983	1987
Right	5.3	4.8	12.7	9.6	6.9	5.8	8.7	6.1	5.9	7.0	5.9
Center	46.3	62.4	49.7	52.3	53.2	52.3	51.1	47.0	47.6	45.0	46.3
Left	42.0	31.0	35.4	37.6	39.3	41.0	40.1	46.6	45.9	45.0	47.8

Source: Parisi and Pasquino (1980); see also Table 5.1.

continues to have some numerical weight, although no bargaining power, in Italian politics, but the now-defunct Monarchists and conservative forces in the DC and the PLI have fared poorly. In recent years there have basically been only two subcultural voting blocs in Italy: the left and the center–right.

Within the period of leftist gains at the expense of the center-right, the only abrupt shift occurred between the elections of 1972 and 1976. As a consequence of a lowered voting age, nearly 10% of the 1976 voters were participating for the first time, a proportion almost twice as large as for the average postwar election (Sani, 1977a, b). This cohort looked much more favorably on the parties of the left than the generation it replaced. It has been estimated that in 1974 the PCI was favored by 38% of the youngest voters (18–21 years old), a proportion more than twice as large as that of any other party. In 1978 the PCI was the party of choice of 39% of those 25 or younger, as opposed to a support rate of only 17% among voters 55 or older (Farneti, 1985: 102–3). The PCI maintained its appeal to the youngest cohorts at least through the 1979 election (Amyot, 1980; Penniman, 1987).

Floating voters and issue voting have become more common over time but still appear to have been much less responsible for the "earthquake" in favor of the PCI than turnover in the electorate. Even between the elections of 1972 and 1975 (regional elections), 91.8% of those voting for the center–right and almost 99% of the supporters of the left at the latter juncture claimed to have made the same choice three years earlier (Sani, 1977a: 83). And although the subcultural basis of Italian party politics is weakening, individual voter volatility remains low, particularly between the two major blocs (Farneti, 1985; Sani, 1980). However, within-bloc vote switching has become a more common occurrence.

The postwar governments

The subcultural nature of political partisanship and the modest volatility of the electorate (except for the constituencies of the minor parties) have had profound consequences for government formation in Italy. The volatility of Italian governments is customarily noted, and the underlying continuity of the postwar record is almost equally commonplace. Italy accounts for a larger number of governments than any other country in my sample, and only Denmark rivals the number of minority governments formed in Italy since the end of World War II (20 of 48). On the other hand, just as evidently partisan composition and personnel have changed very little from government to government (Calise and Mannheimer, 1979, 1982; Marradi, 1982). In fact, the large number of cabinets can be reduced to a modest number of phases or formulas. The Christian Democrats have been a pivotal member of every postwar government, and between 1946 and 1981 every Italian cabinet was headed by a DC premier. Even the partisan distribution of the various ministerial departments has remained remarkably stable, and particular individuals have retained the same portfolios for extended periods of time (Marradi, 1982: 60–6).

As Table 5.3 indicates, there have been 28 majority coalitions, 16 substantive minority governments, and 4 formal minority governments in Italy since June 1946. Note the absence of majority party governments, despite DC majorities in both houses between 1948 and 1953. The cabinets formed in this five-year period thus violate the strong expectation of majority party governments in majority situations. Since the 1953 election, however, no majority situation has ever occurred. In the 43 postwar minority situations, undersized governments have formed in almost half the cases. On the other hand, numerically unnecessary coalition members are an equally persistent characteristic of Italian governments.

The mean parliamentary basis of postwar Italian governments is 51.7%, with extrema of 35% and 81%. Fourteen cabinets have enjoyed less than 45% support, whereas seven have been in a position to count on more than 60% of the legislators. The mean parliamentary basis of majority coalitions is as high as 58%. These figures confirm the tendency for Italian governments to diverge rather markedly from minimum winning size (Marradi, 1982; Pappalardo, 1978). Most oversized Italian governments have in fact included several unnecessary parties, and several of the smaller parties have hardly been pivotal to any coalition in which they have participated. At the extreme, the PRI has been pivotal in only 1 of the 23 governments in which it has taken part.[2]

The number of governments formed per legislative term has remained fairly constant, but the distribution of cabinet types has varied rather sharply from one legislature to the next.[3] During most legislative periods majority coalitions have predominated, typically with only one or two undersized aberrations. However, during the second, third, and seventh legislatures minority cabinets were rife. These were transitional periods between different coalition patterns or formulas: from centrism to the center-left in the second and third legislatures, and from the center-left to the brief period of "governments of national solidarity" in the seventh. Only in the first legislature and after 1987 have there been no minority governments. The absence of minority governments in the first legislature is easily explained by the absolute parliamentary majority enjoyed by the Christian Democrats during these years.

Formal minority governments have formed according to no easily discernible pattern. No more than one has formed during any legislature. There has been a slight tendency for formal minority governments to form during legislatures when substantive minority governments have also been numerous. Half of the 16 substantive minority cabinets have formed in the four legislatures that also have featured a formal minority government, with the other 8 substantive minority governments spread over the remaining seven legislative terms.

External support

Not all 16 substantive minority governments have lacked support agreements with parties outside the cabinet. On the contrary, most

---

[2] Even in the single case where the PRI was pivotal (Fanfani IV), its necessity was more apparent than real, since the cabinet was externally supported by the Socialists.
[3] The first legislature met from 1948 to 1953, the second from 1953 to 1958, and so forth. The assembly that met from 1946 to 1948 is referred to as the Constituent Assembly.

Table 5.3. *Italian governments, 1946–87*

Government	Formation date	Demission date	Tenure (months)	Parties	Parliam. base	Formation attempts	Type
De Gasperi II	Jul 46	Jan 47	6	DC, PCI, PSIUP, PRI	81	2	MC
De Gasperi III	Feb 47	May 47	3	DC, PCI, PSI	69	1	MC
De Gasperi IV	May 47	Dec 47	7	DC	37	5	SM
De Gasperi V	Dec 47	May 48	5	DC, PLI, PSLI, PRI	56	1	MC
De Gasperi VI	May 48	Oct 49	17	DC, PLI, PSLI, PRI	63	1	MC
De Gasperi VII	Nov 49	Jan 50	2	DC, PLI, PRI	58	1	MC
De Gasperi VIII	Jan 50	Apr 51	14	DC, PSLI, PRI	60	2	MC
De Gasperi IX	Apr 51	Jul 51	3	DC, PRI	54	1	MC
De Gasperi X	Jul 51	Jun 53	23	DC, PRI	54	2	MC
De Gasperi XI	Jul 53	Jul 53	0	DC	44	4	SM
Pella	Aug 53	Jan 54	5	DC	44	2	SM
Fanfani I	Jan 54	Jan 54	0	DC	44	2	SM
Scelba	Feb 54	Jun 55	16	DC, PLI, PSDI	50	2	MC
Segni I	Jul 55	May 57	22	DC, PLI, PSDI	50	2	MC
Zoli	May 57	Jun 58	13	DC	44	2	SM
Fanfani II	Jul 58	Jan 59	7	DC, PSDI	49	2	SM
Segni II	Feb 59	Feb 60	12	DC	45	2	SM
Tambroni	Mar 60	Jul 60	4	DC	45	4	SM
Fanfani III	Jul 60	Feb 62	19	DC	45	1	FM
Fanfani IV	Feb 62	May 63	15	DC, PSDI, PRI	50	1	MC
Leone I	Jun 63	Nov 63	5	DC	41	2	SM
Moro I	Dec 63	Jun 64	7	DC, PSI, PSDI, PRI	61	1	MC
Moro II	Jul 64	Jan 66	18	DC, PSI, PSDI, PRI	61	2	MC
Moro III	Feb 66	Jun 68	27	DC, PSI, PSDI, PRI	61	2	MC
Leone II	Jun 68	Nov 68	5	DC	42	2	SM
Rumor I	Dec 68	Jul 69	7	DC, PSU, PRI	58	1	MC
Rumor II	Aug 69	Feb 70	6	DC	42	2	FM
Rumor III	Mar 70	Jul 70	3	DC, PSI, PSDI, PRI	58	4	MC

Colombo I	Aug 70	Mar 71	7	DC, PSI, PSDI, PRI	58	MC
Colombo II	Mar 71	Jan 72	10	DC, PSI, PSDI	56	MC
Andreotti I	Feb 72	Feb 72	0	DC	42	SM
Andreotti II	Jun 72	Jun 73	12	DC, PSDI, PLI	50	MC
Rumor IV	Jul 73	Mar 74	8	DC, PSI, PSDI, PRI	58	MC
Rumor V	Mar 74	Oct 74	7	DC, PSI, PSDI	56	MC
Moro IV	Nov 74	Jan 76	14	DC, PRI	44	FM
Moro V	Feb 76	Apr 76	3	DC	42	SM
Andreotti III	Jul 76	Jan 78	18	DC	41	SM
Andreotti IV	Mar 78	Jan 79	11	DC	41	FM
Andreotti V	Mar 79	Mar 79	0	DC, PSDI, PRI	46	SM
Cossiga I	Aug 79	Mar 80	8	DC, PSDI, PLI	46	SM
Cossiga II	Apr 80	Sep 80	6	DC, PSI, PRI	54	MC
Forlani	Oct 80	May 81	7	DC, PSI, PSDI, PRI	57	MC
Spadolini I	Jun 81	Aug 82	13	PRI, DC, PSI, PSDI, PLI	58	MC
Spadolini II	Aug 82	Nov 82	3	PRI, DC, PSI, PSDI, PLI	58	MC
Fanfani V	Nov 82	Apr 83	5	DC, PSI, PSDI, PLI	56	MC
Craxi	Aug 83	Apr 87	45	PSI, DC, PRI, PSDI, PLI	58	MC
Fanfani VI	Apr 87	Apr 87	0	DC	35	SM
Goria	Jul 87	NA	NA	DC, PSI, PRI, PSDI, PLI	59	MC

Abbreviations
MC Majority coalition
SM Substantive minority
FM Formal minority
See Table 5.1 for party abbreviations.
Source: Keesing's Contemporary Archives.

minority governments have enjoyed some sort of outside support. We shall explore these relationships more closely later. But the critical point is that most Italian support agreements have differed from *formal minority* arrangements in the following ways:

1. In some cases the support parties have not been pivotal; that is, their votes have not sufficed to put the government over the majority threshold. This was the case for Segni's second cabinet, formed in February 1959. Even with the external support of the PLI, the government fell eight votes short of a majority in the Camera dei Deputati. Aldo Moro's fifth government, externally supported by the Social Democrats, represents a similar case of more recent vintage.

2. Some support agreements had not been negotiated prior to the formation of the government and are therefore discounted. The Zoli government of 1957–8 is one such case, in which this DC *monocolore* found itself dependent upon the unnegotiated and undesirable support of the extreme right.

3. Finally, there have been cases where the commitment of outside parties has been insufficiently strong and explicit. The Andreotti III government of *non sfiducia* (lack of no confidence) came to power after a vote of investiture in which it received no more than 152 favorable votes from the 605 deputies present. Most parties abstained on this vote, however, making it possible for Andreotti's *monocolore* to accede to power with a minimum of positive support.

In sum, although many Italian governments have lacked a precommitted legislative majority, it would be a mistake to conclude that they have had to seek parliamentary support on a purely ad hoc basis. The latter option has occasionally been attempted, but without much success.

The government formation process

The process of government formation begins with the president's designation (*incarico*) of a prime ministerial candidate. Normally the designate has been a DC representative (though not necessarily the effective leader of that party), although in recent years there have been exceptions, such as La Malfa (PRI) in 1979 (Manzella, 1980), Craxi (PSI) in 1979 and 1983, and Spadolini (PRI) in 1981 and 1982. Among these, Spadolini was the first to succeed. Yet, the selection of a new premier is at the discretion of neither the DC leadership nor the president of the Republic. The president has been most in- fluential when the prospective coalition partners have been dead- locked over their choice, something that most recently occurred with the designation of Tambroni in 1960 (Marradi, 1982). Even then, candidates handpicked by the president have faced considerable dif- ficulties in their relations with Parliament. Nor have the Christian Democrats effectively been able to determine the choice of prime minister. With the fractionalization of the DC in the 1960s and 1970s, its smaller alliance partners became increasingly effective in picking a prime minister from among the factional contenders within the DC. At the very least, the minor parties have often succeeded in blocking unwanted candidates (Lombardo, 1977: 185–90).

With the designation of a prime-ministerial candidate, negotiations begin between the designate and the "permissible" parties in Parlia- ment. During this phase, portfolio distributions and cabinet policy are negotiated, and even party factions may have to be accommodated in this bargaining process. The final negotiated draft of the govern- ment's policy program then needs the ratification of each party in the coalition. Portfolio distributions, however, quickly boil down to in- traparty squabbles between factions that often represent little more than different political clienteles (Zuckerman, 1979).

When agreement has been reached and ratified, the premier- designate approaches the president with a list of ministers, whereupon the latter nominates the new government. The subsequent inaugu- ration legally marks the formation of a new government and must be distinguished from the preceding designation of a prime-ministerial candidate (Galizia, 1972). Within 10 days the government must pre- sent itself to Parliament with an address (*indirizzo*), in which it spells out its program. Each house of Parliament then proceeds to a vote of investiture. Even if the government fails the vote of investiture, as happened with De Gasperi XI, Fanfani I and VI, and Andreotti I and V, its official status is not negated (Mannino, 1973; Manzella, 1977: 218, 262–4). Hence, even governments that never gained the confidence of Parliament are included in the official record (see Table

Table 5.4. *Italian cabinet crises, 1946–1987: crisis duration and formation attempts (mean values)*

Cabinet type	Crisis duration (days)	Formation attempts
Majority coalition	27.1	1.56
Formal minority	36.0	2.00
Substantive minority	33.7	2.75
All governments	30.0	2.02

5.3). The vote of investiture is essentially a manifestation of the battle lines facing the new administration.

As one would expect, government formation takes time. Table 5.4 presents the average crisis duration and formation attempts for the various cabinet types since 1946. The duration of a cabinet crisis is measured from the date of resignation of one government to the date of nomination for the next. Formation attempts are, as usual, counted on the basis of sets of designated prime ministers *and* intended parties.

There is clear evidence that minority governments have tended to follow longer crises and more formation attempts than majority co-alitions. Evidently, Italian political leaders almost invariably look for a majoritarian solution initially. Only one undersized government has formed in a first attempt, namely, the formal minority government headed by Amintore Fanfani in July 1960. The political situation that occasioned this cabinet was especially precarious, given the explosive civil unrest that provoked the resignation of the preceding Tambroni government.

Cabinet types differ less in crisis duration, but there is a clear evolution over time. During the first legislature, it took an average of 8.8 days to compose a new government. By the seventh legislature (1976–9), the corresponding figure had risen to no less than 64 days. Every cabinet crisis from November 1974 through the 1970s lasted a good month or considerably more. Incidentally, all governments formed during this period were undersized. In the 1980s the record has been more mixed, with the cabinet crises preceding Craxi and Goria each lasting more than three months but other crises much less protracted. On the whole, crisis duration has varied more over time than between different cabinet types. Before the watershed elections of 1963, majority governments took an average of 10.5 days to form and minority governments 16.7. After that date, the averages have been 37.8 versus 48.4 days.

Have Italian minority governments formed in the wake of particularly severe political crises? The data indicate that the answer is no. Minority cabinets have often succeeded governments that had resigned for innocuous reasons. For example, undersized administrations account for 6 of 11 governments formed immediately after general elections. In most of these cases, the preceding government had resigned simply because the legislative term had expired. In conclusion, Italian minority cabinets hardly ever emerge as a first choice, and their formation takes time. But their occurrence is not necessarily a symptom of systemic crisis.

Explaining minority governments: the party system

The high frequency of minority governments in Italy has often been associated with the "Italian crisis," which so dominated scholarship on Italian politics in the 1970s. Toward the middle of the turbulent half-decade of continuous minority rule (November 1974 to April 1980), Giuseppe Di Palma observed that Italy was facing "the most prolonged and sustained period of social conflict, turmoil, and even violence in its postwar history" (1977b: xi). Although the diagnoses of the crisis have varied widely, minority governments have commonly been viewed as a symptom. Let us therefore investigate some specifically *political* circumstances that may help account for these symptoms. *Fragmentation* and *polarization* of the party system are two such factors.

Fragmentation

Polarization and fragmentation are intuitively plausible candidate explanations of minority government formation.[4] Table 5.5 presents

[4] Throughout this chapter, I make reference to *extremist* parties. This label is a conventional way to refer to certain parties toward the ends of the Italian left–right dimension, which have not been considered "permissible" for government participa-

Table 5.5. *Polarization and fractionalization in Italian elections, 1946–87*

Election	Polarization		Fragmentation (Rae's F)	Cabinets
	Seats	Votes		
1946	.299	.306	.722	3 MC, 1 SM
1948	.268	NA	.652	5 MC
1953	.359	.375	.718	2 MC, 4 SM
1958	.319	.329	.710	1 MC, 1 FM, 3 SM
1963	.321	.327	.733	3 MC, 1 SM
1968	.365	.376	.717	4 MC, 1 FM, 2 SM
1972	.375	.391	.719	3 MC, 1 FM, 1 SM
1976	.425	.420	.683	1 FM, 2 SM
1979	.378	.371	.710	5 MC, 1 SM
1983	.392	.382	.751	1 MC, 1 SM
1987	.349	.342	.754	1 MC

Note: No vote polarization score for 1948 can be computed since the PCI and the PSI presented joint lists in that election.
Abbreviations
MC   Majority coalition
SM   Substantive minority
FM   Formal minority.

polarization and fragmentation measures for all postwar Italian leg-islatures.[5] There is little evidence that fragmentation of the party system has been a particularly severe problem in Italy, or that frag-mentation bears any causal relation to the formation of undersized governments. Only four elections have produced F scores above the 15-country mean (.720), and between 1953 and 1979 fractionalization remained remarkably stable. In the mid-1970s, the share of the poll won by the two largest parties was almost equal to the corresponding figure for Great Britain. The average F score under which majority coalitions have formed is .714, that for minority governments a vir-tually identical .716. Moreover, the legislatures that have experienced a high incidence of minority governments show no deviation in fractionalization.

tion. I do not mean to imply that these parties are revolutionary or extremist in any absolute sense.
  [5] I have counted the PCI, the MSI, the Monarchists, and some minor leftist and rightist parties as extremist. Figures are for the Chamber of Deputies.

Polarization

Polarization is much more obviously a problem and a probable cause of minority cabinets. Until 1976 the percentage of seats held by "non-permissible" parties varied between 27 and 44, with a clear upward trend. What these figures mainly reflect, of course, is the steady growth of the Italian Communist party. As the PCI gained at the expense of the smaller parties of the political center, fractionalization scores declined, reflecting a trend toward party duopoly. However, the decline of the two-party share after 1976 has gone hand in hand with a decrease in polarization and reduced support for the PCI.

This simple scrutiny of polarization and fragmentation levels reveals their inadequacy as explanations of minority government formation in Italy. Not only do we need knowledge of the *format* of the party system, but it is also necessary to understand the *dynamics* of party strategy and government formation. The structure of the Italian party system is not responsible for its pattern of government formation in any straightforward and deterministic way. True, the payoff structure facing the parties has been generated by the institutions, the policy space, and the preferences of the electorate. But these payoffs, and the resulting incentives facing the parties, have varied widely between parties and over time. Besides, government formations in Italy have less often been mutually independent events than pieces of longer-term interparty bargains. For these reasons we need to understand the nature of party competition in Italy in historical context. In other words, we are required to "take the historical cure" (Almond, Flanagan, and Mundt, 1973).

The history of Italian coalition formulas

Most government formations in postwar Italy can best be understood as realizations of distinct longer-term coalition formulas, reached in an ongoing process of bargaining between a relatively large number of players at several levels (parties and factions). This bargaining environment has been complex and the players constrained, more by the parties' internal commitments than by such external forces as the constitution or foreign states. For a variety of reasons that will become clearer as we proceed, the solutions that have been reached have rarely been very stable, and government formation therefore has often taken place in an environment characterized by uncertainty and testing of the bounds of existing relationships.

Roughly, the history of government formation in postwar Italy can be divided into the following periods:

1. Emergency coalitions of the major parties (1945–7);
2. Centrism (1947–53);
3. Crisis of centrism (1953–62);
4. The center-left (1962–72);
5. Crisis of the center-left (1972–6);
6. Governments of national solidarity (1976–9); and
7. Five-partyism (*pentapartio*) (1979–).

The early postwar years brought the DC, the PSI, and the PCI together in government, in a type of grand coalition that has never been attempted since 1947. With the onset of the Cold War, the Marxists were excluded from power, initiating a period of centrist governments, including the DC, the PLI, the PSDI, and the PRI. Centrism was under attack from 1953 on, when the Republicans withdrew from cabinet participation. In 1955 and 1956 PSI participation in government began to look increasingly feasible, but only in 1962 was centrism replaced with another stable formula, the center-left. This "opening to the left" ushered in the PSI, whereas the Liberals left the government majority. Before the breakthrough of the center-left there had been attempts (most notably Pella, Zoli, and Tambroni) to construct a center-right coalition with the support of the PNM, the MSI, or both. Neither of these two parties was ever brought into the cabinet or the official parliamentary majority, however, and the center-right was finally abandoned after the polarizing effects of Tambroni's government. The center-left reigned supreme until the withdrawal of the PSI from the majority in 1972 (Tamburrano, 1973). The 1970s witnessed a variety of unstable coalitions, including a half way version of the historic compromise between the Christian Democrats and the Communists, as well as renewals of centrism and the center-left. After the 1979 elections, a new five-party coalition was gradually developed, which for the first time included both Socialists and Liberals. In a departure from previous coalitions, governments in the 1980s have typically been headed by prime ministers from one of the smaller coalition parties, or from a new generation of Christian Democrats.

The existence of one dominant coalitional formula has critically affected most Italian cabinet formations. Old formulas have been abandoned because they have been perceived as politically ineffective, or, more important, because their majorities have been eroded. Thus, centrism ceased to be a majority alternative in 1968. Successive stages or formulas have taken the form of a continuous search for broader-based and more stable majorities. Clearly this quest has been a reaction to the centrifugal (center-fleeing) character of electoral competition, that is, the gradual electoral erosion of the centrist parties, particularly from the early 1950s to the late 1970s. This unfavorable electoral trend was particularly evident under the center-left formula.

When minority governments form in the Italian system, it is occasionally because not all members of the dominant coalition wish full government participation. Very rarely is such exclusion forced upon the parties; it is normally a matter of voluntary abstention. But although some undersized cabinets have formed due to the withdrawal of certain members of an established coalition formula (Leone II and Rumor II are cases in point), minority governments have been much more frequent when there has been no established formula. The years from 1953 to 1962 and from 1972 to 1980 exemplify this tendency. During these two periods combined, 15 of a total of 20 governments were undersized. During all other periods, only 5 of 28 governments have been below the majority threshold. Minority governments thus have formed most frequently when the parties have not been overconstrained by any specific coalition formula. Oversized governments, on the other hand, have prevailed when one formula has been dominant. Interestingly, then, bargaining constraints seem to *diminish* the likelihood of undersized cabinets.[6]

The search for broad majorities has coincided with the electoral

[6] It is of course possible that longer-term coalition formulas can be established only when the participating parties are relatively *unconstrained* in their behavior by factional demands, prior commitments, etc. If so, it would be misleading to associate minority governments with a lack of such constraints. See, however, the later discussion of why the smaller parties in particular may face substantial electoral incentives to bolt from existing coalitions.

erosion representative of "centrifugal" electoral competition (Sartori, 1976). Note the poor performance of the centrist parties in the 1953 elections and the similarly distressing fate of the parties of the center-left in 1968. Both of these elections took place in situations of particularly broad coalition formulas. Have oversized coalitions therefore caused centrifugal competition? The answer may well be yes. In polarized polities, where parties have very diverse policy positions, the construction of broad, oversized majorities has two obvious and fateful consequences. One is that such coalitions necessarily bring together parties with highly divergent policy objectives. Presumably, this increases the likelihood that each party will behave inconsistently with its previous policy positions, as well as the probability of policy-based tension or even deadlock in the governing coalition. Both of these effects are likely to be electoral liabilities. The second important implication of oversized coalitions under these circumstances is that all reasonably moderate parties are likely to be in government, which renders the opposition fairly extremist. Hence, the first consequence is policy compromises, a circumstance that easily leaves the supporters of all coalition parties disaffected. The second consequence is that these disgruntled voters have nowhere to go but to an extremist opposition. To the extent that voters punish inconsistent parties, oversized policy-diverse coalitions are particularly vulnerable.

This pattern of government formation and its electoral consequences help us understand the progressive polarization of the Italian party system between the 1950s and the 1970s. More than electoral politics, it was governmental politics that pulled voters away from the political center. The lack of a loyal and responsible opposition among the "permissible" parties propelled disaffected voters toward the extremist parties. Thus, these parties (particularly the PCI and the MSI, but also some of the smaller left-wing parties) gradually gained in strength. The gains of the PCI were halted only when that party too became tainted with the ploys, corruption, and ineffectiveness of government.

This Italian form of polarization is compatible with trends toward convergence between centrist and extremist parties (e.g., the DC and the PCI). As a matter of fact, syncretism through co-optation and enlargement of the governing area is the classical Italian response to polarization (Di Palma, 1978), as well as a cause of its perpetuation.

As the PCI has moved toward the governing area, new parties such as the Demoproletarians and the Radicals have emerged as contenders for its favored position on the left (McCarthy, 1981).

My point is that *centrifugal electoral competition is a consequence of certain patterns of coalition formation rather than an inherent tendency in party systems of a particular format.* If this is correct, there may be an alternative to voter flight from the political center, even in a party system such as the Italian one. If government coalitions were constructed more narrowly, policy compromises would be less electorally damaging, and there would be a more credible loyal opposition to absorb the losses of the incumbents. In the Italian case, this possibility seems realistic enough, given the large number of minority governments in situations with no compelling coalition formula. If the Christian Democrats had continued the practice of "pendular" coalitions from the late 1950s and alternated between left-leaning and right-leaning coalitions, then perhaps some of the crises of the 1970s could have been avoided. Of course, for such a scenario to be plausible, the effectiveness of minority cabinets must not have been too seriously questioned, and the pendular solution must have been in the interest of the dominant players, especially the DC leadership. We shall consider these issues in later sections of this chapter.

Italy as a captive government system

In the cross-national analysis, I classified Italy as a *captive government* system, which means that both the policy benefits and the electoral costs that follow from government incumbency are comparatively low. In other words, the stakes of government formation are low. I have argued that minority governments tend to form where there are substantial disincentives to office holding, that is, where the costs exceed the benefits. Since both costs and benefits are low in captive government systems, we should expect an intermediate frequency of minority governments.

The classification of Italy as a captive government system was based on two assessments. First, I found that the potential policy influence of the Italian parliamentary opposition was comparatively high. Second, I concluded that parliamentary elections in Italy were characterized by low competitiveness and in particular that elections did not appear decisive for subsequent bargaining power. These assessments were necessarily based on somewhat sketchy evidence. We shall now investigate these variables in greater detail, beginning with the influence of the opposition in the Italian national assembly.

Opposition influence

My characterization of the Italian Parliament as one in which the opposition can exercise substantial policy influence was based on four characteristics of the parliamentary committee structure that generally favor the opposition:

1. There is a relatively large number of standing legislative committees.
2. These committees have fixed areas of jurisdiction.
3. Their jurisdictions generally correspond to those of the ministerial departments.
4. There are restrictions on the number of committee assignments each legislator can receive.

This image of the Italian Parliament is reinforced as we take a more comprehensive look at the institution. There are several formal differences in structure between the two chambers, but these are more apparent than real. Most notably, the number of committees differs between the two legislative chambers, as the lower house has 14 and the Senate 12. However, their respective areas of jurisdiction are very similar, in that the Chamber of Deputies simply has two committees (Internal Affairs and Transportation) in addition to those found in the Senate. Every Italian parliamentarian is given a committee assignment by his parliamentary group (caucus). With a couple of minor exceptions, every representative serves on one and only one committee, and, at least in the lower house, strict interparty proportionality is maintained.

All legislative bills, government or private, must go through a three-stage process of deliberation. In both chambers, parts of this process may take place on the floor and parts in committee. Normal parliamentary procedure requires that article-by-article approbation and the final comprehensive vote take place on the floor, but there also exists a decentralized procedure, which delegates the whole process to committee. Certain critical legislation, such as constitutional amendments and international treaties, much go through the ordinary procedure and be reported to the floor, but otherwise there is no clear relationship between type of legislation and procedure (Manzella, 1977: 317–18). Interestingly enough, government bills tend to be enacted in committee more often than private bills. In numerical terms, approximately two-thirds of all legislation goes through the decentralized (committee) procedure (Di Palma, 1977).

There are several distinguishing features of the decentralized procedure, as opposed to the ordinary route. One is that the extremist opposition always has enough strength for provocations and obstructionism on the floor, whereas such behavior is unthinkable in committee. The floor is thus the best arena for oppositional blockage and grandstanding, although overt obstructionism was rare until the 1970s.[7] However, the decentralized procedure offers better opportunities for constructive policy influence. As Di Palma notes, "The committees are not only the place where most legislation is enacted, but also the place where the smaller parties, and to some extent the PCI, have the best opportunity, through amending, to influence even government legislation" (1977: 63).

On the whole, the decentralized procedure also offers better prospects for legislative passage. Hence, the strength of the opposition is strategically located. In sum, the legislative procedure of the Italian Parliament is clearly conducive to oppositional influence.

Yet such legislative influence may be illusory if Parliament is a weak and inefficient institution, as is commonly argued (e.g., Di Palma, 1977; Galli and Prandi, 1970). Allegedly Parliament has been able to reach decisions only on minor and innocuous matters. So although most legislation proposed by Italian governments traditionally has been approved in relatively short time (Mortara, 1976; Motta, 1985), the vast majority of legislation consists of what Italians call *leggine* (literally, "small laws," legislation of minor significance). Yet this weakness on the part of Parliament has not caused a gravitation

---

[7] This is not to say that obstructionism has been nonexistent. The Communists could make life difficult for their adversaries during the height of the Cold War, and in the 1970s and 1980s the Radical party and the extreme right have engaged in various forms of filibustering. See Bartolini (1982) and Manzella (1977).

of power to other political institutions. The shortcomings of the Council of Ministers (cabinet), for example, are every bit as evident as those of the Parliament (Cassese, 1980). The "Italian crisis" may have weakened the effectiveness of the political system, but, if anything, it strengthened the hand of Parliament. To the PCI, a stronger national assembly was a keystone of the democratization process the party wanted Italian political institutions to undergo. The growing influence of the PCI in the 1970s therefore meant a parliamentarization of Italian political life (Bartolini, 1982; Pappalardo, 1978). And the parliamentary reforms of 1971 arguably improved the decisional efficacy of the national assembly (Leonardi et al., 1978: 167–9). The potential policy influence of the legislative opposition is enhanced by the prevailing subculture among Italian political leaders. Politicians favor the decision rule of proportionalism over majoritarianism, and the former is of course much more compatible than the latter with oppositional influence (Fisichella, 1975; Putnam, 1973).

Elections without choice

We have now found substantiation for half of the classification of Italy as a captive government system. We next need to consider the extent to which Italian elections affect coalitional bargaining power. As noted previously, in a captive government system the linkage between electoral fortunes and legislative bargaining power should be tenuous. In operational terms, electoral decisiveness should be low. Recall that electoral decisiveness has four components: (1) identifiability of pre-electoral government alternatives, (2) electoral competitiveness, (3) responsiveness of government formations to electoral verdicts, and (4) temporal proximity of government formations to elections. Let us consider these variables successively.

Identifiability

The identifiability of Italian government options has generally been low. Although certain parties clearly have been identified with the government (e.g., the DC) and others with the opposition (e.g., the

PR), most parties have eschewed commitments concerning participation in specific cabinets, and the minor parties have often entered and left government rather unpredictably over the course of
the legislative term. Yet identifiability has varied from election to
election. It reached its peak in 1948 and 1953, when the parties of
the center coalition sought to demarcate themselves sharply from
the Marxist opposition. The 1953 election was contested under the
so-called *legge maggioritaria* (majoritarian law), which would have
given 65% of the parliamentary seats to any electoral coalition
with a popular vote majority. This electoral scheme, promoted by
Mario Scelba and referred to by its detractors as the *legge truffa*
(swindle law), became tremedously unpopular even among some
of its intended beneficiaries and was abandoned shortly after the
centrist coalition narrowly failed to capture the anticipated majority prize.

But the 1953 election was atypical in the clarity of choices presented. Even though the elections of 1963 and 1968 were in some
sense referenda on the center-left coalition, the link between partisan and governmental choice was far from clear, as evidenced by the
fact that DC *monocolori* (rather than organic center-left coalitions)
followed both elections. In the elections of 1958, 1972, and 1976,
government identifiability was extremely low, and over time identifiability has declined markedly. Even in the early postwar period,
however, Italy ranked low by cross-national standards (Corbetta and
Parisi, 1986).

Electoral competitiveness

The levels of electoral volatility in Italian postwar elections are presented in Table 5.6.[8] Recall for comparative purposes that the cross-
national mean is .11. Only two Italian elections have exceeded this
level, whereas the remaining eight have fallen below, in many cases
by considerable margins. The only high scores are in fact those of
the two earliest elections. As soon as the party system was consolidated, electoral volatility dropped dramatically, and it has remained

---

[8] No volatility scores are available for 1946, since there is no prior basis point for
calculation.

Table 5.6. *Volatility in Italian elections, 1948–87*

Election	Volatility
1948	0.215
1953	0.131
1958	0.044
1963	0.079
1968	0.068
1972	0.054
1976	0.094
1979	0.052
1983	0.068
1987	0.075

Sources: Adapted from Mackie (1988: 580); Mackie and Rose (1982; 1984: 339); Marradi (1982: 40–1).

moderate to low ever since.[9] Recall from Table 5.2 that the size of the major voting blocs also has been quite stable from election to election. The exceptional cases here are 1948, 1953, and 1976. Thus, Italian elections have rarely produced drastic changes in the numerical balance between competing party coalitions (Corbetta and Parisi, 1986).

Responsiveness

Electoral responsiveness is the third element of electoral decisiveness we shall consider. On the responsiveness scale from zero (only losers forming cabinets) to 1 (winners exclusively) Italy scores .48 for the postwar period as a whole. This means that recent electoral losers are slightly overrepresented among governing parties. In most countries, gainers are somewhat more likely to take office than losers, and such a tendency is certainly a requisite for electoral responsiveness. Comparatively, Italy ranks 11th among 15 countries in electoral responsiveness.

Although Italy is not the only country to exhibit "negative" responsiveness, this perverse relation detracts seriously from overall electoral decisiveness. Table 5.7 breaks the Italian responsiveness

[9] Using a different volatility measure, Giacomo Sani arrives at substantially the same conclusion (1977b: 91–93).

Table 5.7. *Responsiveness and proximity by decade, 1946–87 (mean values)*

Variable	1940s	1950s	1960s	1970s	1980s	CN Mean
Responsiveness	.29	.30	.66	.47	.62	.58
Proximity	.33	.18	.20	.23	.25	.49

Abbreviation: CN mean = mean value for cross-national sample.

score down by decade of government formation. Note that responsiveness has varied considerably, from exceptionally low values in the 1940s and 1950s to substantially higher levels in the 1960s and 1980s. The difference is again in large part due to the inclusion or exclusion of the smaller lay parties. Their regular inclusion in the cabinet boosts the scores for the 1960s and 1980s, especially compared to the 1950s.

Proximity

On the last component of electoral decisiveness, the temporal proximity of government formations to elections, the Italian score is as low as .22. This puts the country ahead only of Fourth Republic France. In the average country approximately half of all governments form directly after elections; the mean proximity score for the 15 countries is .49. As Table 5.7 demonstrates, Italy falls well below this level for every decade of the postwar period. From the 1950s through the 1970s Italian proximity was exceptionally low. Keep in mind also that the modest temporal increase in proximity since the 1960s has been caused primarily by increasing recourse to premature elections.

As we have seen, Italy scores low to moderate on all four dimensions of electoral decisiveness. Hence, overall Italian elections are minimally determinative of coalition bargaining power. This, of course, is primarily a comparative statement. Indeed, for its low electoral decisiveness, Italy is rivaled only by France, Finland, and the Netherlands. The classification of Italy as a *captive government* system thus holds up well under closer scrutiny. Captive government systems provide little potential for alternation in power, but also offer no substantial policy-making advantages for governing parties. These circumstances are hardly conducive to political responsibility, as the Italian experience amply demonstrates (Pasquino, 1980b).

The players: Italian political parties

The previous sections have described the structure of the Italian political system in terms of the theory developed in Chapter 2. The next task is to consider the applicability of its behavioral assumptions. As discussed in Chapter 2, all deductive coalition theories make a number of simplifying assumptions about the players in the game of cabinet formation. Although I have relaxed several of these assumptions and sacrificed some rigor for greater explanatory power, my explanation still rests on a number of stylized assumptions about the players in the game of government formation. Among these critical assumptions are the following:

1. Political parties are the primitive actors. I assume that parties can be regarded as *unitary actors* in the cabinet formation game.
2. These players are capable of strategic behavior. This means that parties are in a position to sacrifice immediate benefits for greater payoffs in the future.
3. I further assume that most relevant parties place a positive value on government participation. That is to say, I retain a weaker version of the common assumption that parties are office seekers.
4. Finally, I assume that these parties seek office in order to *influence national policy making*. In other words, office-seeking behavior is at least partly instrumental toward policy pursuits.

As we shall see, the validity of these assumptions cannot be taken for granted in the Italian case. Three recognized features of Italian politics seem to argue against these assumptions, namely polarization, factionalism, and clientelism. Polarization, the presence of strong "antisystem" parties, seems to contradict the supposition that Italian parties are office seekers. Factionalism appears to undermine the plausibility of assuming that they are unitary, much less strategic, actors. Clientelism flies in the face of any depiction of Italian parties as policy seekers.

Polarization

Consider first the problem of polarization, since it has already been discussed in a different context. According to Sartori's (1976) analysis, Italy is (or was in the mid-1970s) the clearest existing case of a party system of *polarized pluralism*. Among other characteristics, such party systems feature parties with widely dispersed policy positions, a significant number of which are "antisystem" in orientation. It may of course be, as a number of observers have argued, that Sartori's description never fit, or no longer fits, the Italian case (e.g., Daalder, 1983; Galli, 1966, 1975a; Pasquino, 1983). However, let us suspend belief and consider the implications of Sartori's description.

At first glance it might appear that high levels of polarization such as Sartori attributes to Italy must mean that large segments of the party system are *not* serious office seekers, especially as Sartori stresses the concomitant irresponsibility of the opposition in this kind of system (1976: 138). However, the Italian problem has only rarely been that too many parties have refused to participate in *any possible government*. This may have been true in the 1950s, but the following decades brought significant changes in the attitudes of the PSI and later the PCI. In recent decades the parties on the left have frequently been willing but unable to join the government.

Moreover, the frequent refusals of the minor centrist parties to participate in specific governments do not contradict the office-seeking assumption. On the contrary, it is precisely the rationale behind such decisions I seek to explain. But the option of participation must be plausible, that is to say, the benefits of office must be sufficiently highly valued that government participation would be chosen for some set of feasible coalitions.

This is a less severe restriction than our measure of polarization in Table 5.5 might suggest. Not all parties there considered *extremist* have rejected all plausible office-holding opportunities. The notable case in point, of course, is the Italian Communist party. Content analysis of the party's electoral pledges has shown the PCI to take consistently more leftist positions than any other major party throughout the postwar period (Mastropaolo and Slater, 1987). Despite its location on the far left. however, the PCI clearly has been an office-seeking party since the early 1970s. At that time the party had abandoned parliamentary obstructionism and the prospect of a dictatorship of the proletariat and had begun seeking a "historic compromise" with the DC.

Yet the high levels of polarization have significantly constrained government formation in postwar Italy. As we have seen, the share of parliamentary seats held by extremist parties rose from about one-fourth to more than two-fifths in the early 1970s, a proportion dramatically higher than in any other contemporary democracy. Such levels of polarization should promote minority government formation, since they are likely to exacerbate the electoral costs of government participation. However, they need not contradict the assumptions upon which my explanation of such cabinets rests.

Clientelism

I have argued that political parties, and Italian ones among them, seek office at least partly as a means toward policy goals. The pervasive *clientelism* and *patronage orientation* of Italian politics, and especially of the DC and its closest allies, render the assumption of Italian parties as policy seekers dubious. Italian parties are frequently described as organizations of political patrons with extensive personalistic exchange-based ties to a network of clients. The clients offer political support, preference votes, and kickbacks, and receive public employment, welfare services, infrastructural appropriations, protection, or otherwise preferential treatment. The roots of these practices go back to, and beyond, the early days of unified Italy and have always been particularly strong in the South. In Parliament, clientelism was intimately intertwined with the development from the 1870s of *trasformismo* (logrolling), a strategy of building ad hoc support legislative support for the government through offers of personal favors and patronage to opposition deputies. In the broader sense of patronage politics, trasformismo has remained a salient feature of Italian party politics ever since.

Political patronage, known as *sottogoverno*, has provided the Christian Democrats alone with an estimated 60,000 well-paying jobs in various public and semipublic agencies and enterprises (La Palombara, 1977: 6). At the same time, more traditional forms of political clientelism remain prevalent at the local level (Belloni, Caciagli, and Mattina, 1979; Chubb, 1982). Different parties practice different forms of clientelism. The Socialists and the Christian Democrats have colonized various public enterprises, the latter party particularly in the areas of agriculture and regional development. The Social Democrats, on the other hand, have relied more on control of pensions and other fiscal instruments.

Factionalism

Italian clientelism is closely related to the pervasive factionalism of many political parties. Factionalism, in turn, violates the aforementioned assumptions even more seriously. In many cases, Italian parties cannot be meaningfully understood as unitary actors in the process of government formation. And of course, if parties do not behave as unitary actors, they are very unlikely to act rationally or strategically. Factionalism has been more prevalent in Italy than in any other contemporary democracy (with the possible exception of Japan), and party factions are intimately involved in the construction of government alliances (Belloni, 1978; Sartori, 1973b; Zuckerman, 1979). As Zuckerman notes:

> The persistence of faction coalitions, which exist within and across the parties of the coalition formula, is the necessary and sufficient condition for the survival of Italian cabinets. It is the dissolution of the interfaction agreements that ends the cabinets. Given the position of the DC factions, their behavior is the prime determinant of the pattern of competition for control of cabinet coalitions in Italy. (1979: 149–50)

Nowhere has factionalism been as extreme as in the Christian Democratic party. The internal disunity of the party could be observed as early as 1946–7, but its disintegration was held in check under the leadership of De Gasperi and during the early years of Fanfani (1954–9). However, as De Gasperi's towering personality receded from the political scene and the DC became institutionalized, factionalization became more difficult to contain. During the early to mid-1960s, the erosion of party unity was accelerated (Galli, 1978; Zuckerman, 1979).

Two developments contributed decisively to this turn of events. One was the introduction of internal proportionalism in the DC in 1964, a reform also adopted by the PSI (Cecchini, 1978; Lombardo, 1977). Factions thus came to be officially recognized and even protected, and competition between them pervaded the party from top to bottom. DC factions began to adopt official names, establish headquarters, publish periodicals, and hold regular meetings, even at regional and local levels (Belloni, 1978).

The second development that promoted the factionalization of Italian parties was the formation of the center-left coalition. The ambitious political program of this coalition caused a significant enlargement of the public sector through the creation and expansion of a large number of *enti pubblici* (public agencies and enterprises). The growth of the public sector had begun in the mid-1950s, but it was accelerated when the PSI entered the governing coalition (Cazzola, 1979; Ferrera, 1984; Lombardo, 1977). This bureaucratization increased the volume of spoils available to governing parties and was accompanied by a change in the nature and motivations of DC (and other) factions. Early postwar factions differed mainly over ideological and even theological issues. Over time, however, debate between DC factions was transformed into a struggle over power within the party and the parastatal institutions it controlled. By the late 1960s, DC factions had become predominantly power oriented, and the organizational integrity of the party seriously undermined.

The Christian Democrats were not the only party beset with factions. In fact, only the MSI and the PCI have generally escaped this fate, and even the latter was organizationally troubled in the aftermath of the social crisis of 1969 (Mammarella, 1978: 449–51). The PSI has experienced as many as seven identifiable factions (Pasquino, 1973), and even minor parties such as the PSDI and the PLI have suffered from factionalism. All in all, the Italian party system harbored more than 20 factions in the early 1970s. Clearly factionalism was a consequence not of party size but rather of access to government patronage (Lombardo, 1977). Factions of opportunity or convenience were in effect promoted by the growth of the spoils system, as well as by the formation of a politically heterogeneous and electorally seemingly invulnerable majority in the center-left coalition.

However, entrenched as they were, Italian factions were not impervious to the forces of the electoral marketplace. The demoralization and electoral debacle of the center-left parties in the elections of 1975 (regional) and 1976 amply demonstrated the limits of public tolerance of patronage politics. In the latter year the DC losses were contained by the tendency of anticommunist voters to "rally round the flag," but the other centrist parties suffered badly. Since that time both Christian Democrats and Socialists have made progress toward party consolidation. After the serious setback of the 1975 elections, the Christian Democrats chose Benigno Zaccagnini as their new party secretary, a post he held for five years. Zaccagnini, a sincere reformer, sought to "refound" the DC by democratizing the party and reducing the power of factions. In the end Zaccagnini enjoyed little success, but his goals were in large part shared and more effectively reached by the forceful Ciriaco De Mita, who took over the secretariat in 1982 (Wertman, 1987, 1988). After 1976 the Socialist party experienced a similar process of consolidation and regeneration under a similarly dynamic leader, Bettino Craxi.

In sum, Italian political parties have approximated the assumption of unitary, policy-motivated actors comparatively poorly. From one point of view, this is precisely what my research design calls for. Italy is a "least-likely" case with respect to these assumptions. If the theory they support performs well in the Italian case, it must therefore be very robust. However, the recent consolidation of the DC and the PSI also demonstrates the remarkable power of electoral competition to constrain the process of intraparty fragmentation. Critical marginal voters reward consistent and effective parties over disunited and corrupt ones. When their one-time supporters are no longer willing to hold their noses, political parties feel the pressure to behave in a consistent fashion and deliver the policy goods. This is what happened to the Italian Christian Democrats and Socialists in the 1970s and early 1980s. Thus, the assumptions I have made about party behavior ultimately depend on more fundamental assumptions about the voters and the effects of electoral competition. In the section that follows, we shall pay particular attention to the electoral incentives faced by the various Italian parties.

The rationality of Italian government formation

The behavioral assumptions underlying my explanation of minority government formation obviously fit the Italian parties rather poorly. The appropriate modifications have important implications for our understanding of Italian party politics. Consider the implications of Italian-style polarization, clientelism, and factionalism. *Polarization* heightens the policy stakes of the cabinet formation game (through spatial dispersion of the parties) and increases the bargaining power of the "permissible" parties and particularly the larger ones (i.e., the DC and the PSI). By restricting the set of such parties, however, polarization may also contribute to minority government formation. *Clientelism* enhances the benefits of office over and above its policy-making opportunities and may therefore reinforce office-seeking behavior. Different forms of clientelism have somewhat different implications for government participation. Parties colonizing the public sector are less dependent on short-term government participation than parties relying on control of government appropriations. *Factionalism* boosts the number of players involved in the process of cabinet formation. Consequently the probability of successfully putting together broad coalitions may diminish. Moreover, factions are less accountable to electoral verdicts than are parties, so the disincentives to government participation (incumbency costs) are likely to be less salient.

The product of these qualifications to the basic theory is not straightforward. Clearly the complexity and uncertainty of the bargaining environment could easily bring about cabinet instability and perhaps frequent deviations from what would otherwise be equilibrium solutions. Perhaps the frequent cabinet crises and the alternation between oversized and undersized governments can be understood in this context (see Dodd, 1976; Riker, 1962). Certain features of the Italian party system propel the parties toward oversized coalitions, whereas others pave the way for minority governments. By implication, the incidence of minimum-winning size coalitions should be relatively modest.

However, this is neither the only possible interpretation of the Italian case nor necessarily the most persuasive one. So far, little has been said to differentiate Italian parties on the basis of their coalitional incentives. Such distinctions are not commonly made in coalition theory, since parties conventionally are assumed to be uniform in their utility functions and interchangeable in government. But this is a convention born of convenience, not necessity, which may be inappropriate in the Italian context. Italian parties are quite dissimilar in objectives, strategic capacity, and electoral vulnerability, and interchangeability may therefore be a particularly ill-fitting assumption. In fact, incentive structures vary greatly among Italian parties, and we shall explore some consequences of these differences.

A party-level analysis of government formation

So far we have focused on the Italian party system as a whole. Next I shall disaggregate the analysis and consider government formation from the perspective of the individual parties. In the process we move closer to an understanding of the particular configurations of goals and strategies that have occasioned the Italian alternation between undersized and oversized cabinets.

Note first that the government status of the two major parties, the DC and the PCI, has been close to constant throughout the postwar period. The Communists have participated in no cabinet since 1947, the Christian Democrats have participated in all. The exclusion of the PCI was originally in large part caused by international events related to the outbreak of the Cold War. Over time, however, keeping the Communists out has become more and more endogenous to the strategies of the Christian Democrats and the Socialists. For the DC exclusion of the Communists has guaranteed that the party would be in government as the leading player. Not only that, but the DC has controlled the prime minister in all but three postwar governments.[10]

The difference between majority and minority governments, then, has been determined by the minor parties. When most of the minor parties have participated in government, the government has been oversized. In the opposite case, minority cabinets have formed. Most undersized governments have been DC *monocolori,* but some have

---

[10] The Christian Democrats also did not hold the premiership in the first provisional government after the war, which was headed by Ferruccio Parri of the Action party. I have discounted the provisional governments formed before the 1946 election to the Constituent Assembly.

also included one or two minor parties. Note finally that, as a consequence of these coalitional choices, minority governments have
been especially prevalent immediately before and after elections.
Since 1948, 11 of 18 governments formed just before or after an
election have been undersized.

Yet, the distinction between government and opposition is too
discrete for Italian reality. Italian party politics is characterized by a
variety of nuances between the "ins" and the "outs." What I have
called "external support" is only the most formalized variety of collaboration between government and parties not represented in the
cabinet. At a minimum, we can also identify a fourth status, namely,
informal participation in the cabinet's legislative coalition. We may
also wish to distinguish between cases of voluntary abstention from
power and those instances in which parties have been excluded from
office against their preference.

Payoffs and strategies: interparty variations

The principal factors that distinguish the incentive structures of the
various Italian parties are *relative position in policy space* and *electoral
vulnerability*. Parties with a centrist policy position obviously have
greater opportunities to enter government than those with more
extremist positions. Given the polarization of the Italian policy space,
centrist parties face unusually attractive opportunities for office holding. Since the set of permissible parties is so restricted, the bargaining
power of each centrist party is enhanced. Also, the pressure for office
exerted within each party increases to the extent that it is factionalized
and engaged in clientelistic practices. Consequently, clientelistic
centrist parties like the Social Democrats face very strong incentives
to participate in government.

These incentives are to a lesser or greater extent counterbalanced
by electoral considerations, which militate against the compromises
involved in government participation. The susceptibility of Italian
parties to electoral sanctions, however, is highly variable, since the
electoral market is so imperfect. Italian voters cannot properly be
understood as rational policy voters, although such assumptions capture critical minorities in the electorate. Students of Italian voters
distinguish between *opinion voters, identification voters* whose be-

havior reflects commitment to a particular subculture (e.g., Catholicism, working-class Marxism), and *exchange voters* involved in clientelistic networks (see, e.g., Parisi and Pasquino, 1977). While the proportion of opinion voters has grown steadily, the other types of voters have by no means been displaced. Opinion voters are much more volatile and more likely to be offended by poor governmental performance than identification voters, whereas exchange voters on the contrary have little patience with a party that is out of power and therefore unable to deliver the pork.

The composition of the electorate differs systematically among parties, with the DC and the PCI having the most identification voters, and the minor centrist parties the greatest proportions of opinion voters. These variations are in turn systematically related to the electoral vulnerability of the various parties. With large proportions of identification and exchange supporters, the Christian Democrats have traditionally (at least until the 1970s) been almost invulnerable electorally. Small middle-class parties like the Republicans and the Liberals, on the other hand, have much more volatile electorates.

Now, consider the joint effects of policy position and electoral vulnerability on a party's willingness to govern. A centrist policy location should propel a party toward government participation, especially if its supporters are also disproportionately identification – or even more so, exchange – voters. Such parties should be expected to be in government regularly. Parties on the "half-wings" have less bargaining power and lesser incentives, especially if their constituencies consist of more sophisticated opinion voters. They should therefore hold office much less frequently and willingly. Parties with centrist policy positions and opinion voters face the clearest dilemmas and should exhibit the most unstable behavior. Let us consider each of the "permissible" parties in these terms and examine the empirical fit of these predictions.

The Christian Democrats

The hegemony of the Christian Democratic party has been based on a combination of central policy position and uncommonly low electoral vulnerability. As a very large center party, the DC in effect has no choice but to be the dominant government party, and has therefore attempted to make a virtue out of this necessity. For large parts of the postwar period the DC has made the most of its predominance by withholding legitimacy (" permissibility") from the only other large party, the PCI.

The traditional subcultural nature of Italian partisanship has been a blessing for the Christian Democrats, since it has limited the number of floating voters who could desert the party on the basis of its performance in office. But the large electoral constituency of the DC may be even more directly beneficial to the party. Being the dominant government party entails additional electoral advantages in crisis situations, when many voters are inclined to "rally round the flag" (Arian and Barnes, 1974). Secure in its predominance, the DC has often found it advantageous to include as many permissible parties as possible in government, so as to preclude a "loyal" opposition. If presented with the stark choice between fundamental social transformation and the status quo, more uncommitted voters may opt for the status quo than otherwise.

On the other hand, a large coalition is not to the advantage of the DC if it means spreading the spoils of office more thinly. But DC leaders have been able to offset concessions to coalition partners by increasing the total volume of spoils. The Italian *partitocrazia* have put few obstacles in the way of powerful parties seeking to enlarge the benefits of political office. However, the DC's strategy of broad alliances and a spoils orientation have had the unintended consequences of enfeebling the party organization and leaving it open to manipulation by its partners in government (Lombardo, 1977).

The lay centrist parties

Unlike the Christian Democrats, the smaller lay parties of the center have frequently faced a real choice of whether or not to participate in government. The choice for these parties has essentially been between power at electoral costs, or self-imposed opposition in the hope of containing the centrifugal drift of the electorate. The smaller parties are much more vulnerable electorally than the DC, since their constituencies are less subculturally insulated and their smaller size leaves them less protected by the electoral system. Also, their efforts to project themselves as pillars of the community are bound to be overshadowed by the DC. Nonetheless, some of the smaller parties have managed to carve out their own niches of responsibility. The best examples are the PSI under Craxi and the well-established role of the Republicans as the financial conscience of government (Barnes, 1977: 31).

In sum, however, the smaller parties face a much less favorable calculus of government participation than the DC. At least the Socialists and the Liberals have a less favorable spatial position, which reduces their bargaining power. All the centrist parties are also more vulnerable than the Christian Democrats electorally. Historically, their voting strength has fluctuated much more (see Table 5.1). Hence, they should abstain from power in proportion to this vulnerability and their distance from the center of the policy space.[11] However, differences between these parties allow us to make more discriminating predictions. As mentioned, the PSI and the PLI have had a less favorable spatial position than the PRI and the PSDI and should therefore be expected to govern less frequently. In terms of electoral vulnerability, the PLI and the PRI appear to have had the greatest proportions of opinion voters (and the greatest historical fluctuations in electoral support), and the PSDI the most clientelistic electorate.

On these grounds, we expect the Social Democrats to be the most willing participants in government and the Liberals the least. The Republicans should experience the most acute dilemmas between their governmental and electoral aspirations. This general tendency is borne out by the results reported in Table 5.8, which summarizes the information on government participation for the smaller centrist parties and for all governments beginning with the first legislature in 1948.[12] Among the four parties, the Social Democrats have most frequently held office, but even the PSDI has participated in only just over half of all postwar governments. The least frequent gov-

[11] The dimensionality of the Italian policy space is not critical to the argument that a centrist position enhances bargaining power and facilitates government participation. However, the empirical application of this argument is implicitly based on the dominance of the left–right dimension, as discussed in the introduction to this chapter.

[12] I have excluded the early emergency governments of national coalition, since interparty relations at this time were rather fluid. The sources of the information summarized in Table 5.8 include *Keesing's Contemporary Archives,* a number of authoritative political histories (e.g. Mammarella, Galli), and such summaries as are presented in Sani (1976), Di Palma (1977), and Pappalardo (1978).

Table 5.8. *Government status by party, 1948–87*

Party	Cabinet participation	External support	Legislative coalition	Opposition	Voluntary abstention	Exclusion
PLI	12	2	5	29	13	23
PRI	23	7	7	11	21	4
PSDI	25	6	3	11	15	5
PSI	18	4	3	23	12	18

Note: Columns 2, 3, and 4 represent different forms of nonparticipation in the cabinet. Columns 5 and 6 constitute a breakdown of the causes of such nonparticipation. See Table 5.1 for party abbreviations.

erning party among the four, the Liberals, has participated in exactly one-fourth of all postwar cabinets. Note that the smaller of the four parties have opted for nonparticipation at a higher rate than the larger parties. This may again reflect the effects of electoral vulnerability.

It is also readily apparent that the lay centrist parties fall into two rough categories: those that have basically only by choice been out of government, and those that have been excluded from the dominant coalition formula for some time. This distinction between excluded and nonexcluded parties coincides with distance from the policy center. The Republicans and the Social Democrats have rarely been excluded from the cabinet, whereas the Socialists and the Liberals have. The PSI was of course in forced opposition between 1947 and 1963 and then in voluntary exile from 1974 to 1980. The PLI was out in the "cold" continuously between 1957 and 1979, except for its participation in Andreotti's second government.

Thus, the PSDI and the PRI have held office much more frequently and been in opposition much less often than either the Socialists or the Liberals. But at the same time, the PSDI and especially the PRI have also voluntarily abstained from power more regularly. Their cycles of participation and withdrawal have been remarkably short and abrupt, particularly during the 1970s. As legislatures have worn on and elections began to loom on the horizon, the Republicans in particular have frequently bolted from the governing coalition. Thus, the PRI withdrew from government almost three years into the fifth legislature, close to four years into the sixth, and about three and a half years into the eighth.[13] In all cases premature elections soon followed. The PLI exhibited a somewhat similar pattern until the "opening to the left," whereas the PSI has operated in longer and more stable cycles of participation and opposition.

The data thus suggest the following pattern of government formation in Italy. The Christian Democrats have been the core party in all postwar governments.[14] Other parties have joined the cabinet to the extent that they have resembled the DC, that is, to the extent that they have been centrist and electorally invulnerable. Minority governments have resulted when few additional parties have found the benefits of office to outweigh its electoral costs. Such cabinet outcomes have been particularly prevalent when elections have been on the horizon. At such times, parties with a large following of opinion voters, such as the PRI, have found it particularly opportune to go into opposition. For more clientelistic parties such as the PSDI, however, the electoral incentives are less powerful. The Social Democrats have fewer opinion voters to lose through embarrassing performance in office and greater need for fiscal pipelines to their clienteles.

So far the argument about the deterrent effect of electoral considerations has been made purely on theoretical grounds. I have argued that government participation tends to stretch the policy consistency of the parties involved and hence to be a liability among voters who prefer consistent parties. This argument has been supported by cross-national data, but not specifically by consideration of the behavior of the Italian electorate. Let us therefore consider whether the electoral fortunes of the four smaller centrist parties in fact have depended on their participation in government.

The overall tendency represented in Table 5.9 is clearly for the minor parties to fare better at the polls when in opposition than when they govern. The average result when in opposition is a minuscule loss of 0.08% of total popular vote. When in the cabinet, on

[13] The Republicans did not participate in any of the cabinets of the seventh legislature.
[14] The term "core" is here used loosely and not in the strict game-theoretic sense as the set of undominated solutions. In a strictly policy-based coalition theory, however, a government of the DC alone could well be in the core in many cases (see Laver and Budge, forthcoming).

Table 5.9. *Minor party electoral gains by government status, 1948–87 (percentage of total vote, mean values)*

Government status	PSI	PSDI	PRI	PLI	All four parties
Government	−1.35	+0.08	−0.65	−1.00	−0.58
Opposition	+0.54	−0.80	+0.25	−0.34	−0.08
All elections	+0.12	−0.45	−0.11	−0.47	−0.24

Sources: Marradi (1982: 40–1); Pasquino (1977a: 185).

the other hand, the average party has lost more than seven times as much. Only the Social Democrats exhibit the opposite tendency, probably due to their more exchange-oriented voters. The clearest contrast is exhibited by the Socialists, who have gained more than half a percentage point when in opposition and lost about one and one-third points when in government. Note also the overall decline of the parties over time. All but the PSI have on the whole lost ground over time, the Liberals most seriously. Even in opposition the PLI has tended to lose rather than gain. These results underscore the predicament of the minor centrist parties in the Italian political system.

There is every reason to believe that the behavior of the various parties has also been influenced by short-term or longer-term learning. Undoubtedly, the reluctance of the PSI to enter government from 1968 to 1976 was in large part caused by its very disappointing electoral results in 1968. Similarly, the defiant attitude of the Liberals in the early 1960s could be attributed to their favorable results in opposition in the elections of 1958 and 1963. The Republicans contested the elections of 1948 and 1953 from a position in government, lost ground in both elections, and did not join another cabinet until 1962. The poor results of the smaller centrist parties in the 1976 election were followed by a legislative term in which none of these parties participated in a single cabinet. The 1983 election, on the other hand, was one in which all four parties gained strength. They subsequently all joined the exceptionally long-lived Craxi government.

But given the electoral costs of governing, why have the minor

parties not decided to abstain from power more steadfastly? At first
sight, the role of responsible opposition would seem a promising
strategy. There are at least two weighty factors that militate against
this option. One is that the minor parties have become caught up in
a game of patronage and factionalism. In this situation, it is difficult
for a party to kick its power addiction. The other obstacle to the role
of responsible opposition has been the rules of the game as defined
by the Christian Democrats. An essential characteristic of Italian
government formulas is that they are defined in terms not of parties
and elections but rather of social forces and long-term alliances. The
designers of Italian coalitions have sought not responsiveness to the
voice of the people but rather insulation from electoral responsibility.
And the successive Italian coalition formulas have been additive and
irreversible, at least by intention (Di Palma, 1977: 116; Sani, 1979).
These characteristics of coalition formulas were most clearly exhibited
by the center-left.

   These DC strategies have served to co-opt certain minor parties
and marginalize others by minimizing short-term bargaining. As a
"captive" governing party the Christian Democrats have little real
bargaining power. By cementing long-term alliances, they have
therefore tried to reduce the ability of other parties to extract disproportionate benefits from bargaining. Parties unwilling to commit themselves and thus relinquish most of their bargaining power
therefore have run the risk of marginalization by the DC. The
less well endowed a party is, in policy positions and votes, the
greater its risk of being chronically cut off from the benefits of
office. And of course, the purpose of voluntary opposition is to
enhance one's bargaining power. Long-term opposition in itself
offers few benefits, and when the situation is involuntary, it can
mean devastation for party recruitment and morale, particularly in
a clientelist party.

   In other words, a party runs a considerable risk by placing itself
outside the ruling coalition, since it may not have a chance to reenter
soon, particularly if its size and spatial location make it expendable.
Successful long-term opposition requires ideological coherence and
organizational capacity, which have often been wanting in the smaller
Italian parties (Zincone, 1977: 212). The fate of the PLI may be
illustrative. From the late 1950s on, the Liberals increasingly opposed

the rapprochement between the other centrist parties and the PSI. Initially this strategy paid off in successful elections in 1958 and 1963. However, the PLI's gains in no way facilitated its return to office. Instead, it was ostracized by the parties of the center-left and ultimately paid dearly for its lack of bargaining power. The PSI, whose larger size makes it "indispensable" as a governing party (Pasquino, 1981), has been able to pursue the oppositional strategy with somewhat greater success. But even the Socialists have displayed considerable paranoia over the prospect of being marginalized in a historic compromise between the DC and the PCI (e.g. Hine, 1980; LaPalombara, 1982; Pasquino 1980a, 1981).

An illustrative case: the Zoli government, 1957–8

Let us now consider a case of how these strategies and considerations have affected Italian government formation in practice. In the early months of 1957, Antonio Segni was well into the second year of his first cabinet, which consisted of Christian Democrats like himself, Liberals, and Social Democrats. The Republicans had committed themselves to supporting the government in Parliament, and Segni thus had a slim legislative majority. Segni's government was already the fifth during the second legislature, whose term would expire in the spring of 1958. The election was thus only just over a year away when the government's controversial land reform bill came up in Parliament in February. At this point, the PRI withdrew its legislative support.

The government was initially able to carry on, thanks to the legislative support of the Monarchists and the MSI. Over the next couple of months, however, the Social Democrats grew increasingly restive in coalition, and on May 5 their leader, Giuseppe Saragat, gave a speech advising his party to withdraw from the coalition. The next day Prime Minister Segni tendered his government's resignation. Giuseppe Mammarella explains the behavior of the Social Democrats in these terms:

By April, the crisis appeared inevitable. The Social Democrats, under the pressure of the Party's left wing and prompted by electoral considerations, took the initiative. In fact, with political elections approaching, for a party that drew its votes from a progressive electorate, such as the PSDI, it would have been dangerous to continue support of the Segni Government, which was by now reduced to carrying on routine business with the parliamentary backing of the right. (1964: 305)

During the ensuing cabinet crisis, prospects for a broad coalition were on the surface auspicious. Despite tensions between the relevant parties, the four-party centrist coalition was still alive and reasonably well. Preparations for an "opening to the left" that would bring the Socialists into government were also underway, though still resisted by powerful factions of the Christian Democratic party. Segni's government had in fact been designed to pave the way for such an expansion of the coalition formula. Finally, although not quite *koalitionsfähig* (coalitionable), the parties of the far right were willing to play a supporting role in Parliament.

Indeed, after Segni's resignation, the leaders of all three parties in the outgoing cabinet expressed their support for a four-party coalition to include the Republicans. On May 12, however, the latter party decided not to accept government responsibility. This reluctance quickly spread to the Social Democrats and the Liberals. On May 19, therefore, after short negotiations Christian Democrat Adone Zoli formed a single-party government. "The refusal of the Republicans and Social Democrats to assume government responsibilities *such a short time before the elections* compelled the DC to form a government composed exclusively of Demo-Christians (monocolor)" (Mammarella, 1964: 305; emphasis added). Or in the succinct summary of Gregory Luebbert (1986: 281), "The PRI and the PLI felt the need to distance themselves from the DC in view of the upcoming elections."

In his investiture Zoli suffered the embarrassment of being dependent on the support of the MSI for his majority. When this became clear, Zoli tendered his resignation, and President Gronchi attempted to establish a coalition government under the premiership of Cesare Merzagora or Amintore Fanfani. Both men encountered the same resistance from Republicans and Social Democrats that had frustrated Zoli and therefore gave up their attempts. Gronchi eventually decided to refuse Zoli's resignation, and the latter assumed office with a precarious minority government. Despite its weak legislative status, Zoli's government actually achieved some notable successes. The nationalization of the telephone network was completed, the development program for the Mezzogiorno (southern Italy) extended, the Superior Council of the Judiciary established, and the Common Market treaties ratified.

Mammarella attributes Zoli's unexpected successes to electoral considerations: "Zoli's major strength lay in the certainty that, in the event of his fall, the President of the Republic would be compelled to dissolve Parliament and call for new elections, an eventuality that all parties feared, in view of their unpreparedness to face the electorate" (1964: 307).

The failure of both the highly respected Merzagora and the DC leader, Fanfani, to construct a broader coalition shows that Zoli's narrow legislative basis was no accident. Electoral strategies seem to be the best explanation of the formation of Zoli's one-party government in a situation where a variety of broader alternatives should have been feasible. There is no evidence that a renewal of the centrist coalition was impossible on policy grounds. Indeed, both Liberals and Social Democrats had declared themselves in favor of the four-party centrist coalition, and Saragat had made this preference clear in the very speech that caused Segni's resignation (*Keesing's Contemporary Archives*, 1957: 15559).

The government was formed in a period of transition, when the DC had no claim on the participation of the minor parties. Factionalism and clientelism were not yet enough of a force to predispose them toward government participation at electoral costs. When the Republicans withdrew, therefore, the whole coalition unraveled. The 1953 election had produced a major setback for all the centrist parties, and the prospect of another contest made them unusually defensive. Each party's major fear may have been a confrontation with another centrist party unencumbered with the compromises of government participation. Hence, when the PRI seemed to position itself to play this role, the other two minor parties quickly defected as well. In fact, in the end even the Christian Democrats attempted to distance themselves from the Zoli government (Mammarella, 1964: 307).

Italian governments in office

In the preceding sections I have sought to illuminate the process of Italian government formation, and especially the causes of under-sized cabinets. I have said little about the fate of these governments after their formation. Obviously, the latter topic demands its own investigation. The remainder of this chapter will address this issue within the framework developed in the cross-national analysis in Chapter 4. Thus, we shall first consider the ways in which Italian minority cabinets have built legislative majorities and then go on to consider their performance in terms of duration, the circumstances of government resignation, electoral fortunes, and legislative success.

Majority construction

We have noted the Italian norm of preconstituted government majorities. Four undersized cabinets have qualified as *formal* minority governments, and several others have enjoyed the prenegotiated support of outside parties, although not enough to put them over the majority threshold. Typically, such support agreements have been *comprehensive*; that is to say, they have not been limited in scope or temporally restricted. The latter does not mean that most support agreements have been durable. On the contrary, the fact that legislative coalitions have been defined without reference to the electoral cycle has imposed few constraints on the early dissolution of such ties.

Italian support agreements have generally been highly formalized. Parties in the legislative coalition have announced their support for an explicit legislative program, or for parts of it. This formalization is at least partly a result of parliamentary procedure: the constitution requires the designated prime minister to go before Parliament with a specific program and ask for its vote of confidence. The various parties have been counted in the government's legislative coalition or the opposition according to their vote on the investiture motion.

The membership of Italian legislative coalitions has tended to be consistent over time and over issues. The obstacles to launching minority governments in the hope of ad hoc support have already been mentioned. Yet, this practice has been attempted by several DC *monocolori*, such as De Gasperi XI, Pella, Fanfani I, Zoli, and Andreotti I, with modest success. Fanfani's first government represents an especially interesting attempt to construct a government around an ambitious legislative agenda rather than a coalition formula. The result was not auspicious for the feasibility of Scandinavian-style ad hoc majorities in Italy: Fanfani was soundly defeated on the vote of investiture (Galli, 1975b: 55–7).

Italian governments have relied on a combination of policy concessions and spoils in their efforts to build legislative coalitions. Increasingly, opposition parties including the PCI have been allowed to share in offices and benefits controlled by the government.

Performance in office

The preceding discussion of majority building suggests problems for the performance of Italian minority cabinets once in office. The Italian institutional setting is not a flexible one that allows minority cabinets much freedom to experiment with informal majority building in the legislature. Battle lines are drawn early and explicitly, and minority governments should not expect much toleration or forgiveness. These restrictions have had consequences for the electoral, policy, and especially office performance of minority governments.

Duration

The average duration of various cabinet types, as presented in Table 5.12, suggests that the institutional environment has indeed been inhospitable for minority cabinets. Italian governments, whether minority or majority, have not proved very durable. The average duration for majority coalitions has been 11.5 months, for minority governments only 6.9 months. Interestingly, formal minority governments have enjoyed the highest average at 12.5 months, but this figure should not be given too much weight in view of the small number of cases. Substantive minority cabinets have lasted no more than 5.4 months on average. All of these figures are well below the cross-national means, most significantly so for substantive minority governments. The average Italian government has in fact been in office only about half as long as cabinets in the other 14 countries.

The most durable Italian government through 1987 has been Bettino Craxi's administration (1983–7), which endured for 45 months. This is the only Italian cabinet that has lasted anywhere near the duration of a normal parliamentary term. The second most durable cabinet, Moro III, lasted only a little more than two years. The durability of Italian governments has varied over time as well as between cabinet types. The governments of the 1950s and 1960s outlasted those formed earlier or later by about 50%. The low average figure for minority governments is partly a function of the total lack of durability of those cabinets that have been denied investiture, but even the longest-lasting minority government (Fanfani III) stayed in office for no more than 19 months.

Government resignations

Let us next consider the circumstances under which Italian governments have resigned. Table 5.10 presents a breakdown of the *causes* of resignation and Table 5.11 one of the *mode* of resignation, as discussed in Chapter 4. In comparison to other Italian governments, minority cabinets have not suffered particularly traumatic resignations. It is true that only minority governments have been defeated on votes of no confidence (four times), but these have all been governments that failed their initial investiture. On the other hand, substantive minority cabinets have resigned slightly less frequently out of internal disarray (although all *formal* minority cabinets have resigned under these circumstances). Moreover, five minority governments have resigned vountarily, unlike any majority coalition.

However, *all* Italian cabinets look bad when compared to governments in other countries. Note that only 13% of Italian governments have resigned for the relatively innocuous electoral reasons (Table 5.10), compared to more than one-third of all governments elsewhere. And the proportion of cabinets that have fallen apart due to internal disunity is about twice as high in Italy (64%) as elsewhere. Moreover, not a single Italian government resignation has been purely technical, as I have defined that term. Hence, the favorable performance of minority cabinets relative to other Italian governments is faint praise.

Table 5.10. *Cause of resignation of Italian cabinets, 1946–87 (percentages by cabinet type)*

Cabinet type	Government disunity	Parliamentary confidence	Parliamentary policy defeat	Electoral	Systemic	Personal/ constitutional	(N)
Majority coalition	67	0	11	19	0	4	(27)
Minority formal	100	0	0	0	0	0	(4)
Minority substantive	50	25	0	6	19	0	(16)
All governments	64	9	6	13	6	2	(47)

Table 5.11. *Mode of resignation of Italian cabinets, 1946–87* *(percentages by cabinet type)*

Cabinet type	Crisis/defeat	Voluntary	Technical	(N)
Majority coalition	100	0	0	(27)
Minority formal	50	50	0	(4)
Minority substantive	81	19	0	(16)
All governments	89	11	0	(47)

Electoral performance

The regularity of elections imposes the most important constraint on the longer-term consideration of political parties in democratic systems. In Italy, however, attention to the electoral cycle is weaker than in most countries. One reason may be that the average alternation for Italian governments is only about one-third of the cross-national mean. Thus, the lack of turnover in Italian politics is powerfully confirmed. Note also that alternation has declined over time. Parties in government presumably favor a low degree of alternation, but for the Italian system as a whole it indicates a fundamental problem.

Alternation scores have been virtually identical for majority and minority governments, as Table 5.12 indicates. This is note worthy, since it suggests that minority cabinets have not significantly alleviated the problem of "captive" governments and irresponsible oppositions. However, minority governments may still have contributed to alternation *potential*, which may simply have gone unexploited. Only in the late 1950s was a limited degree of turnover in office attained through a series of "pendular" minority governments, which alternated between left-wing and right-wing legislative support.

In electoral terms Italian governing parties in majority coalitions have lost an average of 2.13% of total popular vote, whereas minority governments have made a small average gain of 0.22%. In both cases, the results are substantially better than the cross-national averages. The small positive figure for minority governments reflects the elec-

Table 5.12. *Government performance by cabinet type (mean values)*

Cabinet type	Duration (months)	Electoral success	Alternation
Majority coalition	11.5 (17.7)	−2.13 (−4.54)	6.9 (19.0)
Minority formal	12.5 (13.2)	−1.18 (− .97)	7.0 (12.4)
Minority substantive	5.4 (14.1)	.57 (−1.30)	7.8 (29.8)
All governments	9.5 (18.0)	−1.13 (−3.12)	7.2 (22.6)

Note: Figures in parentheses represent cross-national means.

toral stability of the Christian Democratic party, which has been the only member of most minority cabinets.

It may come as a surprise that Italian governments have fared comparatively well with the voters, since the centrifugality of political competition could be assumed to produce very different results (Sartori, 1976). The crucial point, however, is that in a nonalternance system like Italy the same parties always absorb the incumbency costs, small as they may seem. Under these circumstances the mean government loss of 1.13% can be serious enough. The averages may also be misleading, since especially large gains were scored by governments formed before 1948. Thus, the average loss of subsequent governments is considerably higher than the entire postwar mean. For example, cabinets formed during the 1960s, the heyday of the center-left, faced an average loss of 2.17%.

Legislative performance

Qualitative evaluations of the legislative effectiveness of Italian minority governments suggest a rather mixed record. Many minority governments have been no more than unambitious holding operations, while others have enjoyed a measure of legislative success. Although hardly ambitious at the outset, the cabinets of Pella, Zoli, and Leone I proved reasonably effective. Giuseppe Pella, somewhat of an outsider in the DC, capitalized on nationalist fervor during the Trieste affair to build support for aggressively right-wing policies. Ironically, it was Pella's strength and independence and the prospect that he might prolong his administration's tenure that prompted Fanfani and the DC leadership to depose him in January 1954 (Mammarella, 1978: 282–7). Zoli's accomplishments have already been mentioned. The life of Leone's first government was clearly more tranquil, but this government introduced legislation at a faster rate and with a higher rate of approval than any other cabinet between 1955 and 1972. Although much of this legislation may have been uncontroversial, it was not necessarily unimportant (Cantelli, Mortara, and Movia, 1974: 304).[15]

There have been a series of quantitative studies of parliamentary legislation in Italy. In a large sample of parliamentary bills over the period from 1948 to 1968, government formula and numerical status were virtually unrelated to legislative success. Average approval rates for five different coalition formulas varied only in the narrow range from 80% to 86% (Cantelli et al., 1974). The first legislature, which had only majority governments, had the lowest average approval rates. The second legislature, with a predominance of minority governments, scored highest among the four legislatures up through 1968. There was a positive correlation between cabinet duration and rates of legislative initiative ($r = .33$).

Similar studies have been conducted up through the eighth legislature (1979–83). Table 5.13 presents aggregate legislation figures broken down by the numerical status of the initiating government. Two different performance measures are included: the mean monthly rate of bills introduced and the percentage of government bills passed. As Table 5.13 shows, majority governments have enjoyed an insignificant advantage in approval rates. On the other hand, there is a much more significant tendency for minority governments to introduce legislation *at a more rapid rate* than majority administrations. This tendency holds up even in the first four legislatures (1948–68), for which we do not have fully comparable data (see Cantelli et al., 1974: 304). However, bills proposed by minority governments were more often amended (59% vs. 52%) (Cazzola, 1974).

A simple count of bills does not necessarily give an adequate representation of legislative effectiveness in a parliament flooded with *leggine*. To control for significance, the investigators divided all bills in the sample into nine categories on the basis of two criteria: gen-

[15] See later in this chapter for further analysis of the data of Cantelli et al. (1974).

Table 5.13. *Legislative performance by legislature and cabinet type, 1948–83*

Performance and cabinet type	Legislature								Total
	I (1948–53)	II (1953–8)	III (1958–63)	IV (1963–8)	V (1968–72)	VI (1972–6)	VII (1976–9)	VIII (1979–83)	
Bills introduced (monthly means)									
Majority	NA	NA	NA	NA	18	27	—	27	24
Formal minority	NA	NA	NA	NA	27	29	30	—	29
Substantive minority	NA	NA	NA	NA	38	16	37	63	39
All governments	40	29	26	26	19	27	29	29	28
Bills approved (%)									
Majority	79.3	94.0	77.3	81.4	72.9	71.6	—	51.1	71.8
Formal minority	—	—	86.4	—	73.6	63.0	37.1	—	65.0
Substantive minority	—	66.8	81.4	93.5	67.1	45.8	64.6	63.5	70.5
All governments	79.1	85.6	81.5	83.9	60.8	69.0	55.3	56.6	74.1

Note: Values for specific cabinet types are means of means. Colombo I and II considered as one government. Data missing for Andreotti I and V. NA indicates inavailability of data; a dash indicates there was no such government at that time.
Sources: Compiled and computed from Cantelli et al. (1974); Motta (1985).

erality and function. Contrary to expectations, there was no significant tendency for minority cabinets to propose less important legislation than majority administrations. Instead, the highest relative production of *leggine* was associated with the majority governments of the center-left (Cantelli et al., 1974: 308–18; Cazzola, 1974: 35–52).

A closer investigation of Table 5.13 reveals that legislative effectiveness has varied more over time than between cabinet types in aggregate. Table 5.14 examines this temporal trend in greater detail. It includes data on government bills in aggregate, as well as on the increasingly important decree laws (*decreti legge*), which were originally intended as emergency legislation, but which over time have become part of the standard legislative process. Decree laws can be promulgated by the government without parliamentary deliberation, but must subsequently be converted into law by Parliament within 60 days to remain in force. In a study of the use of decree laws during the first five legislatures, Franco Cazzola reports that DC *monocolori*, and particularly those leaning toward the right, have resorted to this type of legislation less frequently, for more pressing reasons, and with higher rates of subsequent parliamentary ratification than majority coalitions. Since the opening to the left, the use of decree laws has increased tremendously, and parliamentary approval has become more problematic (Cazzola, Prediero, and Priulla, 1975; Cazzola and Morisi, 1981a, b; Della Sala, 1988).

Table 5.14 clearly illustrates the secular decline in legislative effectiveness, as well as the increasing recourse to decree legislation. These trends have had little to do with the numerical status of the governments involved. Thus, there is no evidence that minority governments have been systematically less effective than other Italian cabinets. Although it would be unwarranted to embellish the effectiveness of minority governments, it would be equally wrong to single them out for criticism. Governability problems can legitimately be blamed on Italian political parties, but not specifically on their predilection for undersized governments.

In sum, the analysis confirms several of the peculiarities of Italian governments. The durability problems of minority governments are abundantly clear, but this cabinet type fares unexpectedly well on other dimensions of government performance. Yet its showing can be considered positive only in comparison to other Italian govern-

Table 5.14. Legislative activity by legislature, 1948–87

	Legislature								
Legislative activity	I (1948–53)	II (1953–8)	III (1958–63)	IV (1963–8)	V (1968–72)	VI (1972–6)	VII (1976–9)	VIII (1979–83)	IX (1983–7)
Government bills									
No. introduced	2,547	1,667	1,569	1,569	940	1,255	1,022	1,358	NA
Monthly approvals[a]	32	24	21	22	12	18	16	16	NA
Never discussed (%)[b]	NA	NA	NA	NA	18	28	30	35	NA
Decree laws									
No. introduced	29	60	30	94	69	124	167	275	283
Conversion rate (%)	97	100	93	95	99	87	81	61	58
Share of approved government legislation (%)	1	4	2	7	12	13	24	22	24

[a]In "real" government time (cabinet crises excluded).
[b]Means of means.
Sources: Della Sala (1988); Motta (1985).

ments, and we may most appropriately conclude that the performance differential between the various cabinet types is small.

Conclusions

In this chapter I have investigated minority government formation and performance in a setting that violates several key assumptions of my explanation of minority cabinet formation, notably party cohesiveness, policy orientation, and interchangeability of party utility functions. These are common and basic assumptions in the coalition-theoretic literature on government formation. Yet, I have shown that even when these assumptions are violated, the incidence of minority cabinets in Italy can be explained through a rational-choice framework. Among the polities where minority cabinets are common, Italy probably deviates most from these fundamental assumptions. Hence, the empirical fit we have found is encouraging. The results in the Italian case testify to the *robustness* of the explanation I have advanced.

The formation of minority governments in Italy is to a large extent due to the vacillation of the minor centrist parties. While the DC as a dominant party may have been able to define the limits of permissible coalition formulas (Arian and Barnes, 1974), the minor parties have been responsible for short-term changes in government participation within those confines. The behavior of the minor parties, in turn, can be explained in terms of their conflict between electoral and governmental incentives.

The performance of Italian minority governments in office has not been all bad. Although minority cabinets have been seriously deficient in viability, they have not been significantly less effective than other governments. On the positive side, minority governments may actually enhance the potential for turnover in Italian politics. However, the historical record gives us little hope that such opportunities will actually be exploited. Note that minority governments have done quite well at the polls. Perhaps more important, so has the "loyal" opposition, since it has been allowed to follow its electoral incentives. Over the period from 1953 to 1963, when minority governments were most frequent, the proportion of extremist party support actually dropped substantially, from .375 to .327. A similar development may have taken place since the late 1970s, following the bankruptcy of the "historic compromise." Periods without a dominant coalition formula may frustrate social reformers, but they appear crucial to the restoration of party system competitiveness and accountability. Minority governments are parts of this restorative process.

Given the trends toward heightened volatility and issue voting in Italian elections, there is likely to be increased pressure to extend the degree of alternation in government. If continuous expansion of the government majority has been the ruling illiteracy in Italian politics (Sartori, 1973a), then a state of greater literacy might incorporate some form of minority rule.

6. Norway: the politics of inclusion

Paradoxically enough, in one sense political systems I have labeled "inclusionary" tend to have the *least* inclusive governments. That is to say, these polities have high frequencies of minority governments with narrow parliamentary bases. This paradox becomes less puzzling in theoretical context. The inclusion of nongovernmental actors in various phases of policy-making reduces the influence differential between government and opposition. Elections offer decisive opportunities for turnover in government. Thus, incentives for short-term government participation are limited.

The Scandinavian countries are the closest approximations to the inclusionary regime type in our sample. But even Scandinavia is not uniform. Oppositional influence has traditionally been high throughout the area, though less so in Denmark than farther north (Arter, 1984; Damgaard, 1977, 1985; Strom, 1986). Electoral competitiveness and decisiveness for government formation have increased in all countries since 1945, most notably in Norway (Maguire, 1983; Pedersen, 1983).

Indeed, Norway is the most typical inclusionary system we can find. Norway also serves two theoretical purposes quite nicely. First, it meets two underlying assumptions of my rational-choice explanation particularly well: Political parties are cohesive and do not seem to discount future benefits too heavily (see Strom, 1986). Second, Norway offers a very clear-cut choice between this theory and the conventional view, since these two explanations yield radically different predictions about the incidence of minority governments. Therefore Norway will serve as a critical case study for the contending explanations of minority cabinet formation.

Our investigation of Norwegian governments will take us back beyond 1945. This is useful both because prior events will help illuminate subsequent ones, and because the earlier Norwegian record is interesting in its own right. Recall that the rationale behind confining the cross-national analysis to the postwar period was to exclude systems with dubious democratic integrity or regime discontinuities. In the Norwegian case, we may safely go back to the interwar period and beyond without encountering a crisis-ridden, undemocratic, or discontinuous political system.

Norwegian democracy: historical background

The political history of modern Norway begins at the conclusion of the Napoleonic Wars in 1814, when a liberal constitution was drafted.[1] At that time, the country was transferred from the Danish to the Swedish monarchy. However, a considerable degree of domestic autonomy was jealously guarded by the newly created national legislature, the Storting.[2] In 1859 a parliamentary alliance was forged between farmers and representatives of the liberal urban intelligentsia under the leadership of Johan Sverdrup. This coalition was the rudiment of the Liberal party (Venstre, V), officially founded 25 years later. The Liberal program called for such reforms as the institution of parliamentary government. The supporters of the king, the union, and the ruling elite of civil servants responded by forming the Conservative party (Høyre, H). After the Liberals triumphed in the bitterly fought electoral campaign of 1884, the conservative Selmer government was impeached and parliamentary government imposed (Derry, 1968).

To this day, parliamentary government has found no place in the written constitution of Norway. Nonetheless, this form of government has been virtually unchallenged since 1884. Parliamentary government came to be regarded as a symbol of several popular causes in the late nineteenth century. One was the assertion of national identity against Sweden. A second was political democratization, which essentially meant the mobilization of newly enfranchised groups, such

[1] Contrary to the cases of Denmark and Sweden, the Norwegian constitution has not been redrawn in the postwar period. It is now the second oldest living constitution in the world, predated only by that of the United States.

[2] Literally, the name of the Norwegian legislature means "The Great Court," an allusion to the popular assemblies of the Viking era.

as the peasantry. Thus, the Storting became entrenched as the defender of national identity and the popular classes, and the government reduced to "a committee of the Storting" (Olsen, 1983).

The party system until World War II

After its victory in 1884, the Liberal party soon fell victim to continuous factionalism, fragmentation, and long-term decline. A succession of new parties, such as the Moderates (Frisinnede Venstre, FV), split off from the Liberal party, but few of these early formations met with any enduring success. The formation of the Norwegian Labor party (Det Norske Arbeiderparti, DNA or A) in Arendal in 1887 signaled a separate development. A reflection of nascent industrialization and urbanization, the Labor party elected its first four representatives to the Storting in 1903. Yet, for all intents and purposes, Norway remained dominated by the two traditional parties well beyond the dissolution of the union with Sweden in 1905 (see Rokkan, 1967).

One factor contributing to the persistence of this political duopoly was the Norwegian electoral system. Direct parliamentary elections were introduced in 1906, along with single-member constituencies. Although the Labor party benefited greatly from rapid industrialization after 1905, its parliamentary representation suffered scandalously under a two-ballot electoral system, where the "bourgeois" parties normally collaborated on the second ballot.[3] In 1915, Labor garnered more than 32% of the popular vote, but only 19 of 123 representatives. With the introduction of proportional representation in 1921 came increased Labor representation, as well as fragmentation of the parliamentary party system.

The Agrarian party (Bondepartiet, BP) was created in 1920 and received 13% of the vote in its first election the following year. The Radical People's party (Radikale Folkeparti, RF), formerly the Labor Democrats (Arbeiderdemokratene, AD), a left-wing Liberal splinter group that remained very closely tied to the mother party, never

---

[3] The terms "bourgeois" and "nonsocialist" are used synonymously in this chapter, as they are in conventional Norwegian usage. The former label is accepted without embarrassment by the nonsocialist parties themselves. Thus, my use of this term is neither derogatory nor indicative of a class-analytic perspective.

captured more than two seats in the Storting and drifted into oblivion in the 1930s. Even the socialist bloc was beset with dissent and fragmentation. Although the Labor party received an immediate boost through the introduction of PR, its gains were to a large extent offset by party schisms in the early 1920s. In 1921 its national convention voted to join the Communist International, only to withdraw two years later. In both instances, a dissenting minority seceded to form a new party: the Social Democratic Labor party (Norges socialdemokratiske Arbeiderparti, SD) in 1921 and the Norwegian Communist party (Norges kommunistiske Parti, NKP) in 1923. The former of these merged with the Labor party again before the 1927 elections, whereas the NKP has remained at the radical fringe of the Norwegian party system (Lafferty, 1974; Nilson, 1981a,b).

In the early 1930s several additional parties began to contest parliamentary elections, although they found little favor, at least at the national level. One was the Christian People's party (Kristelig Folkeparti, KRF), which remained strictly a west coast fundamentalist movement until after World War II. Another newcomer was the fascist National Union (Nasjonal Samling, NS), which was to collaborate with the German occupation forces during the war. In electoral terms, the NS was utterly insignificant and never managed to elect a single representative to the Storting (Brevig, 1979; Larsen, Hagtvet, and Myklebust, 1980).

The interwar period saw a rapid succession of mostly nonsocialist governments up to 1935. In that year, a Labor government came to power with the external support of the Agrarians. This was not the first socialist government in Norway, but it was the first viable one. After Labor gains in the elections of 1927, a socialist minority government had been formed under the premiership of Christopher Hornsrud. However, this government was promptly ousted by the bourgeois majority after less than three weeks in office. The Labor premier of 1935, Johan Nygaardsvold, was to remain in office for 10 years.

The postwar period

After Norway had been liberated in the spring of 1945, an interim national coalition government was formed by Einar Gerhardsen (Labor). The 1945 election gave a majority of Storting seats (though not of the popular vote) to Labor, which formed a majority party government under Gerhardsen. The Communists and the Christian People's party also scored substantial gains, whereas the remaining nonsocialist parties suffered drastic setbacks compared to the 1936 election. The next 20 years witnessed remarkable electoral stability. Labor retained its parliamentary majority until 1961, although it never managed to capture a majority of the popular vote. With the advent of the Cold War, the Communists entered a period of drastic decline, whereas the electoral fortunes of the four nonsocialist parties (H, V, BP, and KRF) remained strikingly stable.

Since 1961, Labor has never been able to regain its parliamentary majority, but has nevertheless been in power more often than not. Part of the explanation lies in the formation of the "new-leftish" Socialist People's party (Sosialistisk Folkeparti, SF) in 1961. The fortunes of this party have fluctuated sharply, but the SF and its successor have often held the numerical balance between Labor and the nonsocialist bloc. In the early 1970s, the SF merged with anti-EEC Laborites and revisionist Marxist groups to form the Socialist Left party (Sosialistisk Venstreparti, SV). On the bourgeois side, the years since 1973 have seen an increasing Conservative dominance over its allies. The continuous decline of the Liberals took a disastrous turn when their pro-EEC faction broke out and formed the New People's party (Det Nye Folkepartiet, DNF) in 1972. In 1985 the Liberals for the first time lost all parliamentary representation.[4] On the far right, the Progress party (Fremskrittspartiet, FRP), originally Anders Lange's Parti (ALP), was founded in 1973. The Progress party, originally purely a tax protest party, has over time broadened its policy base to take in many conservative and libertarian positions. Through 1985 the party has never captured more than four Storting seats. However, its popular appeal has been highly volatile, and in 1988 some opinion polls gave the party the support of more than 20% of the electorate.

Elections and government, 1905–87

Let us now turn to the electoral and governmental record in greater detail. Table 6.1, which gives the composition of the Storting from independence until World War II, demonstrates the remarkable long-

---

[4] Det Nye Folkepartiet only elected one member of parliament (1973). Later the party rapidly declined to insignificance and in 1988 rejoined the Liberals.

Table 6.1. *Composition of the Storting, 1906–36*

Party	1906	1909	1912	1915	1918	1921	1924	1927	1930	1933	1936
NKP	0	0	0	0	0	0	6	3	0	0	0
A	10	11	23	19	18	29	24	59	47	69	70
SD	0	0	0	0	0	8	8	0	0	0	0
AD/RF	4	2	6	6	3	2	2	1	1	1	0
V	64	46	70	74	51	37	34	30	33	24	23
KRF	0	0	0	0	0	0	0	0	0	1	2
LF/BP	0	0	0	0	3	17	22	26	25	23	18
SFP	0	0	0	0	0	0	0	0	0	1	1
FV	0	23	4	1	10	15	11	2	5	1	0
H	45	41	20	20	40	42	43	29	39	30	36
Others	0	0	0	3	1	0	0	0	0	0	0
Total	123	123	123	123	126	150	150	150	150	150	150

Abbreviations
NKP   Norges kommunistiske Parti (Communists)
A   Det Norske Arbeiderparti (Labor party)
SD   Norges socialdemokratiske Arbeiderparti (Social Democrats)
AD/RF   Arbeiderdemokratene/Radikale Folkeparti (Radical People's party)
V   Venstre (Liberals)
KRF   Kristelig Folkeparti (Christian People's party)
LF/BP Landmandsforbundet/Bondepartiet (Agrarian party)
SFP   Samfundspartiet (Society party)
FV   Frisinnede Venstre (Moderates)
H   Høyre (Conservatives)
Sources: Björnberg (1939); Furre (1976); Kaartvedt et al. (1964); *Keesing's Contemporary Archives.*

term growth of the Labor party and the corresponding Liberal decline. For the Conservative party, no clear long-term trend is discernible. The Agrarians experienced significant expansion up through 1927 and steady setbacks later. As a whole, the party system suffered considerable fragmentation during the 1920s, but consolidation was well on its way by 1940.

Table 6.2 presents the postwar figures. Note the remarkable stability in the left half of the table. Only the short-lived electoral success of the Communist party stands out. However, since the mid-1960s electoral fortunes have changed much more abruptly. The Liberals have declined precipitously. The other parties of the political center, the KRF and the Agrarians, in 1959 renamed the Center party (Senterpartiet, SP), experienced steady gains until the early 1970s, but have more recently lost ground. Despite heightened volatility, the

Table 6.2. *Composition of the Storting, 1945–85*

Party	1945	1949	1953	1957	1961	1965	1969	1973	1977	1981	1985
NKP	11	0	3	1	0	0	0	0	0	0	0
SF/SV	0	0	0	0	2	2	0	16	2	4	6
A	76	85	77	78	74	68	74	62	76	66	71
V	20	21	15	15	14	18	13	2	2	2	0
DNF/DLF	0	0	0	0	0	0	0	1	0	0	0
KRF	8	9	14	12	15	13	14	20	22	15	16
BP/SP	10	12	14	15	16	18	20	21	12	11	12
H	25	23	27	29	29	31	29	29	41	53	50
ALP/FRP	0	0	0	0	0	0	0	4	0	4	2
Total	150	150	150	150	150	150	150	155	155	155	157

Abbreviations (see also Table 6.1)
SF/SV   Sosialistisk Folkeparti/Sosialistisk Venstreparti (Socialist People's party/
          Left Socialist party)
DNF/DLF   Det Nye Folkeparti/Det Liberale Folkeparti (Liberal People's party)
BP/SP   Senterpartiet (Center party)
ALP/FRP   Anders Langes Parti/Fremskrittspartiet (Progress party).
Sources: Torp, various editions.

overall balance between the socialist and nonsocialist blocs has remained very close. In fact, since 1933 the socialist share of the popular
vote has never been lower than 42% or higher than 53% (Strom,
1986).

Norway has had 47 peacetime governments since independence:
26 in the 35 years up to the outbreak of World War II, and 21 between
1945 and the end of 1987 (see Table 6.3).[5] Table 6.4 demonstrates
that *more than two-thirds of all Norwegian cabinets have been undersized.* The incidence of minority governments was greatest before
1940, but even in the more recent period a majority of all governments
have been undersized. Of all majority governments, eight have been

---

[5] The rules of counting in Table 6.3 are those presented in Chapter 3. Thus, the
record does not fully correspond to Norwegian conventions. The Labor Democrats/
Radical People's party (AD/RF) have been counted as part of the Liberal party. The
AD/RF cooperated closely with the Liberals in both the electoral and the parliamentary
arenas, and may more profitably be regarded as a faction than as a separate party.
The figures for parliamentary basis exclude external support and do not always correspond to the party alignments in the Storting in the early decades, since party
cohesiveness was in some cases low. Table 6.3 does not include the national coalitions headed by Nygaardsvold and Gerhardsen during and immediately after World
War II.

Table 6.3. *Norwegian governments, 1905–87*

Government	Formation date	Demission date	Tenure (months)	Parties	Parliam. base	Formation attempts	Type
Michelsen I	Nov 05	Jan 07	14	Nat'l Coal.	97	1	MC
Michelsen II	Jan 07	Oct 07	9	Nat'l Coal.	91	1	MC
Løvland	Oct 07	Mar 08	5	V, FV, Mod	55	1	MC
Knudsen I	Mar 08	Feb 10	22	V	43	2	SM
Konow	Feb 10	Feb 12	25	FV, H	52	2	MC
Bratlie	Feb 12	Jan 13	11	H	33	2	SM
Knudsen II	Jan 13	Jan 16	36	V	61	1	MP
Knudsen III	Jan 16	Jan 19	36	V	65	1	MP
Knudsen IV	Jan 19	Jun 20	17	V	42	2	SM
Halvorsen I	Jun 20	Jun 21	12	H, FV	39	3	SM
Blehr I	Jun 21	Jan 22	7	V	42	2	SM
Blehr II	Jan 22	Mar 23	14	V	26	1	SM
Halvorsen II	Mar 23	May 23	2	H, FV	38	2	SM
Berge	May 23	Jul 24	14	FV, H	38	1	SM
Mowinckel I	Jul 24	Jan 25	6	V	26	1	SM
Mowinckel II	Jan 25	Mar 26	13	V	24	1	SM
Lykke	Mar 26	Jan 28	23	H, FV	36	4	SM
Hornsrud	Jan 28	Feb 28	1	A	39	2	SM
Mowinckel III	Feb 28	Jan 31	35	V	20	1	SM
Mowinckel IV	Jan 31	May 31	4	V	22	1	SM
Kolstad	May 31	Mar 32	10	BP	16	1	SM
Hundseid	Mar 32	Mar 33	12	BP	16	2	SM
Mowinckel V	Mar 33	Jan 34	10	V	22	2	SM
Mowinckel VI	Jan 34	Mar 35	15	V	16	1	SM
Nygaardsvold I	Mar 35	Jan 37	22	A	46	1	FM
Nygaardsvold II	Jan 37	Apr 40	39	A	46	1	SM
Gerhardsen I	Nov 45	Oct 49	47	A	50	1	MP
Gerhardsen II	Oct 49	Nov 51	25	A	56	1	MP

Torp I	Nov 51	Oct 53	23	A	56	1	MP
Torp II	Oct 53	Jan 55	15	A	51	1	MP
Gerhardsen III	Jan 55	Oct 57	33	A	51	1	MP
Gerhardsen IV	Oct 57	Sep 61	47	A	52	1	MP
Gerhardsen V	Sep 61	Aug 63	23	A	49	1	SM
Lyng	Aug 63	Sep 63	1	H, V, KRF, SP	49	1	SM
Gerhardsen VI	Sep 63	Oct 65	25	A	49	1	SM
Borten I	Oct 65	Sep 69	47	SP, H, V, KRF	53	1	MC
Borten II	Sep 69	Mar 71	18	SP, H, V, KRF	50	2	MC
Bratteli I	Mar 71	Oct 72	19	A	49	3	SM
Korvald	Oct 72	Oct 73	12	KRF, SP, V	26	1	SM
Bratteli II	Oct 73	Jan 76	27	A	40	1	SM
Nordli I	Jan 76	Sep 77	20	A	40	1	SM
Nordli II	Sep 77	Jan 81	41	A	49	1	SM
Brundtland I	Jan 81	Oct 81	8	A	49	1	SM
Willoch I	Oct 81	Jun 83	19	H	34	2	SM
Willoch II	Jun 83	Sep 85	28	H, KRF, SP	51	1	MC
Willoch III	Sep 85	May 86	7	H, KRF, SP	49	1	SM
Brundtland II	May 86	NA	NA	A	45	1	SM

Abbreviations

MC Majority coalition
SM Substantive minority
MP Majority party
FM Formal minority

See also Tables 6.1 and 6.2.
Sources: Björnberg (1939); Furre (1976); Kaartvedt et al. (1964); Torp (various editions); *Keesing's Contemporary Archives.*

Table 6.4. *Norwegian governments by type and period*

Type	Period 1905–40	1945–87	Total
All majority	6	9	15
Coalition	4	3	7
Party	2	6	8
All minority	20	12	32
Coalition	4	3	7
Party	16	9	25
Total	26	21	47

majority party cabinets and only seven coalitions. In other words, *of the 39 cabinets formed in minority situations, 32 have been minority governments,* a proportion of more than 82%. Norway experienced an uninterrupted series of minority governments from 1918 until the German invasion in 1940. In all probability, this is the longest record of continuous democratic minority rule in world history. The Borten administrations (1965–71) and Willoch II are the only cases of majority governments in minority situations after 1912. Since Borten's fall in March 1971 there have been 9 minority governments and only 1 with a parliamentary majority.

Minority governments have been in office for 513 of 920 months from 1905 through 1987, or 57% of the time. In minority situations, minority governments have accounted for almost 80% of cabinet duration. Yet Norwegian minority governments have rarely been majority governments in disguise. Only 1 of 32 has been a formal minority government, with a secure and prenegotiated majority in the Storting (Nygaardsvold I). Occasionally, minority governments have enjoyed some form of outside support (e.g., Bratlie, Mowinckel III, and Willoch I), but rarely has such support been pivotal for majority status.

Norwegian governments have not only been undersized; many have been radically below the majority threshold. Sixteen governments have had a parliamentary basis of less than 40%, though only two since 1945. None of the six cabinets from February 1928 to March 1935 had the support of even one-fourth of the members of the

Storting. The mean parliamentary basis for all Norwegian governments is 43.3%, which breaks down to 40.4% for governments prior
to 1940 and 47.5% for postwar cabinets. For the interwar period
alone, the average is no higher than 30.8%.

The missing malaise

The overall prevalence of minority governments in Norway, in conjunction with the conventional view of such cabinets, could generate
any of the following expectations about Norwegian politics:

1. Norway is a particularly unstable or crisis-ridden society.
2. Norway is a deeply divided society.
3. Norway has a political culture that impedes political cooperation
   and coalition building.
4. Norway has a highly fragmented and/or polarized party system,
   which makes the formation of majority governments difficult.
5. Norwegian cabinet crises are exhausting and protracted.

In fact, it would be difficult to defend any of these propositions. We
shall address them successively.

Stability and crises

By any international standard Norway is an extremely stable and
peaceful society. In cross-national comparisons the country ranks near
the very bottom in political protest and domestic violence. Taylor
and Jodice (1983) report only one riot and one death from domestic
political violence over a 30-year period. More than 100 other nations
have higher rates of armed attacks and governmental sanctions, and
almost three-fourths of the world's nations have larger internal security forces relative to their populations.[6] As noted by Johan Galtung
and Nils Petter Gleditsch (1975), Norway is a country where violent
forms of aggression are uncommonly well controlled. Norwegian stability and peacefulness are reflected in the economic sphere as well
as in elite politics. Serious labor conflicts have been rare, especially
in the postwar period (Galtung and Gleditsch, 1975).

---

[6] The latter datum is from Taylor and Hudson (1972).

Nor has Norway experienced cabinet instability of noteworthy proportions. We shall examine cabinet durability data in a later section of this chapter. Let us therefore here confine our discussion to the most turbulent period since independence, the interwar period. As Table 6.3 demonstrates, the succession of undersized cabinets between 1918 and 1940 was also a series of short-lived ones. However, two exogenous factors contributed to the rapid rate of turnover. First, Storting elections were held every three years until 1936 (as against every four years thereafter), thus guaranteeing a triennial change of governments. Second, two prime ministers (Otto B. Halvorsen and Peder Kolstad) had the misfortune of dying in office. Between them, elections and deaths account for 7 of 14 cabinet changes between 1918 and 1933. Moreover, three governments in the 1920s resigned over the prohibition issue. With all due respect for the significance Scandinavians attach to alcohol, the predominance of this issue does not indicate fundamental social discord or instability. Berge Furre concludes in his assessment of political stability in Norway in the 1920s: "Thus, there were criticism and attacks on the system from many sources, but the system withstood. Essentially, it was never very seriously threatened. Even if governments changed, the government *system* remained stable" (1976: 170; emphasis in the original).[7] Norway, then, has been remarkably stable throughout this century. Although its stability was at an ebb in the interwar period, even then the country was indisputably among the most stable in Europe. Whatever the sources of government minoritarianism in Norway, surely political instability and crises should not be blamed.

Cleavages, division, and cohesion

It would be far-fetched to speak of Norway as a divided or plural society. According to a variety of social indicators, Norway is one of the most homogeneous societies in the world. There are virtually no ethnic, racial, or linguistic minorities, although the Norwegian lan-

---

[7] Here, as elsewhere, I am responsible for translations from original sources in the Norwegian language.

guage exists in two competing versions.[8] Likewise, not only are the majority of Norwegians Protestants, but over 90% of the total population belong to the Lutheran state church. Income distribution is more egalitarian in Norway than in the great majority of capitalist countries.

This social homogeneity does not translate into a lack of discernible political cleavages. Studies of Norwegian electoral behavior and political history identify at least six dimensions of cleavage (Urwin, 1987, Valen, 1981; Valen and Rokkan, 1974; Valen and Urwin, 1985):

1. A *territorial* cleavage between center and periphery (see Aarebrot, 1982; Rokkan, 1970);
2. A *sociocultural* cleavage between the defenders of the two different versions of the Norwegian language;
3. A *moral* cleavage that primarily concerns the production and consumption of alcohol;
4. A *religious* cleavage between fundamentalist groups on the one hand and more liberal or secular groups on the other;
5. A *sectoral* cleavage between the primary sector of the economy (agriculture, fisheries) and other industries; and
6. A *class* cleavage between unionized workers and private employers.

Historically, these conflicts developed in the order listed here. All were politically well defined by the early 1920s and have remained more or less salient, thus generating a cumulative pattern of cleavages. However, for recent political history this picture of Norwegian cleavage patterns could be simplified. The sociocultural, moral, and religious cleavages tend to overlap and can be collapsed into a moral-religious dimension. In recent decades, class and moral-religious cleavages have dominated Norwegian politics (Strom and Leipart, 1989; Valen, 1981). The development of the Norwegian party system reflects the underlying cleavage structure quite nicely, since Norwegian parties tend to be socially articulative rather than aggregative. Only the Liberals have consistently assumed an aggregative role, and

[8] The only genuine minorities are the relatively small number of Lapps (Samis) and, since the early 1970s, a modest number of Asian immigrants.

their dismal long-term record testifies to the difficulties of this endeavor.[9] Until the early 1970s, Norway remained a good example of a "frozen" party system (Lipset and Rokkan, 1967).

The severity of Norway's political cleavages should not be overestimated. In a sense, these political conflicts dominate the scene by default, since there exist no truly fundamental divisions. In any case, they clearly pose no threat to Norwegian social or political integrity. Norwegian borders have been virtually unchanged since the early eighteenth century. Separatism and expansionism are unknown phenomena,[10] and Norwegians have a strong sense of national identity. Harry Eckstein provides an amusing observation on the strength of Norwegian national identity versus internal divisions:

> During my stay in Norway I saw two soccer matches in Oslo's Ulleval [sic] Stadium. One was between local teams and generated about as much partisanship in the crowd as an academic lecture (and some visible withdrawal symptoms among the players). The other was between Norway and Sweden, on which occasion many rude things about Norwegian savagery were quite rightly said in the Swedish press. (1966:94)

Political culture and coalescence

Norwegians put a premium on consensus building, negotiations, and implicit trust in the public sphere. It is revealing that most civil servants see their role not as that of judges, managers, or scientists, but rather as negotiators or mediators (Olsen, 1983: 134–7). This consensus-happy orientation is marvelously reflected in the multitude of mediational and consultative institutions that have been constructed in the Norwegian system of "corporate pluralism" (Rokkan, 1966). Hence, the lack of government coalescence in Norway can hardly be culturally determined, since it contrasts with a system of highly institutionalized cooperation in virtually all other social do-

[9] Even the Labor party has sought to aggregate a fairly broad range of interests, but the party has remained strongly class based.

[10] The only arguable case of expansionism is the so-called Greenland issue of 1931, when the Norwegian government openly challenged Danish sovereignty over Greenland. The issue was ultimately decided in Denmark's favor by the World Court.

mains. Even with respect to the very parliamentarians who are reluctant to share governmental office, Lægreid and Olsen note that "there is a striking contrast between this willingness to cooperate within the Storting and the unwillingness to make cooperation formal and to signal it to the environment" (1986: 201). We must conclude, then, that the scarcity of formal coalitions at the governmental level is due neither to inability to cooperate nor to disinclination. Instead, it represents a calculated effort to minimize the appearances of coalescence.

Fragmentation and polarization

We have already focused a good deal of attention on the Norwegian party system and rightly so, since properties of the party system are indisputably critical factors in government formation. Two such characteristics, fragmentation and polarization, are especially plausible explanatory variables. Table 6.5 presents fragmentation and polarization measures for all Storting elections since 1906, along with the corresponding cabinet solutions. In computations of polarization scores, extremist parties include not only the NKP and the NS, but even the SF/SV and the ALP/FRP, which in many other countries would be considered quite *"koalitionsfähig."*

There is certainly no alarming degree of polarization. The total vote share of extremist parties has normally been well below 10% and their portion of parliamentary seats even smaller. Polarization of this magnitude is unlikely to impose serious constraints on parliamentary majority building. Note the low levels of polarization in the interwar period, when minority cabinets were rife.[11]

The Norwegian party system has been more fragmented than polarized, and fragmentation and short-lived governments coincided in the 1920s. Yet undersized cabinets have formed even under the more common situations of modest fragmentation. For 17 of 22 Storting elections, Rae's F has been lower than the cross-national mean (.720). Only one postwar election (1973) has resulted in fragmentation above this level. Moreover, in all but three legislatures (those elected in

---

[11] The disputable democratic commitment of the Labor party in the 1920s is a complicating factor in the analysis of polarization. However, since the early 1930s the party has been clearly reformist.

Table 6.5. *Polarization and fractionalization in Norwegian elections, 1906–85*

Election	Polarization		Fractionalization (Rae's F for seats)	Cabinets
	Seats	Votes		
1906	0	0	.588	2 MC, 1 SM
1909	0	0	.709	1 MC, 1 SM
1912	0	0	.611	1 MP
1915	0	0	.585	1 MP
1918	0	0	.707	3 SM
1921	0	0	.798	4 SM
1924	6	.061	.809	2 SM
1927	3	.040	.737	2 SM
1930	0	.017	.757	4 SM
1933	0	.040	.699	1 SM, 1 FM
1936	0	.021	.687	1 SM
1945	11	.119	.685	1 MP
1949	0	.058	.626	2 MP
1953	3	.051	.677	2 MP
1957	1	.034	.666	1 MP
1961	2	.053	.689	3 SM
1965	2	.074	.715	1 MC
1969	0	.044	.680	1 MC, 2 SM
1973	20	.166	.758	2 SM
1977	2	.067	.663	2 SM
1981	8	.104	.687	1 SM, 1 MC
1985	8	.092	.676	2 SM

Note: See Table 6.3 for abbreviations.

1924, 1973, and 1981), it has been possible to construct an ideologically connected majority coalition of no more than two nonextremist parties (see Strom and Leipart, 1989, in press).[12]

Norwegian parliaments have been dominated by the five major traditional parties (A, H, V, BP/SP, and KRF). Each of these has participated in at least four cabinets, and all but the Christian People's party have held the premiership three times or more since 1925. Thus, "a priori unwillingness to bargain" for government participation has been no impediment to majority governments in Norway.

---

[12] For this purpose, the parliamentary parties were ranked in the following order (left to right) in unidimensional space: NKP, SF/SV, A, V, DLF, BP/SP, KRF, H, FRP. This ordering is conventional (see Strom and Leipart, 1989).

Formation processes

A quick look at Table 6.3 reveals that Norwegian cabinet crises have not been long and exhaustive. Of 47 governments, 33 have resulted from a successful first formation attempt. Only 3 governments have required more than two attempts (Halvorsen I, Lykke, and Korvald). The average number of formation attempts has been 1.38, for the postwar period 1.19, as against 1.87 for the entire cross-national sample. The actual process of negotiation has rarely taken more than a few days.

The highest number of unsuccessful attempts preceded the formation of Ivar Lykke's Conservative government in 1926. This was the only serious attempt in Norwegian history to install a nonpartisan government. After Lykke had failed to secure the support of the Agrarians for a two-party coalition, there was an attempt to draft polar explorer Fridtjof Nansen for the premiership. However, the nonsocialist party leaders balked, and after the Liberals had declined a Conservative–Liberal coalition, Lykke eventually formed a single-party minority government. The previous prime minister (Johan L. Mowinckel) had resigned February 27, 1926, and as Lykke's government took office on March 5, the crisis was in reality less than protracted (Björnberg, 1939).

Norwegian oppositions:
the power of powerlessness

The analysis so far has sought to shed some light on the role of minority governments in Norwegian political history. I have also demonstrated that Norway exhibits few characteristics conventionally associated with political systems in which such cabinets are common. But we have not yet seen which *other* structural conditions facilitate minority government formation. In this section, we shall discuss one such critical feature, the role and resources of Norwegian parliamentary oppositions.

The strength of parliamentary oppositions is, of course, highly dependent on the decisiveness of the national assembly as a decision-making arena. Some students of the Storting have questioned its importance. One of the characteristics of the "European Polity Model" is a decline of the relative institutional role of parliaments. Norway is cited as one of the closest approximations to this ideal type (Heisler and Kvavik, 1974). In his seminal analysis of corporate pluralism, Stein Rokkan (1966) stressed the dependence of governmental politics on the extraparliamentary bargaining processes between the giant alliances of associations and corporations. And more traditional students of the Storting have also sounded the familiar theme of the decline of parliament (e.g., Stavang, 1968: 96).

It is important to note that these laments over the emasculation of the Storting are historically bounded propositions. No informed observer would have found the Storting of the 1880s or the 1920s lacking in effectiveness. In fact, the Storting of the interwar period was frequently accused of being too "interventionist" (Kaartvedt, Danielsen, and Greve, 1964). The alleged decline of the Storting refers temporally to the period from 1945 to the early 1960s, and the academic theme had its heyday in the sixties.

In recent years, Norwegians have again witnessed a period of parliamentary resurgence (Arter, 1984; Olsen, 1983). In interviews conducted during the spring of 1981, eight leading parliamentarians and officers in the major parties were asked a variety of questions about legislative–executive relations.[13] Seven of the eight believed that the Storting had increased its power since the early 1960s. Olsen (1983) sees a similar trend and expects the Storting to become a more significant political institution. This expectation is based on the nature of the dominant political issues as well as on the organizational characteristics of the Storting. In times of economic stagnation and contraction, reinterpretation, coordination, and compromises become more important, and these are tasks at which the Storting excels. Also, changing recruitment patterns have brought to the Storting more educated and less parochial politicians, who, with more adequate staffing, are better able to assert themselves (Eliassen, 1985).

---

[13] The following persons participated in semistructured interviews, lasting one to two hours on average: Odd Bye (SP), John Dale (SP), Rolf Fjeldvær (A), Jens Flå (KRF), Berge Furre (SV), Astrid Gjertsen (H), Helge Seip (V/DLF), Svenn Stray (H), and Johannes Vågsnes (KRF). Some of these individuals gave of their time on more than one occasion. I am grateful to all of them for their insight and time. I also had shorter conversations with several other individuals. Most interviews were conducted in May 1981.

In the postwar period, the debate about the decline of the Storting has been focused not so much on the relationship between the legislature and the cabinet as on the bypassing of the numerical-territorial channel of representation altogether. The main challenge has been the development (and subsequent decline) of a corporatist structure, at times encompassing more than 1,000 government committees and boards. The Storting has never been closely connected to this corporatist-functional network, and this has been taken as an indication of the political impotence of parliament.

This interpretation could be challenged on several grounds. Cabinet members have no more extensive ties with corporatist institutions than do legislators, yet the suggestion is rarely made that the cabinet is powerless. Also, one of the reasons Storting members have not been particularly well represented in the corporatist channels may be that corporatist decision making is inimical to their electoral incentives. Norwegian politicians are deeply concerned about their electoral fortunes. Corporatist representation implies a real danger of co-optation and impedes electioneering. Hence, parliamentarians may seek to avoid electorally damaging commitments and alliances by eschewing participation in corporatist networks (Olsen, 1983).

The role of the parliamentary arena in Norwegian politics has been subject to ebbs and flows rather than continuous decline (Lægreid and Olsen, 1986). Periods of extended minority rule have coincided with institutional growth. Minority rule and parliamentary influence are mutually reinforcing. Minority governments strengthen the role of the Storting, and parliamentary strength facilitates minority cabinets. However, even when the opposition has not fully utilized the parliamentary arena, the institutional potential has remained intact.

Legislative structure

Let us now consider the parliamentary settings in which the opposition can press its claims. For this purpose, the most important structures of the Storting are (1) the Board of Presidents, (2) conferences between the parliamentary leaders of the respective parties, and (3) the permanent legislative committees.

The six presidents do not wield great power in their own right, but they do form an important communications center.[14] The opposition is always represented on the Board of Presidents, which is normally composed of seasoned and respected parliamentarians. In 1961, the ruling Labor party increased the number of opposition members from 2 to 3, as a gesture designed to facilitate cooperation in a minority situation. This attests to the fact that the Board of Presidents is a site where compromises are made. Occasionally, the presidents may also become directly involved in government formation. Such was the case when the first Labor cabinet was formed in 1928. In 1971, Conservative Storting president Bernt Ingvaldsen was a key figure in attempts to patch up the ailing coalition of nonsocialist parties (Stavang, 1976).

Conferences between the parliamentary leaders of the various parties are another channel of oppositional influence. More or less formal, such meetings have become quite common in the postwar period. The first conferences of this kind were reportedly convened in 1948, with mainly economic issues on the agenda. Subsequent conferences in the early 1950s dealt with such issues as defense and electoral reform (Stavang, 1968). The utilization of this forum has varied over time and between governments. In 1960–1, conferences between the parliamentary leaders of the three center parties were crucial parts of an effort to establish a centrist government option before the 1961 election. On the whole, however, party leaders have been somewhat wary of institutionalizing such meetings.

These leaders, of course, must always balance the need for top-level interparty cooperation against commitments to their respective parties and caucuses. The high degree of party cohesiveness in parliamentary divisions is a prerequisite for effective top-level negotiations, but too many compromises over the heads of backbenchers will jeopardize party unity and deference. Although party discipline may have suffered somewhat in the Storting in recent years, most parties were still cohesive on more than 90% of the issues in the early 1970s (Bjurulf and Glans, 1976).

It was the growth of party cohesiveness in the interwar period that

---

[14] The Storting is a quasi-bicameral legislature, which constitutes itself as two separate divisions on legislative bills. Hence, the Board of Presidents has no less than six members: one president and one vice-president for each division, as well as one pair for the Storting as a whole.

decisively shifted the locus of effective decision making in the Storting
to the permanent committees (Stavang, 1968). Anybody who has
witnessed a plenary debate in the Storting knows that this is neither
where issues are decided nor great entertainment, despite reforms in
1954 and 1959 to facilitate a looser and livelier form of exchange
(Stavang, 1968). It is very rare that a unanimous or majority committee opinion is not adopted, and as Gudmund Hernes notes, "What
Woodrow Wilson said of congressional government – that it is committee government – is also very much the case for the parliamentary
government in Norway" (1971: 37).

In Chapter 3, we noted that the committee structure in the Storting
has the following characteristics, all of which contribute to the
strength of these bodies and thereby the opposition:

1. There is a relatively large number (12) of standing committees
   concerned with the constitutional functions of the Storting.
2. These committees have fixed areas of specialization.
3. With a couple of minor exceptions, their areas of specialization
   correspond to ministerial departments.
4. Each representative is a member of one and only one committee.
5. Committee assignments and chairs are proportionately distributed among the parties.

Norwegian parliamentary committees were first established soon after
1814. Between 1870 and 1890, they developed many of the features
that characterize them today. Membership was made stable for the
electoral period, jurisdictions were specified, and the election of a
committee rapporteur (*saksordfører*) on each bill was institutionalized. Formerly, the chairman had always represented the committee
on the floor. Thus, this reform strengthened the influence of
backbenchers.

Among the current permanent committees in the Storting, Foreign
and Constitutional Affairs is indisputably the most highly regarded
assignment. Membership tends to be restricted to parliamentarians
of high seniority and status. However, this committee is not the most
important site for political compromises, since the work load is light
and foreign policy normally consensual. In the view of the representatives, the Finance committee has the greatest legislative impact and
constitutes the most important forum for political majority building

(see Hernes, 1971; Rommetvedt, 1984). Accordingly, this is where the parties put their workhorses.

Committees prepare all decisions for the Storting, although they have no authority to legislate in their own right. All committees meet several days per week while the Storting is in session, some every day. Despite the fact that they do not conduct hearings, the permanent committees are in frequent and intimate contact with their respective cabinet members. In a 1975 survey of the members of the Bratteli II cabinet, every minister reported daily or weekly contacts with the corresponding Storting committee (Olsen, 1980: 229).

The capacity of representatives to effect changes in legislation outside their respective committee is severely constrained. In a 1964 survey, 74% of the parliamentarians felt ill-informed about issues outside their committee jurisdictions, and 54% reported that outsiders seldom have a possibility of influencing the outcome of issues under deliberation in their committees. The powerlessness of outsiders apparently extends to cabinet members, since 82% believed that their committees would prevail in case of a difference of opinion with the government (Hernes, 1971).

The fact that all committee proceedings are closed to the public facilitates compromise and committee effectiveness. So do the high degree of intracommittee specialization and the informal and egalitarian work routines. Although Storting representatives are not as wedded to their committees as members of the U.S. Congress, there is a strong tendency for them to stick with their original committee assignments. Over the years from 1950 to 1969, two-thirds of all reelected representatives retained their committee memberships. Those who changed were typically trying to secure more prestigious or otherwise attractive assignments. Thus, 77% of returning members left the dreaded (and now abolished) Protocol committee (Hellevik, 1969).

The emerging picture of the Storting is that of a pragmatic, decentralized, consensus-building institution, where the opposition has ample opportunity to influence policies. But the ways in which this happens are by design subtle and not highly visible. Interestingly, a survey of civil servants and interest group representatives found the highest estimates of the influence of the opposition among top civil

servants, presumably the respondents most attuned to the inner workings of the national assembly (Egeberg, Olsen, and Roness, 1980).

Thus Norwegian political parties do not, in comparative terms,
sacrifice a great deal of policy influence when they forgo government
participation. Yet, before abstention from power and thus minority
governments emerge as rational choices, we need to establish the
validity of the following propositions in the Norwegian context:

1. The great majority of Norwegian parliamentary parties are willing and able to participate in government.
2. Policy effectiveness is a major objective of these parties.
3. Government participation generally entails electoral costs, especially if it involves coalition governments.
4. Elections can significantly alter the relative bargaining power of
   the relevant parties.

Electoral decisiveness: deferring gratification

Several of the preceding propositions require little elaboration. We
have already seen that all five major parties have participated in
government on numerous occasions and that the strength of extremist
parties has generally been negligible. Nor is it controversial to classify
Norwegian parties as highly policy oriented. Norwegian parties have
never performed significant patronage functions, and in modern times
they have been too well organized to be mere vehicles for office-
seeking elites. Besides, the supply of political appointments has never
been very plentiful. Until World War II, cabinet portfolios (10 in
1939–40) were the only political appointments a governing party had
at its disposal. With the introduction of undersecretaries of state and
personal secretaries, the number of political appointments has increased to 22 in 1947, 33 in 1967, and 50 in 1977. However, this is
still a fairly meager electoral prize (Olsen, 1980; Roness, 1979).

Identifiability

Let us now examine the four components of electoral decisiveness in
order. As regards the identifiability of government alternatives, Nor-

way has seen significant historical fluctuations. From the introduction of parliamentary government until the early 1920s, a single-party Liberal government was an obvious option. The alternative was almost equally clearly a Conservative government, possibly in coalition with the Moderates. This bipolarity was undermined by the growth of the Labor party and the introduction of PR. Whereas the Conservatives began advocating bourgeois coalescence fairly early, the Liberals continued to invest in themselves as a government alternative in their own right until after World War II, with notable success until 1935. A nonsocialist coalition has been recognized as a distinct possibility since the mid-twenties, but the first such government only materialized in 1963. Labor presented itself as an alternative in 1928 and has remained one ever since. The party is the only social democratic party in Northern Europe that has never participated in a coalition government with any other party.

In sum, the Norwegian party system has been fully bipolar between 1884 and the early 1920s, and again most of the time since 1936 (see Christophersen and Hirsti, 1980). During the intervening period, there was at least one identifiable alternative, namely, the Labor party. Certain elections break the pattern. The choices of 1924 and 1927 were among the least interpretable in Norwegian history. In 1973, cooperation between the four nonsocialist parties had broken down, and it was not clear whether an alternative to a Labor government existed. In the 1981 election, the Conservative party emerged as a potential governing party, with or without the KRF and the SP. Yet the election was clearly bipolar. This case is particularly interesting since there was a widespread expectation that neither alternative would command a majority. Thus, in 1981 the Norwegian electorate was faced with *a fairly clear choice between two minority governments,* a situation not widely perceived as traumatic.

Electoral volatility

Table 6.6 presents volatility scores for all Norwegian elections from 1909 to 1985. For comparative purposes, recall that the cross-national mean is .11. Ten Norwegian elections have fallen below this level,

Table 6.6. *Volatility (for seats) in Norwegian elections, 1909–85*

1909:	.171	1945:	.153
1912:	.333	1949:	.087
1915:	.057	1953:	.093
1918:	.257	1957:	.027
1921:	.290	1961:	.040
1924:	.080	1965:	.054
1927:	.267	1969:	.059
1930:	.107	1973:	.167
1933:	.160	1977:	.194
1936:	.053	1981:	.123
		1985:	.051
Means			
1909–18:	.205		
1921–36:	.160		
1945–85:	.095		
Overall:	.134		

and ten have exceeded it. But cases of very high volatility have been more common than extreme deviations on the low side, so that the overall Norwegian mean approaches 14. Volatility was notably low in the 1950s and the 1960s, but has been comparatively high in all other decades.[15] For the postwar period as a whole, the score is higher than in most countries.

Competitiveness is also a function of the relative probabilities of the existing government alternatives. In the Norwegian case, note the close balance between Labor and the nonsocialist bloc (the main governmental alternatives) in most postwar elections (see Strom, 1986). In 1961, 1969, 1973, and 1977 a single seat would have tipped the parliamentary balance between socialists and nonsocialists. As volatility has decreased somewhat over the years (until the 1970s), the balance has become closer, so that overall electoral competitiveness has remained high.

[15] Consider, however, the difficulties of comparing the mature party systems of the postwar period with the less consolidated Norwegian system of the beginning of the century.

Table 6.7. *Electoral decisiveness in Norway*

Period	Identifiability	Volatility	Responsiveness	Proximity
1905–18	High	.205	1.00	.50
1919–40	Medium	.160	.44	.39
1945–87	Medium/high	.095	.69	.52

Responsiveness and proximity

The figures for electoral responsiveness and proximity are presented in Table 6.7. Recall that responsiveness measures the extent to which governments tend to be formed by parties that have gained seats in the most recent elections. Cross-nationally, responsiveness averages .58. Norway is well above this level for two of three time periods. However, responsiveness was rather low in the interwar years.

Proximity is the proportion of government formations that immediately follow elections. Here, the Norwegian scores are fairly average. The cross-national mean is .49, and Norway falls very close to this value in every time period, although again the score is notably lower in the interwar period than at other times.

Elections and strategies

Table 6.7 summarizes these results for the four dimensions of electoral decisiveness broken down by the three time periods. As we can see, electoral decisiveness has clearly been high in the earliest period and also since 1945. In the intervening years, the picture is more complex and overall electoral decisiveness lower. Elections were still highly competitive and volatile in those years, but electoral fortunes tended to be ignored in government formation (Christophersen, 1965). Because of the predominance of the left–right dimension, centrist parties such as the Liberals had disproportionate bargaining power. The interwar period was the longest period of continuous minority rule in Norwegian history, a fact seemingly at odds with the explanation I have advanced.

However, although electoral decisiveness was somewhat lower between the wars than at other times, oppositional influence, the other predictor of cabinet minoritarianism, was particularly high. Second, there is very little variation in the frequency of Norwegian minority governments over time. Apart from the governments of national coalition immediately after the 1905 secession, there have been only four majority coalitions in this century, namely Konow, Borten I and II, and Willoch II. Thus, there is only modest variation in either independent or dependent variables over the course of Norwegian history, whereas Norway in both respects stands out vis-à-vis most other political systems. Hence, the Norwegian data are more interesting for intersystem than for intrasystem comparisons. *Norway constitutes a clear and persistent case of an inclusionary system.*

Let us then reinterpret Norwegian government formation on the basis of the theory that underlies this classification. This analysis is constrained by a lack of available data on party preferences and strategies. However, this shortage is not fatal. We do not need explicit statements of the preferences and strategies of party leaders. In fact, party leaders need not even be aware of their preference structures. All that is required is that they respond consistently and predictably to given incentive structures.

Norway presents some particular problems of data availability and interpretation. Some of these have to do with the relationship between the information certainty of party leaders and the ambiguity of their public policy positions. High levels of certainty concerning cabinet options need not be associated with clear statements of preference. Obversely, uncertainty should not be deduced from ambiguity in policy positions. Interparty relations in Norway are characterized by good information. Exceptionally short and uncomplicated formation processes attest to the high quality of information relating to cabinet participation. Partly as a consequence of this certainty however, party strategies often remain implicit, since there is no need to spell out to other parties what is already clear. *Elite-level politics in Norway is high on certainty and low on explicitness.* Lawrence Dodd (1976) argues that the likelihood of minimum winning coalitions should covary positively with the certainty of information available to political parties. Norway is hardly a confirming case for Dodd's theory.

Norwegian political culture lessens the explicitness of partisan strategies. Until very recently, the mass media have been highly protective of politicians and the confidentiality of their interactions. This attitude has made it possible for political leaders to project an image to the electorate starkly at odds with their interaction in the parliamentary arena. Publicly, politicians stress their differences on the issues and their commitment to policy objectives. These commitments are undoubtedly sincere, but they are tempered by less publicized strategic considerations.

In so doing, they help project the preferred image of political life. But, as Lægreid and Olsen observe:

> Actually, Norwegian parties invest heavily in the belief that their platforms present a clear political alternative to the voters, and that elected representatives will try strenuously to realize the program. *To mobilize voters* and to keep up party activists' enthusiasm *parties forego policy benefits* in order to preserve their identity. This is typically done in situations of greatest visibility: formal coalition building and electoral cooperation. In a way, *if conflict did not exist,* it would have to have been invented. (1986: 201; emphases added)

In general terms, Norwegian scholars have also suggested that politicians primarily concern themselves with vote maximization, and that this consideration moderates their legislative behavior (Berg, 1978: 67; Østerud, 1979: 20). However, this perspective has generated few empirical investigations of cabinet-level politics (Kuhnle and Rokkan, 1977). With broad brush strokes, and focusing on selected cases, the next section presents such an interpretation of Norwegian cabinet formation.

Policies and electioneering: illustrative cases

Government formation was fairly unproblematic in Norway under the modified parliamentary two-party system that existed until 1921. The large national coalitions formed immediately after the secession from Sweden were not viable solutions in the long run. When Liberal leader Gunnar Knudsen formed the first Norwegian minority gov-

ernment in 1908, it occasioned some trauma (Björnberg, 1939; Stavang, 1971), but the prevalent fears were not borne out by subsequent
events. The bipolarity of the system was strengthened by the rapprochement between the Conservatives and the Moderates. Their
alliance became progressively less of a coalition and more of a party.

The introduction of PR complicated party strategies considerably.
Yet, the various parties soon developed parliamentary strategies to
which they generally remained faithful until the 1935 watershed.
Roughly, the Conservatives and Agrarians pressed for broad nonsocialist coalitions as a bulwark against Labor, whereas the Liberals
insisted on either a grand coalition of all parties (which was quite
unrealistic) or a government of the Liberals alone. Both options, of
course, were likely to yield policies close to the Liberals' ideal point.
Labor refused to participate in any coalition.

All these positions made sense as electoral strategies and as credible
avenues to power. The Conservatives recognized that a majority of
the electorate remained nonsocialist throughout the interwar period.
This majority could be mobilized, as indeed it was in 1930, whenever
the bourgeois parties made a joint effort to stress their differences
with the socialists as the fundamental cleavage in Norwegian politics.
Being the most vehemently antisocialist party, the Conservatives
stood to gain the most from this kind of mobilization. This is exactly
what happened in 1930. On the other hand, up through 1928 the
Conservatives had bad experiences with single-party governments.
On all three occasions when they had been in power, the Conservatives had suffered subsequent electoral reverses, and in two cases
the setbacks had been stunning. Electorally the Lykke government
(1926–8) was a veritable *ulykke* (disaster) for the Conservatives,[16]
who lost 24 of their 54 representatives in 1927.[17] Hence, the Conservatives pressed primarily for a nonsocialist coalition. When this
invariably foundered due to Liberal resistance, the Conservatives did
not press their own claims to power too vigorously.

The Agrarians had similar objectives, but their interests were narrower in scope. As an articulative party with a narrowly defined

---

[16] I ask the reader to excuse this play on words. *Lykke* in Norwegian means fortune,
ulykke misfortune.
[17] These figures include the Moderate representatives, who were by this time an
integral part of the Conservative party.

constituency, they did not have the same electoral designs as the other nonsocialist parties. Yet they did want the recognition that government participation entailed, and they were concerned about their electoral competitors. Despite the fact that a large number of Agrarians were former Liberals, the new party felt much more comfortable in alliance with the Conservatives. And when the bourgeois bulwark against Labor caved in, in 1935, it was a feud between the Agrarians and the Liberals that precipitated the event. The Agrarians and the Liberals were direct competitors for the rural vote, particularly in western Norway, whereas the urban and business-oriented Conservatives were no threat to the Agrarian constituency (Kaartvedt et al., 1964: 323–4).

By assuming government responsibility in 1928 Labor showed its willingness to play by the parliamentary rules. As the socialists harbored no illusion that their cabinet would endure, they presented a radical government program (Björnberg, 1939: 298–321). The assumption of office had been divisive in the Labor party, and government responsibility remained a controversial issue over the next few years. It was only after the electoral victory of 1933 that Labor again began to press its claim to power seriously. At that time, Labor wanted recognition as a legitimate governing party, while at the same time it did not want to compromise itself by entering a coalition with the bourgeois parties. Time was demonstrably on Labor's side throughout the interwar era, and it could therefore confidently turn down Liberal overtures. When the socialists finally assumed power in 1935, the price they had to pay was low. The Agrarians were willing to provide external support in exchange for a "crisis accord" including government relief for the agricultural sector, hard hit by the depression. These measures were easily incorporated into the "New Deal" legislation initiated by Labor. The program of the Nygaardsvold government was much more moderate than that of 1928. Time was ripe for effective Labor government. From 1935 to the early 1970s Labor generally faced low incumbency costs, and since Nygaardsvold the party has been remarkably willing to govern, but equally unwilling to enter any coalition.

The Liberals played one of the most interesting roles in the interwar period. No party was more frequently in office, and none had a more disastrous electoral development. The Liberal party

continued to invest in itself as a government alternative despite drastic electoral losses. Its claims remained credible due to what Herbert
Tingsten called the "point-of-gravity parliamentarism," in which the
parties of the political center could balance off the oppositions on
both wings (Tingsten, cited in Seip, 1963: 15). In game-theoretic
terms, the Liberals were consistently in the one-dimensional core between the wars, since they controlled the median legislator along the
dominant left–right dimension. This "privileged position" of the Liberals had been recognized by Gunnar Knudsen in 1921, and both
Knudsen and his successors refused to commit themselves to any coalition toward the right (see Björnberg, 1939). Seemingly, this strategy even made electoral sense. The Liberals were the only party to
draw support from all segments of society, and being associated
firmly with either working-class or middle-class parties could only
cost votes in the opposite camp. Moreover, as the government party
par excellence, the Liberals could conceivably become a rallying
point for all defenders of a besieged system. In 1924, the Liberals ea-
gerly accepted government responsibility in the expectation that this
would be to their advantage in the election that fall (Björnberg,
1939). They were wrong in 1924, and they were even more wrong
later. Being identified as the government party was no boon during
the Great Depression. The Liberals' predicament became desperate
as the contradiction between their electoral and parliamentary goals
became more and more obvious. This dilemma was accentuated in
the chain of events that led to the demise of the last Liberal government in 1935.

1935: Mowinckel and the Agrarians

By 1935 relations between the Liberals and the Agrarians had already
been strained for some time. The Agrarians had been instrumental
in defeating Mowinckel's previous government in 1931, and the Liberals had retaliated by bringing down the Agrarian Hundseid government less than two years later. Under the ensuing Mowinckel
government tensions persisted. The noninterventionist austerity policies of the powerful Liberal minister of agriculture, Haakon Five,
were clearly at odds with Agrarian desires. During 1934 and 1935 the
Agrarians twice seemed ready to topple Mowinckel over his lack of

positive measures to combat the depression in Norwegian agriculture. Both times the Agrarians retreated, after Conservative mediation and government promises of forthcoming legislation. After all, the Agrarians were not anxious to bring a Labor government to power. But when the promised government legislation materialized, the Agrarians were bitterly disappointed. On the first occasion, the government delivered only a modest appropriation to combat cattle disease. This was a direct provocation to the Agrarians. The second time, the government delivered nothing at all. That was even worse.

In the winter of 1935, it was obvious that the Mowinckel government was in imminent danger. Yet, Mowinckel neither sought an accommodation nor resigned voluntarily. Instead, on March 14 the prime minister moved for a vote of confidence *on the government's proposed budget as a whole.* If there ever was a sure-fire way for a government to commit suicide, Mowinckel had found it. His government was promptly defeated, and Nygaardsvold's Labor cabinet took over with Agrarian support.

Jorunn Bjørgum (1970) has offered a persuasive interpretation of Mowinckel's puzzling behavior. In her opinion, the embattled prime minister was initially faced with two equally undesirable options. On the one hand, he could try to keep the government afloat until the 1936 elections through ad hoc majorities. But the Liberals had again lost ground in the municipal elections of 1934 and saw the prospects of a continued downward trend if they remained in office. On the other hand, the Agrarians had not pressed an unambiguous motion of no confidence, and Mowinckel feared that if he resigned the Liberals would be held responsible for the accession of a Labor government. Thus, the Liberals would again stand to lose in future elections. So Mowinckel decided to force the Agrarians to vote down his government. The prime minister was willing to give up his office in the hope of electoral victory in 1936, and his strategy was based on three assumptions:

1. The Agrarians would be compromised with their nonsocialist voters for bringing a socialist government to power.
2. The Labor party would be unable to alleviate the depressed economy and would lose the faith of many supporters.

3. There would be no logical place for these disgruntled Laborites and Agrarians to go but to the Liberals.

Unfortunately for the Liberals, only one of Mowinckel's predictions came true. The Agrarians did suffer in the 1936 elections, but so did the Liberals. For whatever reason, the economy began to improve under Nygaardsvold, and the Labor party was even more successful in 1936 than in 1933.

1963: Lyng and Kings Bay

For the postwar period, the tumultuous events of 1963 serve as an illustration of similar political designs. During the early 1960s, Labor was preoccupied with its socialist challenger to the left, the Socialist People's party (SF). Most SF voters and activists were former Laborites, and between them the two parties held a socialist parliamentary majority after the 1961 elections. However, the Labor attitude toward the SF was one of intense hostility and noncooperation. In the words of the SF leader, his party was treated as if it were "worse than any bourgeois party, and worse even than the Communists" (Gustavsen, 1968: 150). By appealing to the traditional Labor constituency, the SF clearly represented a more serious electoral competitor than any nonsocialist party. The Labor response was one of ostracism and humiliation. By snubbing the SF and seeking compromises with the centrist parties, Gerhardsen in effect sought to reduce the former to size, from pivot to political impotence. After the initial shock of the electoral defeat of 1961, Labor leaders reasoned that they could safely ignore the left socialists, since these would never want to suffer the electoral consequences of toppling a socialist government (Finstad, 1970; Karmly, 1975).

Labor's conciliatory posture created a dilemma for the nonsocialist parties. On the one hand, they were given unprecedented opportunities to influence Labor government policies. On the other hand, the situation contained a potential for co-optation. Since the mid-1950s there had been serious efforts to facilitate nonsocialist cooperation and a future coalition government, with or without the Conservatives. Any flirtation with Labor could easily jeopardize the fragile bourgeois unity that had been attained. However, a premature and unsuccessful nonsocialist minority government might be just as detrimental to the longer-term prospects for a bourgeois majority. The center-right parties were therefore not unwilling to let Labor buy time. The Liberals in particular were courted by Gerhardsen, but the Liberal leader, Bent Røiseland, was only too conscious of the lessons of 1935. He knew that if he moved too close to the government and the nonsocialist alliance floundered, the Liberals would be vilified by the other bourgeois parties (Bergh and Pharo, 1981: 439). Such a stigma could be very costly in elections to come.

In the first half of 1963, a number of issues came up in which the opposition perceived government mismanagement and arrogance. The Kings Bay issue, where the government seemed to withhold damaging information from the Storting, was the final straw.[18] The nonsocialist parties had found a symbolic issue on which to confront the government. This was an ideal situation because it provided the bourgeois parties with an opportunity to present a united front against Labor without ironing out their own policy differences. After considerable soul-searching, even the SF decided to oppose the government. The fear of defeating a socialist government remained strong, but the countervailing sentiment was that the party could not allow itself to be kicked around by Labor indefinitely. If future bargaining power required retaliation for these snubs, SF leaders were willing to take such action. The SF eventually helped bring down Gerhardsen's government in August 1963, but paid the price in the local elections in September.

The four bourgeois parties were happy to install Conservative John Lyng as the new prime minister because it gave their coalition credibility as a governmental alternative. But the government was never expected or intended to be anything but transitory (Karmly, 1975). Instead, the nonsocialists set their sights on the 1965 election. When it became clear that Labor would defeat the government at the earliest opportunity, Lyng responded in a fashion remarkably similar to that

---

[18] The Kings Bay issue concerned a fatal mining accident in a government-operated coal mine in Spitsbergen. An investigative report that was critical of the government's safety precautions was released immediately after the Storting adjourned for the summer in June. Opposition leaders believed the government had deliberately withheld the report until adjournment to prevent, or at least postpone, parliamentary consideration.

of Mowinckel in 1935. Labor and the SF presented separate motions of no confidence, so the government found itself confronted with a negative majority. Under these circumstances, there was a precedent for the government to remain in office (Stavang, 1971). However, Lyng asked the Storting for a positive vote of confidence, a move that effectively sealed his fate. Again, this apparently self-defeating behavior made electoral sense. After 28 years of Labor government, a credible alternative had been presented. However, the nonsocialists had not had sufficient time to iron out their policy differences, and they were anxious to avoid the embarrassments of trial and error. The year 1965 would be the time to try to govern.

My interpretation of these events has stressed electoral strategies as a determinant of government participation. The purpose is not to deny the importance of policy conflicts in government formation. On the contrary, a key argument in this chapter is that Norwegian parties are strongly policy motivated. But their pursuit of policy objectives is constrained by electoral concerns. Also, the importance of policy motivations does not imply that the party system is unable to accommodate conflict. The curious fact is that such a large number of Norwegian governments, both before and after 1945, have been formed and defeated over *foreign policy* issues (Christophersen and Hirsti, 1980), despite the fact that the party system has developed around domestic cleavages. As Lægreid and Olsen point out, "Most cabinet crises in Norway in this century have not been struggles over large substantive stakes. They have rather been linked to issues that in a specific situation were redefined and given great political significance" (1986: 187).

Norwegian governments in office

Norwegian parties are office seekers as well as policy seekers and vote seekers. Since the late 1920s, all major parties have been willing and legitimate governing parties. All have had considerable government experience. Government performance thus concerns them all fairly directly. In this section, we shall investigate the performance of Norwegian governments from the perspective of the participating parties as well as from a more systemic point of view.

Majority construction

Since most Norwegian governments have been undersized, building legislative majorities has been a challenge. Seemingly, Norwegian minority cabinets have succeeded very well in this endeavor without trying too hard. Norwegian minority governments have attained respectable durability, but without formal support agreements with parties outside the cabinet. Only two governments, Nygaardsvold I and Willoch I, have enjoyed external support. Even these cases have been marginal, since their support agreements have lacked the explicit precommitment required of formal minority cabinets. Based on the relative commitment of the supporting parties, however, Nygaardsvold, but not Willoch, can be classified as a formal minority government. Nygaardsvold had had negotiations with the Agrarians prior to this accession to power, but the concrete contents of their "crisis accord" were hammered out only after Labor had come to power. Nygaardsvold agreed to crisis appropriations for agriculture, local government, and road construction, but the Agrarians made few other policy demands (Furre, 1976).

Kåre Willoch's first government took office after unsuccessful efforts to construct a majority coalition of the three major nonsocialist parties (H, KRF, and SP). The subsequent commitment of the centrist parties to the conservative cabinet was never very explicit, although the government seemed secure. A joint three-party legislative program for the 1981–5 period had been promulgated prior to the 1981 elections, and this formed a rough basis for Willoch's policies. However, when the Conservatives presented their first budget in October 1982, the consent of the Christian People's party and the Center party had not been prenegotiated. The three parties reached a compromise during the Storting budget deliberations, but Labor attempts to interject itself into the process suggest that this agreement was no foregone conclusion.

None of the remaining 30 minority governments since 1905 have enjoyed formal external support. The typical practice has been ad hoc and disaggregated legislative coalitions, often involving different opposition parties on different issues. In the postwar period, the need for parliamentary coalition building first presented itself when Einar Gerhardsen's government lost its majority in 1961. At that time, many in the Labor party, and especially within the unions, favored resignation. But Gerhardsen quickly discovered that he could exploit the reluctance of the pivotal Socialist People's party to bring him down. The limits of this strategy were of course demonstrated in the Kings Bay crisis of 1963. However, the electoral costs of toppling Labor were not lost on the left socialists, who have struggled with a "Kings Bay complex" ever since.

Labor's minority governments have rarely been forced to choose between a leftist and rightist strategy. Trygve Bratteli's first cabinet (1971–2) was in the most precarious bargaining position, since it had no preliamentary opposition to the left. Thus, all deals had to be cut with the opposition on the right, and Labor's bargaining power was reduced. But the EEC membership issue secured the government until the referendum in September 1972. Given their internal disagreements over this issue, the nonsocialists were in no mood to be in charge at that time. Bratteli could cooperate with the Conservatives on the EEC issue, and with the Liberals on budgetary matters.

Labor reached a more critical juncture when Bratteli returned to power in 1973. The party had been badly split and demoralized over the EEC issue and humiliated by the voters (Hellevik, 1979). It was therefore a cautious and diffident Bratteli who resumed the tasks of prime minister. His party was 16 votes short of a parliamentary majority, and there was considerable internal dissension over the choice of partners in majority building. Former premier Gerhardsen suggested future cooperation toward the left (Kielland, 1972), whereas party secretary Ronald Bye and others wished a rapprochement with the Center party or the Christian People's party (Ørvik, 1977: 80–3). Yet no formal coalition or agreement with any party was ever envisioned and no consultations were undertaken before Bratteli faced the Storting (Gustavsen, 1979; Larsen, 1980). Nor did any of the opposition parties desire a formal agreement, although the nonsocialists clearly preferred a rightward-leaning government (Langslet, 1974: 93–4).

Bratteli's shifting legislative coalitions were continued by his successors, Odvar Nordli and Gro Harlem Brundtland. They were sufficiently successful to keep Labor in power until 1981. In general, Labor's ad hoc majorities have included the Left Socialists on many domestic issues of ideological significance, the centrist parties in budgetary matters, and the Conservatives on foreign and defense policy, as well as on industrial and environmental issues. Brundtland's second government, which has had to operate under a nonsocialist majority, has tilted more toward the centrist parties than most Labor governments. In particular, the period from 1986 to 1989 saw a rapprochement between Labor and the Center party. Over the longer haul, it is indicative of the success of this balancing act that each opposition bloc has perceived Labor to be leaning excessively in the opposite direction.[19]

The centrist and radically undersized Korvald government enjoyed a privileged position, since its main purpose was to reach a trade agreement with the EEC. Until this task was accomplished, the government was fairly secure. Since no pro-EEC party was interested in government participation after the referendum, Korvald had the positive support of only 39 representatives (see Allen, 1979). Korvald was not challenged on foreign policy matters. In domestic politics, the government performed another balancing act. On tax issues, Korvald was supported by the Conservatives, whereas in other economic matters he sought majorities to the left. Korvald also chose to ignore a number of parliamentary defeats, which he could have interpreted as sufficient reasons for resignation.[20] Thus, the Korvald government was less successful than most in building legislative majorities.

Lyng's government saw even less success and never had a chance to build any kind of majority for its legislative program. Willoch's single-party Conservative government from 1981 to 1983 rested on a fairly secure three-party majority. This coalition was formalized when the Christians and the Center party entered the government in June 1983. When this three-party coalition lost its majority in 1985, it became dependent on the two votes of the Progress party. However, the two minor governing parties refused to enter any legislative agreement with these two right-wing parliamentarians. Despite this snub,

---

[19] See, e.g., Gustavsen (1979: 186); Larsen (1980: 233–7); and Lars Korvald, cited in *Nordisk Kontakt* (1976: 112–13). This tendency was borne out in my conversations with leading parliamentarians.

[20] Prominent Labor parliamentarian Guttorm Hansen, later to become president of the Storting, saw this unresponsiveness to parliamentary defeats as a threat to parliamentary democracy. Hansen, *Fri Fagbevegelse* (1973), no. 8; cited in Stavang (1976: 442). The context of Hansen's remarks should be taken into consideration – the statement was made during the 1973 election campaign.

Table 6.8. *Mean duration of Norwegian cabinets, 1905–87 (months)*

	1905–40	1945–87	1905–87
All majority	20.8	31.9	27.1
Coalition	13.3	31.0	20.9
Party	36.0	31.7	32.8
All minority	14.5	18.4	15.9
Coalition	12.8	6.7	10.1
Party	14.9	22.8	17.5
All governments	15.9	24.3	19.5

FRP leader Carl I. Hagen initially pledged to support the nonsocialist coalition. But in the spring of 1986 Hagen voted with the socialist opposition against increased gasoline taxes, the government lost, and Willoch resigned.

Majority building by Norwegian minority cabinets has thus taken a variety of forms, but all have been characterized by a low level of aggregation and commitment. The role has been played most easily by Labor governments, which have generally benefited from both internal unity and bilateral oppositions.

Performance in office

In the preceding section we have discussed *how* Norwegian minority governments have maintained themselves in power. We now turn to an analysis of *how well* they have succeeded. Let us first consider cabinet duration. Table 6.8 presents average duration figures for Norwegian governments since 1905, broken down by form and time period. The longevity of Norwegian governments, particularly in the postwar period, is amply demonstrated. With a mean duration of 24.3 months, Norwegian cabinets have been almost 40% longer lived than the average for all 15 countries (17.5 months). The prewar figures are markedly lower but should not be compared to postwar measures for other countries.[21] Two series of minority governments were ini-

---

[21] The lower pre-1940 figures are partly explained by the fact that until 1936 the term of the Storting was only three years. Consequently, maximum cabinet longevity is also 36 months in the earlier period, as against 48 months since 1936.

tiated in 1961 and 1971, respectively. There is no indication that these were particularly troubled times in terms of executive stability.

Minority governments have been less durable than majority governments, but postwar minority cabinets have enjoyed approximately 17% greater longevity than the cross-national mean for *all* governments. Over this century as a whole, coalition governments have been substantially less durable than single-party cabinets, but since 1945 this difference shows up only for minority governments. The two minority coalitions have lasted a meager average of 6.5 months, whereas minority party governments post a very respectable 23.3 months. The overall picture is far from embarrassing for Norway's undersized administrations. Apart from Lyng's four-week interlude, minority governments have endured long enough to surprise knowledgeable observers and sometimes even the participants themselves (as seems to have been the case with Gerhardsen V and Korvald) (Dale, 1980; Lie, 1975). At the extreme, Odvar Nordli's second cabinet soldiered on for 41 months before the prime minister suddenly resigned for health reasons.

Government resignations

Table 6.9 reports the *causes* of resignations (in percentage terms) for the various types of Norwegian cabinets since 1905. Due to the small number of cases, we should not attach too much significance to the numerical results. However, several tendencies in the material present themselves quite strongly. Three of the seven majority coalitions have resigned because of internal fission, whereas this fate has befallen no majority party or minority government. On the whole, the pattern of majority party government resignations is much more benign than that of majority coalitions, with minority governments falling in between. Majority party governments have resigned only for electoral or personal reasons. Minority governments have resigned for the widest range of reasons. Nine such administrations have fallen on votes of no confidence (seven of these prior to World War II), but this indication of vulnerability is offset by the sizable proportion of resignations caused by less severe factors (e.g., electoral and personal resignations).

Table 6.10, which reports the *mode* of resignation broken down in

Table 6.9. *Causes of resignation of Norwegian cabinets, 1905–87 (percentages by cabinet type)*

Cabinet type	Government disunity	Parliamentary confidence	Parliamentary policy defeat	Electoral	Systemic	Personal/ constitutional	(N)
All majority	20	7	0	60	0	13	(15)
Coalition	43	14	0	43	0	0	(7)
Party	0	0	0	75	0	25	(8)
All minority	3	29	10	39	6	13	(31)
Coalition	0	29	29	29	0	14	(7)
Party	4	29	4	42	8	13	(24)
All governments	9	22	7	46	4	13	(46)

Table 6.10. *Mode of resignation of Norwegian cabinets, 1905–87 (percentages by cabinet type)*

Cabinet type	Crisis/defeat	Voluntary	Technical	(N)
All majority	47	7	47	(15)
Coalition	57	0	43	(7)
Party	38	13	50	(8)
All minority	65	6	29	(31)
Coalition	86	0	14	(7)
Party	58	8	33	(24)
All governments	59	7	35	(46)

a similar manner, confirms the superiority of majority party governments, but reveals no significant difference between the other cabinet types. Note that *no Norwegian majority party government has ever been removed from office through electoral defeat or in any other direct manner*. Such cabinets have tended to retain their parliamentary majorities. In the two cases when they have not (1918 and 1961), the incumbents have soldiered on as minority cabinets. This is a remarkable standard of governmental stability. Even majority coalitions and minority cabinets have performed very well by cross-national standards. About one-third have suffered only technical resignations, as compared to no more than 14% cross-nationally.

Electoral performance

Table 6.11 shows how much Norwegian governments have tended to gain (or lose) in the next subsequent election. While pre-1940 governments tended to lose heavily, the tendency has been different in the postwar era. Majority governments have on average gained in the latter period, and the mean losses of minority governments have been cut by almost half. Since 1945, then, Norway has experienced strong electoral performance by governing parties.

Note that the usual electoral advantage of minority governments is reversed in the Norwegian case. However, the relationship between minority governments and electoral losses may well be spurious, since it is arguably the greater electoral volatility since the 1960s that is at

Table 6.11. *Subsequent electoral gain by cabinet type, 1905–87*
(percentage points of total vote, mean values)

	1905–40	1945–87	1905–87
All majority	−8.30	0.06	−3.29
Coalition	−12.60	−2.67	−8.34
Party	−4.00	1.42	0.06
All minority	−3.03	−1.68	−2.61
Coalition	−1.80	−0.45	−1.35
Party	−3.34	−2.03	−2.94
All governments	−3.61	−0.86	−2.84

the root of both government minoritarianism and electoral erosion. Table 6.12 gives a breakdown of average alternation scores by cabinet type and period of formation. Alternation in the Norwegian system has since 1945 been high and increasing. Among our 15 countries, only Iceland and Ireland exhibit higher turnover rates. Three other tendencies are evident in the data:

1. Minority governments have been followed by substantially more alternation than majority governments.
2. Coalition governments have led to greater turnover in office than those of a single party.
3. Prewar cabinets exhibit somewhat less subsequent alternation than those formed after 1945.

Table 6.12. *Subsequent alternation by cabinet type, 1905–87*
(mean values)

	1905–40	1945–87	1905–87
All majority	11.3	11.1	11.2
Coalition	17.0	33.3	24.0
Party	0	0	0
All minority	39.2	57.2	45.6
Coalition	52.0	87.3	67.1
Party	35.9	50.0	40.2
All governments	32.7	36.5	34.3

Table 6.13. *Legislative performance by cabinet type, 1945–87 (mean annual figures)*

Cabinet type	Laws enacted	Budgetary amendments (as % of total budget)
All majority	92.1	1.30
Coalition	91.0	0.25
Party	93.3	1.89
All minority	88.6	1.03
Coalition	110.0	0.35
Party	87.1	1.08
All governments	90.2	1.19
	($N = 28$)	($N = 41$)

Note: Breakdown by cabinet type in power during the greater part of the annual session of the Storting.
Source: Stortingstidende.

The Norwegian political system is therefore aptly described as *alternational,* in the sense that the potential for extensive turnover is present, although not always actualized.

Legislative performance: quantitative analysis

While the enactment of laws and the budgetary process do not exhaust the activity of the Storting, they clearly constitute essential tasks, which we shall now scrutinize for a more direct measure of the effectiveness of different Norwegian governments. The two measures of legislative performance we shall examine are the total number of laws enacted annually, and the proportion of change in the government budget during its passage through the Storting.[22] The latter measure was developed by Per Stavang (1968) in his study of parliamentary government in Norway. Apart from its centrality in parliamentary work,[23] the budgetary process is a regular and inevitable undertaking which lends itself to time series analysis.

[22] Specifically, budgetary amendments are measured as the sum of the absolute values of all additions and deductions introduced during the Storting deliberations as a percentage of the sum of revenues and appropriations in the final budget.
[23] The Storting spends the greater part of its autumn session on budgetary proceedings.

Table 6.13 presents a breakdown of these measures of legislative
performance by cabinet type. Note one problem with the data. Although the budgetary data are complete for the 1945–87 period thanks
to annual overviews reported in *Stortingstidende,* the record on law
enactment is much more spotty.[24] A considerable number of observations, particularly for the 1940s and 1950s, are missing. However,
since legislative output has rarely varied dramatically from one year
to the next, the reported means are not likely to be grossly misleading.

In comparative terms, the Norwegian Storting produces a fairly
average amount of legislation (Di Palma, 1977: 48). Historically the
volume of legislation increased steadily from the turn of the century
to the early postwar period, but it has since remained stable (see
Aubert, 1976). Table 6.13 shows only minor differences in legislative
and budgetary effectiveness between majority and minority governments. Majority coalitions have been the least productive legislatively, but the most effective type of government in securing passage
for their budgets. Majority party governments exhibit the exact opposite pattern. Minority governments do not deviate significantly
from the national mean on either count. Their budgetary effectiveness
is slightly above the mean, whereas legislative effectiveness is marginally below average.[25]

The most obvious interpretation of these results is that only insignificant performance differences exist between the various cabinet
types. Certainly Table 6.13 contains few significant differences. Only
the counterintuitive difference in budgetary effectiveness between
majority coalitions and majority party governments seems to call for
interpretation. The best way to understand these results is to examine
some influential cases. The relatively poor budgetary performance of
majority party governments can be traced largely to the period 1952–
5, when parliamentary amendments exceeded 3% of the overall
budget for three of four years. This period corresponds almost perfectly to the premiership of Oscar Torp. Torp did not preside over
a precarious parliamentary majority, but his personal authority was

[24] *Stortingstidende* is the official record of the Storting. The number of laws enacted
is not published as a separate statistic in these records. Our measure is based on figures
commonly quoted in the speech given by the president of the Storting at the time of
its annual adjournment.
[25] Since minority coalitions are represented by a single case, no comparison between
single-party and coalition minority cabinets makes sense.

clearly the weakest of all Labor prime ministers. Torp struggled with fiscal policies throughout his tenure and was finally deposed by his own party for his inability to address these problems effectively (Heradstveit, 1981; Larssen, 1973; Lie, 1975; Ørvik, 1977).

The strong budgetary performance of majority coalitions is similarly understandable in historical context. The figures largely represent the Borten cabinets, the first of which came to power in 1965. This was the first viable nonsocialist government in 30 years. The Labor campaign against the nonsocialist parties had been based on the premises that (1) the four bourgeois parties could not effectively govern in coalition, and (2) these parties, and especially the Conservatives, would seek to dismantle the welfare state.

Borten's coalition set out to prove Labor wrong on both counts. Thus, the government initially put a premium on internal unity and took care to avoid drastic departures from past government policy (Finstad, 1970; Lyng, 1978; Vassbotn, 1971). It is this strategy that shows up in the high budgetary effectiveness of majority coalitions. Note that there was a steady increase in legislative activity and a corresponding decline in budgetary effectiveness over Borten's first four-year term. Presumably the need to gain legitimacy decreased over time.

In conclusion, there is little evidence that Norwegian majority cabinets have differed to any meaningful extent in legislative performance. The effectiveness of minority cabinets has been remarkably stable, with the poorest showing put in by the first such cabinet in its first year (1961–2). There is no evidence that minority cabinets have been systematically inferior to other governments.

It seems fair to conclude that despite the high frequency of minority cabinets, Norway has enjoyed comparatively successful and effective governments. Ungovernability has not been a favorite concern among observers of Norwegian politics, and the recent predominance of minority governments has not seriously intensified such fears (see, however, Christophersen and Hirsti, 1980). Norwegian majority party governments have performed exceptionally well, but even majority coalitions and minority governments have acquitted themselves remarkably well by international standards. Between the latter two cabinet types, the comparative advantages of minority governments appear more pronounced than in most other countries.

The lengthy periods of minority rule in Norwegian history raise the question of the effects of sustained government minoritarianism. Doubtless, in recent years this situation has made the task of governing more complicated and taxing (Lægreid and Olsen, 1986; Olsen, 1983). Former prime minister Lars Korvald, among others, has testified to this effect (Rommetvedt, 1980: 35). But the power of Norwegian governments has been influenced by a number of variables besides parliamentary basis. The personal authority of the prime minister and other cabinet members is one such factor of considerable weight. Gerhardsen and Torp presided over cabinets with identical parliamentary bases, yet Gerhardsen's governments were much more effective. Similarly, Bratteli was widely perceived as a stronger leader than Nordli.

Norwegian political institutions have been affected by minority governments in a variety of ways. In personal interviews, leading Norwegian politicians were nearly unanimous in their opinion that government minoritarianism had increased the power of the Storting vis-à-vis the government and that of the committees within parliament. With some qualifications, they also held that the strength of the parliamentary parties relative to their respective extraparliamentary organizations had been enhanced. Most of these parliamentarians saw no meaningful decline in the stability and effectiveness of the Norwegian political system as a consequence of the minoritarian experience, and those who did, tended to mention offsetting advantages of minority governments. Government minoritarianism in Norway has inaugurated institutional as well as behavioral changes, but these are rarely seen as ominous or detrimental (see also Stavang, 1976). In fact, in 1988 former prime minister Willoch introduced a constitutional amendment to allow premature dissolution of the Storting. Willoch's premise for this proposal was that minority cabinets would continue to be a regular feature of Norwegian political life. Given this situation, it would make sense to give them this potential sanction against parliament.

Conclusions

Norway has served as a crucial test case for my theory of minority government formation and performance. The country is our clearest case of an inclusionary system. At the same time, Norway has very few of the properties conventionally associated with minority governments. The exceptionally high frequency of minority governments in minority situations (83%) is therefore compatible with only one of the contending explanations, namely, the one advanced in Chapter 2. The generalizability of this finding has not been addressed in this chapter, but at least the other Scandinavian (and inclusionary) countries would seem to have much in common with Norway.

Although the patterns of government formation I have described are widely recognized in Norwegian scholarship, my interpretation of the cabinet formation game is not a common one. This is at least partly due to a lack of intensive and theoretically ambitious scholarship on Norwegian government formation. Thus, my analysis can only claim plausibility where more extensive empirical substantiation would have been desirable. As usual, further empirical investigation should be encouraged.

In terms of government performance, Norwegian minority cabinets make a very respectable showing. Although not as effective as Norwegian majority party governments, undersized administrations have on balance performed as well as majority coalitions, and in some areas considerably better than average for all governments in the cross-national material. The Norwegian political system has been able to endure prolonged periods of minority rule with little apparent stress. Here is the best evidence that we need not fear or discount minority governments.

7. Reassessing minority governments

We have concluded our empirical investigation of minority governments in parliamentary democracies. Let us summarize what we have learned in the process:

1. Minority governments are common in parliamentary democracies, and in the postwar period such governments have formed in substantial numbers across a broad range of political systems.
2. Our understanding of minority cabinets has tended to be superficial and incomplete. Ambitious scholarship on the subject has been rare, and the phenomenon typically has been treated as an anomaly.
3. Conventionally, minority government formation is explained as a consequence of political instability, conflict, and malaise. The empirical analysis in Chapter 3 has demonstrated that these explanations are erroneous.
4. On the other hand, I have shown that it is possible to explain minority governments as the results of rational choices made by party leaders under certain structural constraints.
5. Minority cabinets form with particular frequency in the Scandinavian and English-speaking democracies. My theoretical explanation also most adequately accounts for the pattern of government formation in these polities.
6. More than anything else, it is the anticipation of future elections that predisposes party leaders to opt for minority governments. Undersized governments are most likely to form in political systems where elections are competitive and decisive for coalitional bargaining power.

7. Also, minority governments are promoted by institutions that enhance the power of the parliamentary opposition vis-à-vis the government.

8. Minority governments need not rely on stable and prenegotiated parliamentary alliances in order to secure legislative majorities. *Formal* minority governments are neither very common nor very successful.

9. In building legislative coalitions, minority cabinets can choose between a variety of strategies. Their choice of legislative strategies depends on institutional conditions, the objectives of the parties in government and opposition, and their relative bargaining power.

10. Highly formalized and membership-consistent coalitions are most likely to be formed by parties that have *weak* bargaining power and that value office highly relative to policy.

11. Contrary to conventional wisdom, minority governments do not perform particularly poorly in office. While minority governments are less durable than majority coalitions, they fare better at the polls and resign under more favorable circumstances.

12. Minority governments perform best in those political systems where they are most common, and least well where they are most rare. The same factors that promote minority government formation also enhance their performance.

13. The legislative record in Italy and Norway suggests that at least in these countries minority governments are just as effective as majority coalitions.

14. Undersized cabinets often serve as vehicles of alternation in power in "imperfect" two-party or two-bloc systems.

15. Under such conditions minority governments preserve the strategies and expectations of two-party politics, and particularly the prospective role of elections.

In the remainder of this book, we shall consider the implications of these results for the way we think about party systems, party behavior, and representative democracy.

Party systems and minority governments

Several of the preceding points suggest a linkage between minority governments and certain types of party systems. Specific kinds of party systems foster minority governments. Conversely, the dynamics of such party systems may be significantly affected by the fact that they often give rise to minority cabinets. Hence, the incidence of minority governments may help us understand how parties interact in these systems. In order to explore the properties of the party system that commonly experience minority governments, we shall consider this question within the frameworks of two leading theorists of parties and party systems, G. Bingham Powell, Jr., and Giovanni Sartori.

According to Powell (1981a, b, 1982b), democratic party systems function as channels of representation and accountability through processes of choice, anticipation, and the building of policy coalitions. Different types of party systems give priority to different processes of representation. *Aggregative majority* systems (e.g., Canada and the United States) favor anticipation, *alternative majority* systems (e.g., Britain) favor choice, and *representational* systems (e.g., Belgium) favor coalition building. These types of party systems differ along two dimensions. First, they differ in the clarity of policy choice they offer the electorate. Individual parties offer more distinct policy platforms in representational and alternative majority systems than they do in aggregative majority systems. Second, party systems differ in whether or not they regularly provide one party with a legislative majority. Aggregative and alternative majority systems regularly produce majority situations, whereas representational systems do not.

Powell's typology includes three cells where four are logically possible. What is missing is the type of party system in which majority situations are not the rule, but where parties nevertheless aggregate opinion and anticipate the reactions of the electorate.[1] Powell further assumes that party systems that fail to produce majority situations also fail to produce clear governmental choices. Representational systems, he argues, elect governments through a two-stage represen-

---

[1] In one version of his work, Powell recognizes the possibility of a fourth type, which he calls "fractionalized." Fractionalized party systems are seen as unstable and associated with less developed societies. See Powell (1981a: 863).

tational process. But this is essentially a question of *electoral decisiveness,* and we have already seen that even multiparty systems with no majority party can score high on this variable. Hence, party systems exist that aggregate opinion and provide fairly clear-cut governmental choices. And these systems are particularly conducive to minority governments.

Such governments are also common when majoritarian systems, whether alternative or aggregative, fail to produce the normal majorities, as the Canadian and British experiences show. The recourse to minority governments preserves the emphasis on choice and accountability in government, while the construction of legislative coalitions remains less formal, less visible, and frequently less secure than what is typical of representational systems.

Party systems can hardly be discussed without reference to the influential work of Giovanni Sartori (1976). Sartori distinguishes between multiparty systems of moderate and polarized pluralism. Systems of moderate pluralism tend to have three to five relevant parties, polarized systems no fewer than five or six. Most countries with a high incidence of minority governments are moderate rather than polarized in Sartori's terms.

Italy and Fourth Republic France are the exceptions in the sense that both polities have been polarized and yet had high numbers of minority governments. However, the absolute numbers of minority governments in Italy and France greatly exaggerate the commonness of such governments for two reasons. First, both countries are unusually well represented in the sample due to cabinet instability. Second, since majority situations have been very rare, the ratio of minority governments to majority coalitions is more modest than the absolute numbers might suggest. For France and Italy collectively, minority governments account for 44% of all minority situations, which is only marginally above average for the 15-nation sample. The corresponding figure for the Scandinavian nations (Denmark, Norway, and Sweden) is 81%, for the three English-speaking democracies (Canada, Ireland, and the United Kingdom) 85%. All of the countries in the latter two categories would be described by Sartori as moderate rather than polarized.

Party systems of moderate pluralism are characterized by relatively modest ideological distance among the relevant parties, centripetal competition, and a bipolar governmental format (Sartori, 1976). Note that these properties also describe the *aggregative minority* type we found missing in Powell's typology. Although some systems of moderate pluralism (e.g., Germany) do not frequently experience minority governments, most do.

The linkage between minority governments and party systems of moderate pluralism may be more than coincidental. In fact, *the formation of minority governments rather than majority coalitions is a major reason why some party systems exhibit the features of moderate instead of polarized pluralism.* The more narrowly constructed governments are, the more favorable the opportunities for the "loyal" opposition. Undersized governments facilitate the formation of two electorally competitive and governmentally credible coalitions even in the presence of extremist parties. Under the same conditions, minimum winning (or worse: oversized) governments could easily reduce the opposition to impotence. Moreover, the smaller the government's parliamentary basis, the less severe the electoral erosion it is likely to experience. And if there is a credible nonextremist opposition, chances are that disaffected voters will not flee to the extremist parties.

The implications of minority rule are clarified only when we consider the dynamics of party systems in which minority governments form, and which these governments sustain. Although there are political systems in which one minority government has succeeded another for extended periods of time, apparently with few adverse effects, the more common pattern is for minority governments to be transitional. Minority governments allow party systems of moderate pluralism to retain the expectation of alternation in minority situations, and they give established parties a breathing space in which they can respond to new electoral demands. Whereas undersized cabinets may be less responsible in the short term, they permit a greater degree of governmental *responsiveness* without jeopardizing stability.

The key point here is that the choice of governments is independent of the central variable in Sartori's schema, the number of parties. When majority situations fail to occur, a preference for minority governments will promote the formation of a credible opposition, centripetal competition for votes, and a bipolar, alternational competition for office. The choice of large coalitions, on the other hand, will reinforce tendencies toward government heterogeneity and immobilism, oppositional impotence, and the growth of protest and extremist parties. These are, of course, the essential characteristics of polarized pluralism (Sartori, 1976).

It is not my intention to argue that the forces that shape democratic party systems flow entirely from the top down, that government formation determines party system properties. That clearly would be an exaggeration. But the opposite error is more commonly committed. Governments in parliamentary democracies are frequently portrayed as little more than reflections of a certain configuration of social and political forces. We have seen that there is a large repertoire of government solutions, and that the type of cabinet chosen has a systematic bearing on government performance. Party leaders are presented with a range of cabinet options, and their choices have important ramifications for the channel of representation they control.

These observations lead us to a more general point. The analysis of party systems requires a clear understanding of party behavior, and the current impasse in our knowledge is in large part due to the weakness of these underpinnings. The party systems literature is heavily structural, whereas its behavioral elements are underdeveloped. Even the simple behavioral models reviewed in Chapter 2 have not in any rigorous sense found their way into the party systems literature.

Our understanding of party systems clearly needs such behavioral foundations. Game-theoretic conceptions based on the assumption of parties as purely office seekers, policy seekers, or vote seekers are one place to start. However, this study has shown that simplistic assumptions of this kind can easily lead us astray. Minority government formation cannot be explained unless political parties are understood as something other than pure short-term office seekers. Moreover, the results suggest that one set of assumptions does not fit all parties. Some parties are more office motivated, others more concerned about the pursuit of votes or policy. Minority governments are likely to form where parties value votes and policy highly compared to office.

The differences in objectives across parties are hardly random.

There is every reason to believe that institutional as well as organizational factors affect these utility functions. In explaining minority governments, I have identified some structural factors that predispose parties toward different forms of behavior. But this is only the beginning of the story. And no attempt has been made to derive behavioral hypotheses from the intriguing world of intraparty politics. However, there should be no doubt that the systematic analysis of parties as organizations will greatly illuminate their behavior in office and in elections.

Finally, we need a much better understanding of how vote-seeking, office-seeking, and policy-seeking behaviors are interrelated. Traditionally, few efforts have been made to link these assumptions in theories of party behavior. Recently, however, some promising theoretical advances have been made (Austen-Smith and Banks, 1988; Laver, 1988). In accounting for minority governments, I have argued that the pursuit of votes is largely instrumental toward coalitional bargaining power. However, much additional work remains to be done before we have a comprehensive and rigorous theory of party behavior on which the analysis of party systems and government formation can rest.

Minority government and democracy

Much of the traditional interest in minority governments was motivated by a concern for the quality of democracy. In this light, minority governments appeared suspect on two grounds. First, they seemed to represent serious threats to democratic stability. Second, minority governments violate the application of the norm of majority rule to executive–legislative relations. Thus, a key link in the representational chain might be broken, and the door to elite minority rule possibly opened.

The concern over democratic stability is in many countries much less prevalent today compared to a few decades ago. However, it is very much alive and relevant in polities that have recently undergone, or are currently undergoing, a transition to democracy. Champions of democracy should be relieved to find that minority governments need not be feared in this respect. The empirical results I have pre-

MINORITY GOVERNMENT AND MAJORITY RULE

sented give us no reason to worry that minority governments might be harbingers of, or even precipitate, democratic breakdown.

Let us therefore close this discussion with a few observations on the second concern. The social-choice literature has not been kind to the principle of majority rule. Yet one might legitimately ask whether minority governments do not give up too much of the linkage between governors and the governed in democratic societies. If everything else is equal, we should prefer governments representing parties supported by a majority of the voters to those representing a minority. At least there seems to be no good reason to prefer the latter.

Consider, however, the typical policy positions of minority governments. We saw in Chapter 3 that in left–right space minority governments tend to be more centrist than majority coalitions. In practice this means that the party that would put the government over the majority threshold is likely to be more extreme than the existing members of the protocoalition. Adding such a party would therefore probably pull the government's policy position away from the median voter. A relatively centrist policy position is indeed almost a precondition for the ad hoc legislative coalitions many minority governments favor. Thus, minority governments may represent the preferences of the voters equally well, although in different ways.

Yet there is a sense in which minority governments represent a radically different notion of popular rule from that which pervades the preceding arguments. We have seen that minority governments form in circumstances in which the anticipation of elections weighs heavily on party leaders. Such governments reflect responsiveness to elections future, rather than to elections past. In this way minority governments represent the workings of *prospective,* rather than *retrospective,* orientations among political leaders. And more than anything else, it is this anticipation of the popular will that makes democracy special.

Appendix A. Governments included in this study

Belgium

Government	Formation date	Demission date	Tenure (months)	Parties	Parliam. basis	Formation attempts	Cabinet type
Spaak I	Mar 46	Mar 46	0	PSB	34	3	SM
van Acker II	Mar 46	Jul 46	3	PSB, PLP, PCB	54	2	MC
Huysmans	Aug 46	Mar 47	7	PSB, PLP, PCB	54	5	MC
Spaak II	Mar 47	Nov 48	20	PSB, PSC	79	2	MC
Spaak III	Nov 48	Jun 49	6	PSB, PSC	79	3	MC
Eyskens I	Aug 49	Mar 50	7	PSC, PLP	63	4	MC
Duvieusart	Jun 50	Aug 50	2	PSC	50	1	MP
Pholien	Aug 50	Jan 52	17	PSC	50	3	MP
van Houtte	Jan 52	Apr 54	27	PSC	50	1	MP
van Acker III	Apr 54	Jun 58	49	PSB, PLP	52	1	MC
Eyskens II	Jun 58	Nov 58	4	PSC	49	2	SM
Eyskens III	Nov 58	Mar 61	29	PSC, PLP	59	1	MC
Lefèvre	Apr 61	May 65	49	PSC, PSB	84	1	MC
Harmel	Jul 65	Feb 66	6	PSC, PSB	66	4	MC
Vanden Boeynants I	Mar 66	Feb 68	23	PSC, PLP	59	5	MC
Eyskens IV	Jun 68	Nov 71	41	PSC, PSB	60	5	MC
Eyskens V	Jan 72	Nov 72	10	PSC, PSB	60	3	MC
Leburton	Jan 73	Jan 74	12	PSB, PLP, CVP, PSC	75	1	MC
Tindemans I	Apr 74	Jun 74	2	CVP, PSC, PLP, PVV	48	5	SM
Tindemans II	Jun 74	Mar 77	33	CVP, PSC, PVV, PLP, RW	59	1	MC
Tindemans III	Mar 77	Apr 77	1	CVP, PSC, PVV, PLP	49	2	SM
Tindemans IV	Jun 77	Oct 78	16	CVP, PSC, FDF, PSB, Vlk	81	2	MC

Government				Parties			
Vanden Boeynants II	Oct 78	Dec 78	2	CVP, PSC, PSB, FDF, Vlk	81	1	MC
Martens I	Apr 79	Jan 80	9	CVP, PSC, BSP, PSB, FDF	71	8	MC
Martens II	Jan 80	Apr 80	3	CVP, PSC, BSP, PSB	66	1	MC
Martens III	May 80	Oct 80	5	CVP, PSC, BSP, PSB, PRL, PVV	80	2	MC
Martens IV	Oct 80	Mar 81	5	CVP, PSC, BSP, PSB	66	2	MC
Mark Eyskens	Apr 81	Sep 81	6	CVP, PSC, BSP, PSB	66	1	MC
Martens V	Dec 81	Oct 85	45	CVP, PSC, PVV, PRL	53	4	MC
Martens VI	Nov 85	Oct 87	23	CVP, PSC, PVV, PRL	54	1	MC
Martens VII	Dec 87	NA	NA	CVP, PSC, PVV, PRL	51	1	MC

Parties

BSP   Flemish Socialist party
CVP   Flemish Christian People's party
FDF   Francophone Democratic Front
PCB   Communist party (KPB/PCB)
PLP   Liberal party (renamed Party of Liberty and Progress in 1961; PVV/PLP until 1972; PVV and PLP established as separate parties in 1972, with the Francophone Liberals renamed the PRL)
PRL   Walloon Liberal party.
PSB   Wallon Socialist Party (BSP/PSB until 1972; BSP and PSB established as separate parties in 1978)
PSC   Wallon Christian Social party (CVP/PSC until 1968 CVP/PSC established as separate parties in 1968)
PVV   Flemish Liberal party
RW   Walloon Rally
Vlk   Volksunie

Canada

Government	Formation date	Demission date	Tenure (months)	Parties	Parliam. basis	Formation attempts	Cabinet type
King	Jun 45	Nov 48	41	Liberals	48	1	SM
St. Laurent I	Nov 48	Jun 49	7	Liberals	51	1	MP
St. Laurent II	Jun 49	Aug 53	49	Liberals	73	1	MP
St. Laurent III	Aug 53	Jun 57	46	Liberals	64	1	MP
Diefenbaker I	Jun 57	Apr 58	9	PC	41	1	SM
Diefenbaker II	Apr 58	Jun 62	51	PC	78		MP
Diefenbaker III	Jun 62	Apr 63	10	PC	43	1	SM
Pearson I	Apr 63	Dec 65	32	Liberals	48	1	SM
Pearson II	Dec 65	Apr 68	28	Liberals	49	1	SM
Trudeau I	Apr 68	Jul 68	3	Liberals	49	1	SM
Trudeau II	Jul 68	Nov 72	53	Liberals	58	1	MP
Trudeau III	Nov 72	May 74	17	Liberals	41	1	SM
Trudeau IV	Jul 74	Jun 79	59	Liberals	53	1	MP
Clark	Jun 79	Mar 80	9	PC	48	1	SM
Trudeau V	Mar 80	Jun 84	52	Liberals	52	1	MP
Turner	Jun 84	Sep 84	3	Liberals	52	1	MP
Mulroney I	Sep 84	NA	NA	PC	74	1	MP

Parties
PC Progressive Conservatives

Denmark

Government	Formation date	Demission date	Tenure (months)	Parties	Parliam. basis	Formation attempts	Cabinet type
Kristensen	Nov 45	Oct 47	23	V	25	3	SM
Hedtoft I	Nov 47	Aug 50	33	SD	38	1	SM
Hedtoft II	Sep 50	Oct 50	1	SD	39	5	SM
Eriksen I	Oct 50	Apr 53	30	V, KF	39	1	SM
Eriksen II	Apr 53	Sep 53	5	V, KF	39	1	SM
Hedtoft III	Sep 53	Jan 55	16	SD	42	3	SM
Hansen I	Feb 55	May 57	27	SD	42	1	SM
Hansen II	May 57	Feb 60	33	SD, RV, RF	53	1	MC
Kampmann I	Feb 60	Nov 60	9	SD, RV, RF	53	1	MC
Kampmann II	Nov 60	Sep 62	22	SD, RV	49	1	FM
Krag I	Sep 62	Sep 64	25	SD, RV	49	1	FM
Krag II	Sep 64	Nov 66	25	SD	43	8	SM
Krag III	Nov 66	Jan 68	14	SD	39	4	SM
Baunsgaard	Feb 68	Sep 71	44	RV, V, KF	56	1	MC
Krag IV	Oct 71	Oct 72	12	SD	40	2	SM
Jørgensen I	Oct 72	Dec 73	14	SD	40	1	SM
Hartling	Dec 73	Jan 75	13	V	12	4	SM
Jørgensen II	Feb 75	Feb 77	24	SD	30	4	SM
Jørgensen III	Feb 77	Aug 78	18	SD	37	2	SM

Denmark (cont.)

Government	Formation date	Demission date	Tenure (months)	Parties	Parliam. basis	Formation attempts	Cabinet type
Jørgensen IV	Aug 78	Sep 79	13	SD, V	49	1	SM
Jørgensen V	Oct 79	Nov 81	29	SD	38	1	SM
Jørgensen VI	Dec 81	Sep 82	8	SD	33	2	SM
Schlüter I	Sep 82	Jan 84	16	KF, V, CD, KRF	37	2	SM
Schlüter II	Jan 84	Sep 87	43	KF, V, CD, KRF	44	1	SM
Schlüter III	Sep 87	NA	NA	KF, V, CD, KRF	40	1	SM

Parties

KF Conservatives
CD Center Democrats
KRF Christian People's party
RF Justice party
RV Radicals
SD Social Democrats
V Liberals

250

Finland

Government	Formation date	Demission date	Tenure (months)	Parties	Parliam. basis	Formation attempts	Cabinet type
Pekkala	Mar 46	Jul 48	28	SKDL, KP, SSDP, SFP	81	1	MC
Fagerholm I	Jul 48	Mar 50	19	SSDP	27	3	SM
Kekkonen I	Mar 50	Jan 51	10	KP, SFP, LKP	37	2	SM
Kekkonen II	Jan 51	Mar 51	2	KP, SSDP, SFP, LKP	64	1	MC
Kekkonen III	Sep 51	Jun 53	21	KP, SSDP, SFP	59	1	MC
Kekkonen IV	Jul 53	Nov 53	4	KP, SFP	33	2	SM
Tuomioja	Nov 53	Dec 53	1	Nonpartisan	—	1	NP
Törngren	May 54	Oct 54	5	SFP, KK, KP, SSDP	72	3	MC
Kekkonen V	Oct 54	Feb 56	16	KP, SSDP	53	1	MC
Fagerholm II	May 56	May 57	15	SSDP, KP, SFP, LKP	66	1	MC
Sukselainen I	May 57	Jul 57	1	KP, SFP, LKP	39	1	SM
Sukselainen II	Jul 57	Sep 57	2	KP, LKP	33	1	SM
Sukselainen III	Sep 57	Oct 57	2	KP, LKP, 3 from SSDP	34	1	SM
von Fieandt	Nov 57	Apr 58	5	Nonpartisan	—	6	NP
Kuuskoski	Apr 58	Aug 58	4	Nonpartisan	—	2	NP
Fagerholm III	Aug 58	Dec 58	3	SSDP, KP, KK, LKP, SFP	73	5	MC
Sukselainen IV	Jan 59	Jun 61	30	KP	24	2	FM
Miettunen I	Jul 61	Mar 62	8	KP	24	1	FM
Karjalainen I	Apr 62	Dec 63	20	KP, SFP, KK, LKP	66	3	MC
Lehto	Dec 63	Sep 64	9	Nonpartisan	—	2	NP
Virolainen	Sep 64	Apr 66	19	KP, KK, SFP, LKP	56	2	MC
Paasio I	May 66	Mar 68	21	SSDP, SKDL, KP, TPSL	76	2	MC
Koivisto I	Mar 68	Mar 70	24	SSDP, SKDL, TPSL, SFP, KP	82	3	MC
Aura I	May 70	Jul 70	2	Nonpartisan	—	4	NP
Karjalainen II	Jul 70	Mar 71	8	KP, SSDP, SKDL, SFP, LKP	72	3	MC

Finland (cont.)

Government	Formation date	Demission date	Tenure (months)	Parties	Parliam. basis	Formation attempts	Cabinet type
Karjalainen III	Mar 71	Oct 71	7	KP, SSDP, SFP, LKP	54	1	MC
Aura II	Oct 71	Feb 72	4	Nonpartisan	—	2	NP
Paasio II	Feb 72	Jul 72	5	SSDP	27	3	SM
Sorsa I	Sep 72	Jun 75	33	SSDP, KP, SFP, LKP	53	3	MC
Liinamaa	Jun 75	Nov 75	6	Nonpartisan	—	1	NP
Miettunen II	Nov 75	Sep 76	10	KP, SSDP, SKDL, SFP, LKP	76	3	MC
Miettunen III	Sep 76	May 77	7	KP, SFP, LKP	29	1	SM
Sorsa II	May 77	Feb 78	9	SSDP, SKDL, KP, SFP, LKP	76	1	MC
Sorsa III	Mar 78	Mar 79	13	SSDP, SKDL, KP, LKP	71	2	MC
Koivisto II	May 79	Jan 82	32	SSDP, KP, SKDL, SFP	66	3	MC
Sorsa IV	Feb 82	Dec 82	11	SSDP, SKDL, KP, SFP	66	1	MC
Sorsa V	Dec 82	Apr 83	3	SSDP, KP, SFP	49	1	FM
Sorsa VI	May 83	Apr 87	47	SSDP, KP, SFP, SDP	61	1	MC
Holkeri	Apr 87	NA	NA	KK, SSDP, SFP, SDP	65	2	MC

Parties

KK   Conservatives (National Coalition)
KP   Center party (before 1965, the Agrarian Union)
LKP   Liberal party
SDP   Finnish Rural party
SFP   Swedish People's party
SKDL Finnish People's Democratic Union
SSDP Finnish Social Democratic party
TPSL Social Democratic League (1958–78)

France (Fourth Republic)

Government	Formation date	Demission date	Tenure (months)	Parties	Parliam. basis	Formation attempts	Cabinet type
Gouin	Jan 46	Jun 46	5	SFIO, PCF, MRP	81	3	MC
Bidault I	Jun 46	Nov 46	5	MRP, SFIO, PCF	77	1	MC
Blum	Dec 46	Jan 47	1	SFIO	16	6	SM
Ramadier I	Jan 47	May 47	3	SFIO, MRP, PCF, RI, RS	84	2	MC
Ramadier II	May 47	Oct 47	5	SFIO, MRP, RS, RI	54	1	MC
Ramadier III	Oct 47	Nov 47	1	SFIO, MRP, RS, RI	54	1	MC
Schuman I	Nov 47	Jul 48	8	MRP, SFIO, RS, UDSR	54	4	MC
Marie	Jul 48	Aug 48	1	RS, SFIO, MRP, RI	54	1	MC
Schuman II	Sep 48	Sep 48	0	MRP, RS, SFIO, RI	54	3	MC
Queuille I	Sep 48	Oct 49	13	RS, SFIO, MRP, PRL, UDSR	60	2	MC
Bidault II	Oct 49	Feb 50	3	MRP, SFIO, UDSR, RS	54	3	MC
Bidault III	Feb 50	Jun 50	5	MRP, UDSR, RS	38	1	SM
Queuille II	Jul 50	Jul 50	0	RS, MRP, UDSR, RI	42	5	SM
Pleven I	Jul 50	Feb 51	7	UDSR, MRP, SFIO, RS, RI	59	3	MC
Queuille III	Mar 51	Jul 51	4	RS, SFIO, MRP, UDSR, RI	59	5	MC
Pleven II	Aug 51	Jan 52	5	UDSR, MRP, RS, AP, RI	43	6	FM
Faure I	Jan 52	Feb 52	1	RS, MRP, UDSR, RI, AP	43	5	SM
Pinay I	Mar 52	Dec 52	10	RI, UDSR, RS, AP, MRP	43	3	SM
Mayer	Jan 53	May 53	4	RS, UDSR, MRP, RI, AP	43	4	FM
Laniel	Jun 53	Jun 54	11	RI, RS, MRP, UDSR, AP, URS, URAS	62	8	MC
Mendès-France	Jun 54	Feb 55	7	RS, URAS, RI, UDSR, MRP, RGR	59	1	MC
Pineau	Feb 55	Feb 55	0	SFIO, MRP, UDSR, RS	46	3	SM
Faure II	Feb 55	Jan 56	11	RS, URAS, ARS, UDSR, AP, RI, MRP	60	1	MC

France (Fourth Republic) (cont.)

Government	Formation date	Demission date	Tenure (months)	Parties	Parliam. basis	Formation attempts	Cabinet type
Mollet I	Feb 56	May 57	16	SFIO, RS, UDSR	27	2	SM
Bourges-Maunoury	Jun 57	Sep 57	4	RS, SFIO, UDSR, RGR	29	6	SM
Pinay II	Oct 57	Oct 57	0	RI, RGR, UDSR/RDA, Neo-radicals	20	3	SM
Mollet II	Oct 57	Oct 57	0	SFIO, RS, MRP, UDSR	39	2	SM
Gaillard	Nov 57	Apr 58	5	RS, SFIO, MRP, DisRS, RI, UDSR	56	1	MC
Pflimlin	May 58	May 58	0	MRP, SFIO, UDSR, RS, RGR, RI	54	6	MC
de Gaulle	Jun 58	Oct 58	4	URAS, MRP, SFIO, UDSR, RS, RGR, RI, DisRS	67	1	MC

Parties
AP   Peasants
ARS   Dissident Gaullists
DisRS   Dissident Radicals
MRP   Popular Republican Movement
PCF   Communist party
PRL   Republican Liberty party
RDA   African Democrats
RGR   Left Republicans
RI   Conservatives
RS   Radical Socialists
SFIO   Socialist party
UDSR   Democratic and Socialist Union of the Resistance
URAS   Gaullists (in 1956, called the Republican Socialists)
URS   Gaullists

Iceland

Government	Formation date	Demission date	Tenure (months)	Parties	Parliam. basis	Formation attempts	Cabinet type
Stefansson	Feb 47	Oct 49	33	SD, IP, P	80	1	MC
Thors III	Dec 49	Mar 50	3	IP	36	NA	SM
Steinthorsson	Mar 50	Jun 53	40	P, IP	69	1	MC
Thors IV	Sep 53	Jul 56	34	IP, P	71	1	MC
Jonasson	Jul 56	Dec 58	28	P, SD, PA	63	1	MC
Jonsson I	Dec 58	Nov 59	11	SD	15	1	SM
Jonsson II	Jun 59	Nov 59	5	SD	11	1	SM
Thors V	Nov 59	Jun 63	43	IP, SD	55	1	MC
Thors VI	Jun 63	Nov 63	5	IP, SD	53	1	MC
Benediktsson I	Nov 63	Jun 67	43	IP, SD	53	1	MC
Benediktsson II	Jun 67	Jul 70	37	IP, SD	53	1	MC
Hafstein	Oct 70	Jun 71	8	IP, SD	53	1	MC
Johannesson I	Jul 71	Jul 74	36	P, PA, ULL	53	1	MC
Hallgrimsson	Aug 74	Jun 78	46	IP, P	70	3	MC
Johannesson II	Aug 78	Oct 79	13	P, SD, PA	66	1	MC
Grøndahl	Oct 79	Dec 79	2	SD	23	1	SM
Thoroddsen I	Feb 80	Apr 83	39	P, PA (3 IP Representatives)	51	5	MC
Hermannsson	May 83	Apr 87	48	P, IP	61	4	MC
Palsson	Jul 87	NA	NA	IP, P, SD	65	1	MC

Parties
IP   Independence party II
P   Progressive party
PA   People's Alliance
SD   Social Democrats
ULL   Union of Liberals and Leftists

Ireland

Government	Formation date	Demission date	Tenure (months)	Parties	Parliam. basis	Formation attempts	Cabinet type
Costello I	Feb 48	Jun 51	40	FG, Lab, NLab, CT, CP	46	1	SM
de Valera II	Jun 51	May 54	35	FF	46	2	SM
Costello II	Jun 54	Mar 57	34	FG, Lab, CT	50	2	MC
de Valera III	Mar 57	Jun 59	27	FF	53	1	MP
Lemass I	Jun 59	Oct 61	28	FF	53	1	MP
Lemass II	Oct 61	Apr 65	42	FF	48	1	SM
Lemass III	Apr 65	Nov 66	19	FF	50	1	MP
Lynch I	Nov 66	Jul 69	32	FF	50	1	MP
Lynch II	Jul 69	Mar 73	44	FF	52	1	MP
Cosgrave	Mar 73	Jul 77	52	FG, Lab	50	2	MC
Lynch III	Jul 77	Dec 79	29	FF	56	1	MP
Haughey I	Dec 79	Jun 81	18	FF	56	1	MP
Fitzgerald I	Jun 81	Jan 82	7	FG, Lab	48	2	SM
Haughey II	Mar 82	Nov 82	8	FF	48	1	SM
Fitzgerald II	Dec 82	Dec 86	48	FG, Lab	51	1	MC
Fitzgerald III	Dec 86	Jan 87	2	FG, Lab	49	1	SM
Haughey III	Mar 87	NA	NA	FF	48	1	SM

Parties
CT   Clann na Talmhan (The People of the Land)
CP   Clann na Poblachta (Republican party)
FF   Fianna Fáil
FG   Fine Gael
Lab Irish Labour party
NLab National Labour

Israel

Government	Formation date	Demission date	Tenure (months)	Parties	Parliam. basis	Formation attempts	Cabinet type
Ben-Gurion I	Mar 49	Oct 50	19	MAP, NRP, PRO, SPR, MIN	60	1	MC
Ben-Gurion II	Oct 50	Aug 51	9	MAP, NRP, PRO, SPR, MIN	60	3	MC
Ben-Gurion III	Oct 51	Sep 52	11	MAP, MIN, SPR, REL	54	2	MC
Ben-Gurion IV	Sep 52	Dec 52	3	MAP, MIZ, WMZ, MIN	50	1	MC
Ben-Gurion V	Dec 52	Dec 53	12	MAP, GNZ, MIZ, WMZ, PRO	72	3	MC
Sharett I	Jan 54	Jun 55	18	MAP, GNZ, MIZ, WMZ, PRO	72	2	MC
Sharett II	Jun 55	Nov 55	4	MAP, PRO, MIZ, WMZ	53	1	MC
Ben-Gurion VI	Nov 55	Dec 57	26	MAP, MPM, AA, PRO, NRP	66	NA	MC
Ben-Gurion VII	Jan 58	Jun 58	6	MAP, MPM, AA, PRO, NRP	66	1	MC
Ben-Gurion VIII	Jun 58	Nov 59	16	MAP, MPM, PRO, AA	57	1	MC
Ben-Gurion IX	Dec 59	Jan 61	13	MAP, MPM, NRP, AA, PRO	71	2	MC
Ben-Gurion X	Nov 61	Jun 63	17	MAP, NRP, AA	55	5	MC
Eshkol I	Jun 63	Dec 64	18	MAP, NRP, AA	55	1	MC
Eshkol II	Dec 64	Nov 65	10	MAP, NRP, AA	55	1	MC
Eshkol III	Jan 66	Jun 67	17	LAB, NRP, MPM, ILP	60	1	MC
Eshkol IV	Jun 67	Feb 69	21	LAB, NRP, MPM, ILP, RAF, GHL	90	1	MC
Meir I	Mar 69	Nov 69	8	LAB, NRP, MPM, ILP, RAF, GHL	90	1	MC
Meir II	Dec 69	Jul 70	8	LAB, MPM, GHL, NRP, ILP	81	1	MC
Meir III	Jul 70	Jan 74	41	LAB, MPM, NRP, ILP	63	1	MC
Meir IV	Mar 74	Apr 74	1	LAB, NRP, ILP, MPM	56	3	MC
Rabin I	Jun 74	Oct 74	5	LAB, ILP, CRM	50	2	MC
Rabin II	Oct 74	Dec 76	26	LAB, NRP, ILP	56	2	MC
Begin I	Jun 77	Oct 77	4	LIK, NRP, SHL	48	3	FM
Begin II	Oct 77	Jun 81	44	LIK, NRP, SHL, DML	64	1	MC
Begin III	Aug 81	Sep 83	25	LIK, NRP, TMI	47	1	FM
Shamir I	Oct 83	Jul 84	9	LIK, NRP, TMI	47	1	FM
Peres	Sep 84	Oct 86	25	LAB, LIK, NRP, SHI, MOR, SHA	81	1	MC
Shamir II	Oct 86	May 87	7	LAB, LIK, NRP, SHI, MOR, SHA	81	1	MC

Israel (cont.)

Government	Formation date	Demission date	Tenure (months)	Parties	Parliam. basis	Formation attempts	Cabinet type
Shamir III	May 87	NA	NA	LAB, LIK, NRP, MOR, SHA	79	1	MC

Parties

AA	Achudut Ha'avoda (Unity of Labor)
LAB	Alliance between MAP, AA, and other parties beginning in 1965; became Israel Labor party in 1968
CRM	Citizens Rights Movement
DML	Democratic Movement for Change
GHL	Gahal
GNZ	General Zionists
ILP	Independent Liberal party
LIK	Likud
MPM	Mapam
MIN	Minority Lists
MIZ	Mizrahi party
MAP	Mapai/Labor party (became Israel Labor party in 1968)
MOR	Morasha
NRP	National Religious party
PRO	Progressive party
RAF	Rafi, Workers List (Reshima Poalei Israel)
REL	Religious parties (includes Agudat Israel, Poalei Agudat Israel, Mizrahi, National Religious party, and Workers Mizrahi party)
SHA	Shas
SHI	Change (Shinui, was incorporated into DML)
SHL	Peace for Zion
SPR	Sephardim party
TMI	Tami, Movement for Israel's Tradition
WMZ	Workers Mizrahi party

258

Italy

Government	Formation date	Demission date	Tenure (months)	Parties	Parliam. basis	Formation attempts	Cabinet type
De Gasperi II	Jul 46	Jan 47	6	DC, PCI, PSIUP, PRI	81	2	MC
De Gasperi III	Feb 47	May 47	3	DC, PCI, PSI	69	1	MC
De Gasperi IV	May 47	Dec 47	7	DC	37	5	SM
De Gasperi V	Dec 47	May 48	5	DC, PLI, PSLI, PRI	56	1	MC
De Gasperi VI	May 48	Oct 49	17	DC, PLI, PSLI, PRI	63	1	MC
De Gasperi VII	Nov 49	Jan 50	2	DC, PLI, PRI	58	1	MC
De Gasperi VIII	Jan 50	Apr 51	14	DC, PSLI, PRI	60	2	MC
De Gasperi IX	Apr 51	Jul 51	3	DC, PRI	54	1	MC
De Gasperi X	Jul 51	Jun 53	23	DC, PRI	54	2	MC
De Gasperi XI	Jul 53	Jul 53	0	DC	44	4	SM
Pella	Aug 53	Jan 54	5	DC	44	2	SM
Fanfani I	Jan 54	Jan 54	0	DC	44	2	SM
Scelba	Feb 54	Jun 55	16	DC, PLI, PSDI	50	2	MC
Segni I	Jul 55	May 57	22	DC, PLI, PSDI	50	2	MC
Zoli	May 57	Jun 58	13	DC	44	2	SM
Fanfani II	Jul 58	Jan 59	7	DC, PSDI	49	2	SM
Segni II	Feb 59	Feb 60	12	DC	45	2	SM
Tambroni	Mar 60	Jul 60	4	DC	45	4	SM
Fanfani III	Jul 60	Feb 62	19	DC	45	1	FM
Fanfani IV	Feb 62	May 63	15	DC, PSDI, PRI	50	1	MC
Leone I	Jun 63	Nov 63	5	DC	41	2	SM
Moro I	Dec 63	Jun 64	7	DC, PSI, PSDI, PRI	61	1	MC

Italy (cont.)

Government	Formation date	Demission date	Tenure (months)	Parties	Parliam. basis	Formation attempts	Cabinet type
Moro II	Jul 64	Jan 66	18	DC, PSI, PSDI, PRI	61	2	MC
Moro III	Feb 66	Jun 68	27	DC, PSI, PSDI, PRI	61	2	MC
Leone II	Jun 68	Nov 68	5	DC	42	2	SM
Rumor I	Dec 68	Jul 69	7	DC, PSU, PRI	58	1	MC
Rumor II	Aug 69	Feb 70	6	DC	42	2	FM
Rumor III	Mar 70	Jul 70	3	DC, PSI, PSDI, PRI	58	4	MC
Colombo I	Aug 70	Mar 71	7	DC, PSI, PSDI, PRI	58	2	MC
Colombo II	Mar 71	Jan 72	10	DC, PSI, PSDI	56	1	MC
Andreotti I	Feb 72	Feb 72	0	DC	42	3	SM
Andreotti II	Jun 72	Jun 73	12	DC, PSDI, PLI	50	2	MC
Rumor IV	Jul 73	Mar 74	8	DC, PSI, PSDI, PRI	58	1	MC
Rumor V	Mar 74	Oct 74	7	DC, PSI, PSDI	56	1	MC
Moro IV	Nov 74	Jan 76	14	DC, PRI	44	3	FM
Moro V	Feb 76	Apr 76	3	DC	42	3	SM
Andreotti III	Jul 76	Jan 78	18	DC	41	2	SM
Andreotti IV	Mar 78	Jan 79	11	DC	41	2	FM
Andreotti V	Mar 79	Mar 79	0	DC, PSDI, PRI	46	3	SM
Cossiga I	Aug 79	Mar 80	8	DC, PSDI, PLI	46	4	SM
Cossiga II	Apr 80	Sep 80	6	DC, PSI, PRI	54	1	MC
Forlani	Oct 80	May 81	7	DC, PSI, PSDI, PRI	57	1	MC
Spadolini I	Jun 81	Aug 82	13	PRI, DC, PSI, PSDI, PLI	58	2	MC
Spadolini II	Aug 82	Nov 82	3	PRI, DC, PSI, PSDI, PLI	58	1	MC
Fanfani V	Nov 82	Apr 83	5	DC, PSI, PSDI, PLI	56	2	MC
Craxi	Aug 83	Apr 87	45	PSI, DC, PRI, PSDI, PLI	58	2	MC

Italy (cont.)

Government	Formation date	Demission date	Tenure (months)	Parties	Parliam. basis	Formation attempts	Cabinet type
Fanfani VI	Apr 87	Apr 87	0	DC	35	2	SM
Goria	Jul 87	NA	NA	DC, PSI, PRI, PSDI, PLI	59	1	MC

Parties
PCI Partito Comunista Italiano (Communist party)
PSI Partito Socialista Italiano (Socialist party)
PSU Partiti Socialista Unificati (United Socialist party)
PSDI Partito Socialista Democratico Italiano (Social Democratic party)
PRI Partito Repubblicano Italiano (Republican party)
DC Democrazia Cristiana (Christian Democrats)
PLI Partito Liberale Italiano (Liberal party)
Note that several of these parties have contested one or more elections under names and labels that differ from those listed here.

261

The Netherlands

Government	Formation date	Demission date	Tenure (months)	Parties	Parliam. basis	Formation attempts	Cabinet type
Beel I	Jul 46	Jul 48	25	KVP, PvdA	61	NA	MC
Drees I	Aug 48	Jan 51	30	PvdA, KVP, CHU, VVD	76	3	MC
Drees II	Mar 51	Jun 52	15	PvdA, KVP, CHU, VVD	76	6	MC
Drees III	Sep 52	Jun 56	46	PvdA, KVP, ARP, CHU	81	3	MC
Drees IV	Oct 56	Dec 58	26	PvdA, KVP, ARP, CHU	85	8	MC
Beel II	Dec 58	Mar 59	3	KVP, ARP, CHU	51	1	MC
de Quay	May 59	May 63	48	KVP, ARP, CHU, VVD	62	2	MC
Marijnen	Jul 63	Feb 65	19	KVP, ARP, CHU, VVD	61	2	MC
Cals	Apr 65	Oct 66	18	KVP, PvdA, ARP	70	4	MC
Zijlstra	Nov 66	Feb 67	3	ARP, KVP	42	2	SM
de Jong	Apr 67	Jul 71	49	KVP, ARP, CHU, VVD	57	2	MC
Biesheuvel I	Jul 71	Nov 72	13	ARP, KVP, CHU, VVD, DS'70	54	2	MC
Biesheuvel II	Aug 72	Mar 77	4	ARP, KVP, CHU, VVD	49	2	SM
den Uyl	May 73	May 81	46	PvdA, KVP, ARP, D'66, PPR	64	2	MC
van Agt I	Dec 77	May 82	41	CDA, VVD	51	7	MC
van Agt II	Sep 81	Sep 82	8	CDA, PvdA, D'66	72	5	MC
van Agt III	May 82	May 86	3	CDA, D'66	43	1	SM
Lubbers I	Nov 82	NA	43	CDA, VVD	54	3	MC
Lubbers II	Jul 86	NA	NA	CDA, VVD	54	1	MC

Parties
ARP   Anti-Revolutionary party
CDA   Christian Democratic Appeal
CHU   Christian Historical Union
D'66   Democrats '66
DS'70   Democratic Socialists '70
KVP   Catholic Peoples party
PPR   Radical Political party
PvdA   Labor party
VVD   Liberal party

Norway

Government	Formation date	Demission date	Tenure (months)	Parties	Parliam. basis	Formation attempts	Cabinet type
Michelsen I	Nov 05	Jan 07	14	Nat'l Coal.	97	1	MC
Michelsen II	Jan 07	Oct 07	9	Nat'l Coal.	91	1	MC
Løvland	Oct 07	Mar 08	5	V, FV, Mod.	55	1	MC
Knudsen I	Mar 08	Feb 10	22	V	43	2	SM
Konow	Feb 10	Feb 12	25	FV, H	52	2	MC
Bratlie	Feb 12	Jan 13	11	H	33	1	SM
Knudsen II	Jan 13	Jan 16	36	V	61	1	MP
Knudsen III	Jan 16	Jan 19	36	V	65	1	MP
Knudsen IV	Jan 19	Jun 20	17	V	42	2	SM
Halvorsen I	Jun 20	Jun 21	12	H, FV	39	3	SM
Blehr I	Jun 21	Jan 22	7	V	42	2	SM
Blehr II	Jan 22	Mar 23	14	V	26	1	SM
Halvorsen II	Mar 23	May 23	2	H, FV	38	2	SM
Berge	May 23	Jul 24	14	FV, H	38	1	SM
Mowinckel I	Jul 24	Jan 25	6	V	26	1	SM
Mowinckel II	Jan 25	Mar 26	13	V	24	1	SM
Lykke	Mar 26	Jan 28	23	H, FV	36	4	SM
Hornsrud	Jan 28	Feb 28	1	A	39	2	SM
Mowinckel III	Feb 28	Jan 31	35	V	20	1	SM
Mowinckel IV	Jan 31	May 31	4	V	22	1	SM
Kolstad	May 31	Mar 32	10	BP	16	1	SM

Norway (cont.)

Government	Formation date	Demission date	Tenure (months)	Parties	Parliam. basis	Formation attempts	Cabinet type
Hundseid	Mar 32	Mar 33	12	BP	16	2	SM
Mowinckel V	Mar 33	Jan 34	10	V	22	2	SM
Mowinckel VI	Jan 34	Mar 35	15	V	16	1	SM
Nygaardsvold I	Mar 35	Jan 37	22	A	46	1	FM
Nygaardsvold II	Jan 37	Apr 40	39	A	46	1	SM
Gerhardsen I	Nov 45	Oct 49	47	A	50	1	MP
Gerhardsen II	Oct 49	Nov 51	25	A	56	1	MP
Torp I	Nov 51	Oct 53	23	A	56	1	MP
Torp II	Oct 53	Jan 55	15	A	51	1	MP
Gerhardsen III	Jan 55	Oct 57	33	A	51	1	MP
Gerhardsen IV	Oct 57	Sep 61	47	A	52	1	MP
Gerhardsen V	Sep 61	Aug 63	23	A	49	1	SM
Lyng	Aug 63	Sep 63	1	H, V, KRF, SP	49	1	SM
Gerhardsen VI	Sep 63	Oct 65	25	A	49	1	SM
Borten I	Oct 65	Sep 69	47	SP, H, V, KRF	53	1	MC
Borten II	Sep 69	Mar 71	18	SP, H, V, KRF	50	1	MC
Bratteli I	Mar 71	Oct 72	19	A	49	2	SM
Korvald	Oct 72	Oct 73	12	KRF, SP, V	26	3	SM
Bratteli II	Oct 73	Jan 76	27	A	40	1	SM
Nordli I	Jan 76	Sep 77	20	A	40	1	SM
Nordli II	Sep 77	Jan 81	41	A	49	1	SM

Norway (cont.)

Government	Formation date	Demission date	Tenure (months)	Parties	Parliam. basis	Formation attempts	Cabinet type
Brundtland I	Feb 81	Oct 81	8	A	49	1	SM
Willoch I	Oct 81	Jun 83	19	H	34	2	SM
Willoch II	Jun 83	Sep 85	28	H, KRF, SP	51	1	MC
Willoch III	Sep 85	May 86	7	H, KRF, SP	49	1	SM
Brundtland II	May 86	NA	NA	A	45	1	SM

Parties

A	Det Norske Arbeiderparti (Labor party)
V	Venstre (Liberals)
KRF	Kristelig Folkeparti (Christian People's party)
BP	Bondepartiet (Agrarian party)
FV	Frisinnede Venstre (Moderates)
H	Høyre (Conservatives)
SP	Senterpartiet (Center party)
Mod.	Moderate Venstre (Moderate Liberals)

Portugal

Government	Formation date	Demission date	Tenure (months)	Parties	Parliam. basis	Formation attempts	Cabinet type
Gonçalves I	Apr 75	Jul 75	3	PSP, PPD, PCP, MDP-CDE	92	1	MC
Gonçalves II	Jul 75	Sep 75	1	Nonpartisan	—	1	NP
Azevedo I	Sep 75	Apr 76	7	PSP, PCP, PPD, Mil	90	1	MC
Azevedo II	Apr 76	Jul 76	3	PSP, PCP, PPD, Mil	83	1	MC
Soares I	Jul 76	Dec 77	17	PSP, Mil, indeps.	40	1	SM
Soares II	Jan 78	Jul 78	6	PSP, CDS	54	3	MC
da Costa	Aug 78	Sep 78	1	Nonpartisan	—	3	NP
Mota Pinto	Nov 78	Jun 79	7	Nonpartisan	—	2	NP
Pintassilgo	Aug 79	Dec 79	5	Nonpartisan	—	1	NP
Sá Carneiro I	Jan 80	Oct 80	9	AD	51	1	MC
Sá Carneiro II	Oct 80	Dec 80	2	AD	53	1	MC
Pinto Balsemão I	Jan 81	Dec 82	23	AD	53	1	MC
Pinto Balsemão II	Jan 83	Apr 83	3	PSD, CDS, PPM	53	2	MC
Soares III	Jun 83	Jun 85	24	CDS, PSP	70	1	MC
Soares IV	Jul 85	Oct 85	3	PSP, CDS	70	2	MC
Cavaço Silva I	Nov 85	Apr 87	17	PSD	35	1	SM
Cavaço Silva II	Aug 87	NA	NA	PSD	59	1	MP

Parties

AD   Center-Right Electoral Alliance (includes PSD, CDS, and PPM)
CDS   Center Social Democrats
MDP-CDE Democratic Movement
Mil   Military
PCP   Communist party
PPD   Popular Democratic party (1975–6)
PPM   Popular Monarchist party
PSD   Popular Democratic party (1976–present)
PSP   Socialist party

Spain

Government	Formation date	Demission date	Tenure (months)	Parties	Parliam. basis	Formation attempts	Cabinet type
Suárez I	Jul 77	Apr 79	21	UCD	47	1	SM
Suárez II	Apr 79	Jan 81	22	UCD	48	1	SM
Calvo Sotelo	Feb 81	Oct 82	22	UCD	48	1	SM
González I	Dec 82	Jun 86	43	PSOE	57	1	MP
González II	Jul 86	NA	NA	PSOE	52	1	MP

Parties
PSOE   Socialist party
UCD   Union of the Democratic Center

267

Sweden

Government	Formation date	Demission date	Tenure (months)	Parties	Parliam. basis	Formation attempts	Cabinet type
Hansson V	Jul 45	Oct 46	14	SD	50	1	MP
Erlander I	Oct 46	Sep 48	23	SD	50	1	MP
Erlander II	Sep 48	Sep 51	36	SD	48	1	SM
Erlander III	Oct 51	Sep 52	12	SD, CP	61	1	MC
Erlander IV	Sep 52	Sep 56	48	SD, CP	59	1	MC
Erlander V	Sep 56	Oct 57	13	SD, CP	54	1	MC
Erlander VI	Oct 57	Jun 58	7	SD	45	3	SM
Erlander VII	Jun 58	Sep 60	28	SD	48	1	SM
Erlander VIII	Sep 60	Sep 64	48	SD	49	1	SM
Erlander IX	Sep 64	Sep 68	48	SD	48	1	SM
Erlander X	Sep 68	Sep 69	12	SD	53	1	MP
Palme I	Oct 69	Sep 70	11	SD	53	1	MP
Palme II	Sep 70	Sep 73	36	SD	46	1	SM
Palme III	Sep 73	Sep 76	36	SD	44	1	SM
Fälldin I	Oct 76	Oct 78	24	CP, FP, M	51	1	MC
Ullsten	Oct 78	Oct 79	12	FP	11	3	SM
Fälldin II	Oct 79	May 81	19	CP, M, FP	50	1	MC
Fälldin III	May 81	Sep 82	16	CP, FP	29	1	SM
Palme IV	Oct 82	Sep 85	36	SD	47	1	SM
Palme V	Oct 85	Feb 86	5	SD	45	1	SM
Carlsson I	Mar 86	NA	NA	SD	45	1	SM

Parties
CP Agrarian party (renamed the Center party in 1957)
FP People's party
M   Moderate Unity party (called Conservatives until 1969)
SD Social Democrats

United Kingdom

Government	Formation date	Demission date	Tenure (months)	Parties	Parliam. basis	Formation attempts	Cabinet type
Attlee I	Jul 45	Feb 50	55	Labour	61	1	MP
Attlee II	Feb 50	Oct 51	20	Labour	50	1	MP
Churchill	Oct 51	Apr 55	41	Conservatives	51	1	MP
Eden I	Apr 55	May 55	2	Conservatives	51	1	MP
Eden II	May 55	Jan 57	19	Conservatives	54	1	MP
Macmillan I	Jan 57	Oct 59	33	Conservatives	54	1	MP
Macmillan II	Oct 59	Oct 63	48	Conservatives	57	1	MP
Douglas-Home	Oct 63	Oct 64	12	Conservatives	57	1	MP
Wilson I	Oct 64	Mar 66	16	Labour	50	1	MP
Wilson II	Mar 66	Jun 70	51	Labour	57	1	MP
Heath	Jun 70	Feb 74	44	Conservatives	52	1	MP
Wilson III	Mar 74	Oct 74	7	Labour	47	2	SM
Wilson IV	Oct 74	Apr 76	18	Labour	50	1	MP
Callaghan I	Apr 76	Nov 76	7	Labour	50	1	MP
Callaghan II	Nov 76	May 79	30	Labour	49	1	SM
Thatcher I	May 79	Jun 83	50	Conservatives	53	1	MP
Thatcher II	Jun 83	Jun 87	49	Conservatives	61	1	MP
Thatcher III	Jun 87	NA	NA	Conservatives	57	1	MP

Appendix B. Extremist parliamentary parties by country

Belgium
Francophone Democratic Front
Walloon Rally
Flemish Nationalists (Volksunie)
Flemish National party (Vlaams Blok)
Communist party

Canada
None

Denmark
Progress party
Left Socialist party
Socialist People's party
Common Course

Finland
Rural Party
Communist party (SKDL and DEVA)

France
Communist party
Gaullists
Poujadists

Iceland
People's Alliance

Ireland
Sinn Féin

Israel
Hadash
Kach
PLP

Italy
Communist party
Proletarian Democracy (PDUP/DP)
Italian Social Movement (MSI)
Monarchists (PNM/PMP/PDIUM)

Netherlands
Communist party
Center party
Pacifist Socialist party

Norway
Socialist Left party (SV)
Socialist People's party (SF)
Progress party
Communist party

Portugal
Communist party

Spain
Communist party
United People (Herri Batasuna)
Basque Nationalist party (PNV)
Basque Left (Euzkadiko Ezkerra)
Aragonese Regionalist party (PAR)
Canaries Independent party (AIC)
Galician Coalition (CG)
Valencian Union (UV)

Sweden
Communist party (VPK)

United Kingdom
Scottish National party
Plaid Cymru

References

Aarebrot, Frank H. "Norway: Center and Periphery in a Peripheral State." In Rokkan and Urwin (1982), 75–111.

Abrams, Robert. *Foundations of Political Analysis.* New York: Columbia University Press, 1980.

Allen, Hilary. *Norway and Europe in the 1970's.* Oslo: Universitetsforlaget, 1979.

Almond, Gabriel A., Scott C. Flanagan, and Robert F. Mundt, eds. *Crisis, Choice, and Change: Historical Studies of Political Development.* Boston: Little, Brown, 1973.

Almond, Gabriel A., and G. Bingham Powell, Jr. *Comparative Politics.* 2nd ed. Boston: Little, Brown, 1978.

Almond, Gabriel A., and Sidney Verba, eds. *The Civic Culture Revisited.* Boston: Little, Brown, 1980.

Ameller, Michel, eds. *Parliaments.* London: Cassel, 1966.

Amyot, Grant. "Voto giovanile e voto differenziato nelle ultime elezioni italiane: Una confutazione di alcune analisi." *Rivista Italiana di Scienza Politica* 10 (1980), 471–83.

Arian, Alan, and Samuel H. Barnes. "The Dominant Party System: A Neglected Model of Democratic Stability." *Journal of Politics* 36 (1974), 592–614.

Arrow, Kenneth J. *Social Choice and Individual Values.* New York: Wiley, 1951.

Arter, David. *The Nordic Parliaments.* London: Hurst, 1984.

Aubert, Vilhelm. *Rettens sosiale funksjon.* Oslo: Universitetsforlaget, 1976.

Austen-Smith, David, and Jeffrey S. Banks. "Elections, Coalitions, and Legislative Outcomes." *American Political Science Review* 82 (1988), 405–22.

Axelrod, Robert. *Conflict of Interest.* Chicago: Markham, 1970.

The Evolution of Cooperation. New York: Basic Books, 1984.

Banzhaf, John F. III. "Weighted Voting Doesn't Work: A Mathematical Analysis." *Rutgers Law Review* 19 (1965), 317–43.

Barnes, Samuel H. *Representation in Italy: Institutionalized Tradition and Electoral Choice.* Chicago: University of Chicago Press, 1977.

Baron, David P. "A Spatial Bargaining Theory of Government Formation in Parliamentary Systems." Unpublished manuscript, Stanford University, Stanford, Calif., 1989.

Barry, Brian. *Sociologists, Economists, and Democracy.* Chicago: University of Chicago Press, 1978.

Bartolini, Stefano. "The Politics of Institutional Reform in Italy." *West European Politics* 5 (1982), 203–21.

Beller, Dennis C., and Frank P. Belloni, eds. *Faction Politics: Political Parties and Factionalism in Comparative Perspective.* Santa Barbara; Calif.: ABC-Clio, 1978.

"Party and Faction: Modes of Political Competition." In Beller and Belloni (1978), 417–50.

Belloni, Frank P. "Factionalism, the Party System, and Italian Politics." In Beller and Belloni (1978), 73–108.

Belloni, Frank P., Mario Caciagli, and Liborio Mattina. "The Mass Clientelism Party: The Christian Democratic Party in Catalonia and in Southern Italy." *European Journal of Political Research* 7 (1979), 253–75.

Berg, Ole. *Hvor demokratisk?* Oslo: Universitetsforlaget, 1978.

Berger, Suzanne D., ed. *Organizing Interests in Western Europe.* Cambridge: Cambridge University Press, 1981.

Bergh, Trond, and Helge Pharo. *Vekst og Velstand: Norsk politisk historie 1945–1965.* 2nd ed. Oslo: Universitetsforlaget, 1981.

Bjørgum, Jorunn. *Venstre og kriseforliket.* Oslo: Universitetsforlaget, 1976.

Björnberg, Arne. *Parlamentarismens utveckling i Norge efter 1905.* Uppsala: Almqvist & Wiksell, 1939.

Bjurulf, Bo, and Ingemar Glans. *Från Tvåblocksystem till fraktionalisering: Partigruppers och ledamöters röstningsmönster i norska Stortinget 1969–1974.* Meddelande no. 1, Statsvetenskapliga Institutionen, Lund University, 1976.

Black, Duncan. *The Theory of Committees and Elections.* Cambridge University Press, 1958.

Blackmer, Donald L. M., and Sidney Tarrow, eds. *Communism in Italy and France.* Princeton, N.J.: Princeton University Press, 1977.

Blondel, Jean. "Party Systems and Patterns of Government in Western Democracies." *Canadian Journal of Political Science* 1 (1968), 180–203.

Comparative Legislatures. Englewood Cliffs, N.J.: Prentice-Hall, 1973.

World Leaders: Heads of Governments in the Postwar Period. London: Sage, 1980.

Bogdanor, Vernon, ed. *Coalition Government in Western Europe.* London: Heinemann, 1983.

Bogdanor, Vernon, and David Butler, eds. *Democracy and Elections: Electoral Systems and Their Political Consequences.* Cambridge: Cambridge University Press, 1983.

Brevig, Hans O. *NS – Fra parti til sekt 1933–1937.* Oslo: Pax, 1979.

Brown, Bernard E., ed. *Eurocommunism and Eurosocialism: The Left Confronts Modernity.* New York: Gyrco, 1979.

Browne, Eric C. *Coalition Theories: A Logical and Empirical Critique.* Sage Professional Papers in Comparative Politics, 4: 1–43. Beverly Hills, Calif.: Sage, 1973.

"Conclusion: Considerations on the Construction of a Theory of Cabinet Behavior." In Browne and Dreijmanis (1982a), 335–57.

"Introduction." In Browne and Dreijmanis (1982b), 1–6.

Browne, Eric C., and John Dreijmanis, eds. *Government Coalitions in Western Democracies.* New York: Longman, 1982.

Browne, Eric C., John Frendreis, and Dennis Gleiber. "An Events Approach to the Problem of Cabinet Stability." *Comparative Political Studies* 17 (1984), 167–97.

"The Process of Cabinet Dissolution: An Exponential Model of Duration and Stability in Western Democracies." *American Journal of Political Science* 30 (1986), 628–50.

Budge, Ian, and Valentine Herman. "Coalitions and Government Formations: An Empirically Relevant Theory." *British Journal of Political Science* 8 (1978), 459–77.

Budge, Ian, and Michael Laver. "Office Seeking and Policy Pursuit in Coalition Theory." *Legislative Studies Quarterly* 11 (1986), 485–506.

Budge, Ian, David Robertson, and Derek Hearl, eds. *Ideology, Strategy and Party Change: Spatial Analyses of Post-War Election Programmes in 19 Democracies.* Cambridge: Cambridge University Press, 1987.

Bueno De Mesquita, Bruce. *Strategy, Risk, and Personality in Coalition Politics: The Case of India.* New York: Cambridge University Press, 1975.

"Coalition Payoffs and Electoral Performance in European Democracies." *Comparative Political Studies* 12 (1979), 61–81.

Butler, David, and Dennis Kavanagh. *The British General Election of February 1974.* New York: St. Martin's Press, 1974.

The British General Election of October 1974. London: Macmillan, 1975.

Butler, David, Howard R. Penniman, and Austin Ranney, eds. *Democracy at the Polls.* Washington, D.C.: American Enterprise Institute, 1981.

Butterworth, Robert L. "A Research Note on the Size of Winning Coalitions." *American Political Science Review* 65 (1971), 741–8.

Calise, Mauro, and Renato Mannheimer. "I governi misurati. Il trentennio democristiano." *Critica Marxista* 17 (1979), 47–62.

Governanti in Italia. Bologna: Il Mulino, 1982.

Cantelli, Franca, Vittorio Mortara, and Giovanna Movia. *Come lavora il Parlamento.* Milan: Giuffrè, 1974.

Carstairs, Andrew McLaren. *A Short History of Electoral Systems in Western Europe.* London: Allen & Unwin, 1980.

Carty, R. K. "Politicians and Electoral Laws: An Anthology of Party Competition in Ireland." *Political Studies* 28 (1980), 550–6.

Party and Parish Pump: Electoral Politics in Ireland. Waterloo, Ontario: Wilfried Laurier University Press, 1981.

Cassese, Sabino. "Is There a Government in Italy? Politics and Administration at the Top." In Rose and Suleiman (1980), 171–202.

Cazzola, Franco. *Governo e opposizione nel Parlamento Italiano*. Milan: Giuffrè, 1974.

Anatomia del potere DC. Bari: De Donato, 1979.

Cazzola, Franco, and Massimo Morisi. "La decretazione d'urgenza continua: da Andreotti a Cossiga." *Laboratorio Politico* 1 (1981a), 123–41.

L'alluvione dei decreti. Il processo legislativo tra settima e ottava legislatura. Milan: Giuffrè, 1981b.

Cazzola, Franco, Alberto Prediero, and Grazia Priulla. *Il decreto legge fra governo e parlamento*. Milan: Giuffrè, 1975.

Cecchini, Vincenzo. *L'Italia nella stretta*. Milan: Pan Editrice, 1978.

Cerny, Karl H., ed. *Scandinavia at the Polls: Recent Political Trends in Denmark, Norway, and Sweden*. Washington, D.C.: American Enterprise Institute, 1977.

Christophersen, Jens A. *Valg og regjeringsdannelse*. Oslo: Universitetsforlagets vitenskapelige pressetjeneste, Kronikktjenesten no. 8, 1965.

Christophersen, Jens A., and Reidar Hirsti. *Norsk politikk foran 1980–årene*. Oslo: Gyldendal, 1980.

Chubb, Judith. *Patronage, Power, and Poverty in Southern Italy*. Cambridge: Cambridge University Press, 1982.

Coombes, David, et al., eds. *The Power of the Purse: The Role of European Parliaments in Budgetary Decisions*. London: Allen & Unwin, 1976.

Corbetta, Piergiorgio, and Arturo Parisi. "The 1985 local government elections." In Leonardi and Nanetti (1986), 11–28.

Cotta, Maurizio. "Classe politica e istituzionalizzazione del Parlamento, 1946–1972." *Rivista Italiana di Scienza Politica* 6 (1976), 71–110.

Classe politica e Parlamento in Italia 1946–1976. Bologna: Il Mulino, 1979.

Daalder, Hans. "Cabinet and Party Systems in Ten Smaller European Democracies." *Acta Politica* 6 (1971), 282–303.

Daalder, Hans, ed. *Party Systems in Denmark, Austria, Switzerland, the Netherlands, and Belgium*. New York: St. Martin's Press, 1987.

Daalder, Hans, and Peter Mair, eds. *Western European Party Systems: Continuity and Change*. London: Sage, 1983.

Daalder, Ivo H. "The Italian Party System in Transition: The End of Polarised Pluralism?" *West European Politics* 6 (1983), 216–36.

Dahl, Robert A., ed. *Political Oppositions in Western Democracies*. New Haven, Conn.: Yale University Press, 1966.

Polyarchy: Participation and Opposition. New Haven, Conn.: Yale University Press, 1971.

Dahl, Robert A., and Edward Tufte. *Size and Democracy*. Stanford, Calif.: Stanford University Press, 1973.

Dale, John. "1960 åra: Spranget framover." In Stortrøen et al. (1980), 113–35.

D'Alimonte, Roberto. "Competizione elettorale e rendimento politico: Il caso Italiano." *Rivista Italiana di Scienza Politica* 8 (1978), 457–93.

Damgaard, Erik. *Folketinget under forandring*. Copenhagen: Samfundsvidenskabeligt Forlag, 1977.

"Folketinget, partigrupperne og de stående udvalg." *Politica* 4 (1985), 536–43.

Della Sala, Vincent, "Government by Decree: The Craxi Government and the Use of Decree Legislation in the Italian Parliament." In Nanetti et al. (1988), 8–24.

Derry, T. K. *A Short History of Norway*. London: Allen & Unwin, 1968.

De Swaan, Abram. *Coalition Theories and Cabinet Formations*. Amsterdam: Elsevier, 1973.

Diesing, Paul. *Patterns of Discovery in the Social Sciences*. New York: Aldine, 1971.

Di Palma, Giuseppe. *Surviving without Governing: The Italian Parties in Parliament*. Berkeley: University of California Press, 1977.

Political Syncretism in Italy: Historical Coalition Strategies and the Present Crisis. Berkeley: Institute of International Studies, 1978.

"Government Performance: An Issue and Three Cases in Search of Theory." *West European Politics* 7 (April 1984), 172–87.

Di Palma, Giuseppe, and Maurizio Cotta. "Cadres, Peones, and Entrepreneurs: Professional Identities in a Divided Parliament." In Suleiman (1986), 41–78.

Dodd, Lawrence C. "Party Coalitions in Multiparty Parliaments: A Game-Theoretic Analysis." *American Political Science Review* 68 (September 1974), 1093–1117.

Coalitions in Parliamentary Government. Princeton, N.J.: Princeton University Press, 1976.

Downs, Anthony. *An Economic Theory of Democracy*. New York: Harper & Row, 1957.

Duverger, Maurice. *Political Parties*. London: Methuen, 1954.

Eckstein, Harry. *Division and Coherence in a Democracy*. Princeton, N.J.: Princeton University Press, 1966.

The Evaluation of Political Performance: Problems and Dimensions. Beverly Hills, Calif.: Sage, 1971.

"Case Study and Theory in Political Science." In Greenstein and Polsby (1975), 79–137.

Egeberg, Morten, Johan P. Olsen, and Paul G. Roness. "Opposisjon og opinion." In Olsen (1980), 55–83.

Elder, Neil C. "The Scandinavian States." In Finer (1975), 185–202.

Eliassen, Kjell A. "Rekrutteringen til Stortinget og regjeringen 1945–1985." In Nordby (1985), 109–30.

Elster, Jon. *Explaining Technical Change*. Cambridge: Cambridge University Press, 1983.

Introduction. In Elster, ed. *Rational Choice*. Oxford: Basil Blackwell, 1986, 1–33.

Epstein, Leon D. *Political Parties in Western Democracies*. New York: Praeger, 1967.

Eulau, Heinz, and Michael Lewis-Beck, eds. *Economic Conditions and Electoral Outcomes: The United States and Western Europe.* New York: Agathon, 1985.

Farneti, Paolo. *The Italian Party System.* London: Pinter, 1985.

Farrell, Brian. "Government Formation and Ministerial Selection." In Penniman and Farrell (1987), 131–55.

Ferrera, Maurizio. *Il Welfare State in Italia.* Bologna: Il Mulino, 1984.

Finer, Samuel E., ed. *Adversary Politics and Electoral Reform.* London: Wigram, 1975.

Finifter, Ada, ed. *Political Science: The State of the Discipline.* Washington, D.C.: American Political Science Association, 1983.

Finstad, Hans C. *Fra drakamp til samspill.* Oslo: Lutherstiftelsen, 1970.

Fiorina, Morris P. *Retrospective Voting in American National Elections.* New Haven, Conn.: Yale University Press, 1981.

Fisichella, Domenico. "The Italian Experience." In Finer (1975), 249–65.

Fitzmaurice, John. *Politics in Denmark.* London: Hurst, 1983.

"Coalitional Theory and Practice in Scandinavia." In Pridham (1986), 251–77.

Franklin, Mark, and Thomas T. Mackie. "Familiarity and Inertia in Formation of Governing Coalitions in Parliamentary Democracies." *British Journal of Political Science* 13 (1983), 275–98.

Friesenhahn, Ernst. "Parlament und Regierung im modernen Staat." In Kluxen (1971), 307–19.

Furre, Berge. *Norsk Historie 1905–1940.* Oslo: Det Norske Samlaget, 1976.

Galizia, Mario. *Studi sui rapporti fra Parlamento e governo.* Milan: Giuffré, 1972.

Galli, Giorgio. *Il bipartitismo imperfetto: Comunisti e democristiani in Italia.* Bologna: Il Mulino, 1966.

Il difficile governo. Bologna: Il Mulino, 1972.

Del bipartitismo imperfetto alla possibile alternativa. Bologna: Il Mulino, 1975a.

Fanfani. Milan: Feltrinelli, 1975b.

Storia della DC. Rome: Editori Laterza, 1978.

I partiti politici in Italia 1861–1983. Turin: UTET, 1983.

Galli, Giorgio, and Alfonso Prandi. *Patterns of Political Participation in Italy.* New Haven, Conn.: Yale University Press, 1970.

Galtung, Johan, and Nils P. Gleditsch. "Norge i verdenssamfunnet." In Ramsøy and Vaa (1975), vol. 2, 742–811.

Gamson, William. "A Theory of Coalition Formation." *American Sociological Review* 26 (1961), 373–82.

George, Alexander. "Case Studies and Theory Development." Paper presented to the Second Annual Symposium on Information Processing in Organizations, Carnegie Mellon University, October 15–16, 1982.

Goldthorpe, John H., ed. *Order and Conflict in Contemporary Capitalism.* Oxford: Clarendon, 1984.

Gordon, C. Wayne, and Nicholas Babchuck. "A Typology of Voluntary

Organizations." *American Sociological Review* 24 (1959), 22–9.

Greenstein, Fred I., and Nelson Polsby, eds. *Handbook of Political Science.* Vol. 7. Reading, Mass.: Addison-Wesley, 1975.

Grofman, Bernard. "A Dynamic Model of Proto-Coalition Formation in Ideological *N*-Space." *Behavioral Science* 27 (1982), 77–90.

Grofman, Bernard, and Arend Lijphart, eds. *Electoral Laws and Their Political Consequences.* New York: Agathon, 1985.

Gurr, Ted R., and Muriel McClelland. *Political Performance: A Twelve Nation Study.* Beverly Hills, Calif.: Sage, 1971.

Gustavsen, Finn. *Rett på sak.* Oslo: Pax, 1968.

Kortene på bordet. Oslo: Gyldendal, 1979.

Hardin, Russell. "Hollow Victory: The Minimum Winning Coalition." *American Political Science Review* 70 (1976), 1202–14.

Heisler, Martin O., ed. *Politics in Europe.* New York: McKay, 1974.

Heisler, Martin O., and Robert B. Kvavik. "Patterns of European Politics: 'The European Polity' Model." In Heisler (1974), 27–89.

Hellevik, Atle. *Det ansvarlige opprør: AIK og EF-motstanden i Arbeiderpartiet.* Oslo: Universitetsforlaget, 1979.

Hellevik, Ottar. *Stortinget – En sosial elite?* Oslo: Pax, 1969.

Heradstveit, Per Øyvind. *Einar Gerhardsen og hans menn.* Oslo: Cappelen, 1981.

Herman, Valentine, ed. *Parliaments of the World.* Berlin: De Gruyter, 1976.

Herman, Valentine, and John Pope. "Minority Governments in Western Democracies." *British Journal of Political Science* 3 (1973), 191–212.

Hernes, Gudmund. "Interest, Influence and Cooperation. A Study of the Norwegian Parliament." Ph.D. diss., Johns Hopkins University, Baltimore, Md., 1971.

Hine, David. "The Italian Socialist Party under Craxi: Surviving But Not Reviving." In Lange and Tarrow (1980), 133–48.

Hirschman, Albert O. *Exit, Voice, and Loyalty.* Cambridge, Mass.: Harvard University Press, 1970.

Holler, Manfred J., ed. *Power, Voting, and Voting Power.* Würzburg: Physica-Verlag, 1982.

Holmstedt, Margareta, and Tove-Lise Schou. "Sweden and Denmark 1945–1982: Election Programmes in the Scandinavian Setting." In Budge et al., (1987), 177–206.

Johnson, Nevil. "Adversary Politics and Electoral Reform: Need We Be Afraid?" In Finer (1975), 79–95.

Kaartvedt, Alf, Rolf Danielsen, and Tim Greve, eds. *Det Norske Storting gjennom 150 år.* Vol. 3. Oslo: Gyldendal, 1964.

Karmly, Dag. *Kings Bay-saken.* Oslo: Gyldendal, 1975.

Katzenstein, Peter J. *Small States in World Markets: Industrial Policy in Europe.* Ithaca, N.Y.: Cornell University Press, 1985.

Kielland, Arne. *All Makt? Dagbok fra Stortinget.* Oslo: Pax, 1972.

King, Anthony. "How to Strengthen Legislatures – Assuming That We Want To." In Ornstein (1981), 77–89.

King, Gary. "How Not to Lie with Statistics: Avoiding Common Mistakes in Quantitative Political Science." *American Journal of Political Science* 30 (1986), 666–87.

Kluxen, Kurt, ed. *Parlamentarismus.* Cologne: Kiepenheuer & Witsch, 1971.

Kornberg, Allan, ed. *Legislatures in Comparative Perspectives.* New York: McKay, 1972.

Kuhnle, Stein, and Stein Rokkan. "Political Research in Norway 1960–1978: An Overview." *Scandinavian Political Studies* 12 (1977), 127–56.

Lafferty, William. *Industrialization, Community Structure, and Socialism: An Ecological Analysis of Norway, 1875–1924.* Oslo: Universitetsforlaget, 1974.

Lægreid, Per, and Johan P. Olsen. "The Storting – A Last Stronghold of the Political Amateur." In Suleiman (1986), 176–222.

Lakatos, Imre. "Falsification and the Methodology of Scientific Research Programs." In Lakatos and Musgrave (1970), 91–196.

Lakatos, Imre, and Alan Musgrave, eds. *Criticism and the Growth of Knowledge.* Cambridge: Cambridge University Press, 1970.

Landshut, Siegfried. "Formen und Funktionen der parlamentarischen Opposition." In Kluxen (1971), 401–9.

Lange, Peter, and Sidney Tarrow, eds. *Italy in Transition: Conflict and Consensus.* London: Cass, 1980.

Langslet, Lars R. *Fra sidelinjen.* Oslo: Cappelen, 1974.

La Palombara, Joseph. "Italian Elections as Hobson's Choice." In Penniman (1977), 1–39.

 "Socialist Alternatives: The Italian Variant." *Foreign Affairs* 60 (1982), 924–42.

 Democracy Italian Style. New Haven, Conn.: Yale University Press, 1987.

La Palombara, Joseph, and Myron Weiner, eds. *Political Parties and Political Development.* Princeton: Princeton University Press, 1966.

 "The Origin and Development of Political Parties." In LaPalombara and Weiner (1966), 3–42.

Larsen, Reidar T. *Styrt fra Moskva? Erindringer 1960–1980.* Oslo: Cappelen, 1980.

Larsen, Stein Ugelvik, Bernt Hagtvet, and Jan Petter Myklebust, eds. *Who Were the Fascists: Social Roots of European Fascism.* Bergen: Universitetsforlaget, 1980.

Larssen, Olav. *Den langsomme revolusjonen.* Oslo: Aschehoug, 1973.

Laver, Michael J. "Dynamic Factors in Government Coalition Formation." *European Journal of Political Research* 2 (1974), 259–70.

 The Politics of Private Desires. Harmondsworth: Penguin, 1981.

 "Party Competition and Party System Change." Paper prepared for presentation at the Annual Meeting of the American Political Science Association, Washington, D.C., 1988.

Laver, Michael J., and Ian Budge, eds. *Party Policy and Coalition Govern-*

ment in Western Europe, forthcoming.

Laver, Michael J., and Norman Schofield. *The Politics of Coalition in Western Europe*. Oxford: Oxford University Press, in press.

Lees, John, and Malcolm Shaw, eds. *Committees in Legislatures: A Comparative Analysis*. Durham, N. C.: Duke University Press, 1979.

Lehmbruch, Gerhard, and Philippe C. Schmitter, eds. *Patterns of Corporatist Policy Making*. London: Sage, 1982.

Leiserson, Michael. "Coalitions in Politics." Ph.D. diss., Yale University, New Haven, Conn., 1966.

Leonardi, Robert, and Raffaella Nanetti, eds. *Italian Politics: A Review*. Vol. 1. London: Pinter, 1986.

Leonardi, Robert, Raffaella Nanetti, and Gianfranco Pasquino. "Institutionalization of Parliament and Parliamentarization of Parties in Parliament." *Legislative Studies Quarterly* 3 (1978), 161–86.

Lepsius, M. Rainer. "From Fragmented Party Democracy to Government by Emergency Decree and National Socialist Takeover: Germany." In Linz and Stepan (1978), 34–9.

Lie, Håkon. *Slik jeg ser det*. Oslo: Tiden Norsk Forlag, 1975.

Lijphart, Arend. *Democracy in Plural Societies: A Comparative Exploration*. New Haven, Conn.: Yale University Press, 1977.

Democracies. New Haven, Conn.: Yale University Press, 1984a.

"Measures of Cabinet Durability: A Conceptual and Empirical Evaluation." *Comparative Political Studies* 17 (1984b), 265–79.

Linz, Juan. *The Breakdown of Democratic Regimes: Crisis, Breakdown, and Reequilibration*. Baltimore: Johns Hopkins University Press, 1978.

Linz, Juan, and Alfred Stepan, eds. *The Breakdown of Democratic Regimes: Europe*. Baltimore: Johns Hopkins University Press, 1978.

Lipset. Seymour Martin. "No Room for the Ins: Elections around the World." *Public Opinion* 5 (October/November 1982), 1–64.

Lipset, Seymour Martin, and Stein Rokkan, eds. *Party Systems and Voter Alignments: Cross-National Perspectives*. New York: Free Press, 1967.

"Cleavage Structures, Party Systems, and Voter Alignments: An Introduction." In Lipset and Rokkan (1967), 1–64.

Lombardo, Antonio. "Il fazionismo eterodiretto. Sistema di correnti e deperimento dei partiti in Italia." In Lombardo, ed., *La crisi delle democrazie industriali 1968–1976*. Florence: Valecchi, 1977, 185–215.

Loewenberg, Gerhard, and Samuel C. Patterson. *Comparing Legislatures*. Boston: Little, Brown, 1979.

Luebbert, Gregory M. "Coalition Theory and Government Formation in Multiparty Democracies." *Comparative Politics* 15 (1983), 235–49.

"A Theory of Government Formation." *Comparative Political Studies* 17 (1984), 229–64.

Comparative Democracy: Policymaking and Governing Coalitions in Europe and Israel. New York: Columbia University Press, 1986.

Lyng, John. *Fra borgfred til politisk blåmandag: Erindringer 1968–1971*. Oslo: Cappelen, 1978.

McCarthy, Patrick. "The Parliamentary and Nonparliamentary Parties of the Far Left." In Penniman (1981), 193–211.

McKelvey, Richard, Peter C. Ordeshook, and Mark Winer. "The Competitive Solution for N-Person Games, without Sidepayments." *American Political Science Review* 72 (1978), 599–615.

Mackie, Thomas T., and Richard Rose. *The International Almanac of Electoral History*. 2nd ed. London: Macmillan, 1982.

Macrae, Duncan. *Parliament, Parties and Society in France 1946–1958*. New York: St. Martin's Press, 1967.

Macridis, Roy. "Oppositions in France: An Interpretation." *Government and Opposition* 7 (1972), 166–85.

Maguire, Maria. "Is There Still Persistence? Electoral Change in Western Europe." In Daalder and Mair (1983), 29–66.

Mair, Peter. *The Changing Irish Party System: Organizations, Ideology, and Electoral Competition*. London: Pinter, 1987.

Mammarella, Giuseppe. *Italy after Fascism: A Political History 1943–1963*. Montreal: Casalini, 1964.

L'Italia della caduta del fascismo ad oggi. Bologna: Il Mulino, 1978.

Mannino, Armando. *Indirizzo e Fiducia nei Rapporti tra Governo e Parlamento*. Milan: Giuffrè, 1973.

Manzella, Andrea. *Il parlamento*. Bologna: Il Mulino, 1977.

Il tentativo la Malfa. Bologna: Il Mulino, 1980.

March, James G., and Johan P. Olsen. "The New Institutionalism: Organizational Factors in Political Life." *American Political Science Review* 78 (1984), 734–49.

Marradi, Alberto. "Italy: From Centrism to Crisis of the Center-Left Coalitions." In Browne and Dreijmanis (1982), 22–70.

Mastropaolo, Alfio, and Martin Slater. "Italy 1946–1979: Ideological Distances and Party Movements." In Budge et al. (1987), 345–68.

Mezey, Michael. *Comparative Legislatures*. Durham, N. C.: Duke University Press, 1979.

Michels, Robert. *Political Parties*. New York: Free Press, 1962.

Moe, Terry M. "On the Scientific Status of Rational Models." *American Journal of Political Science* 23 (1979), 215–43.

The Organization of Interests. Chicago: University of Chicago Press, 1980.

Morgan, Michael-John. "The Modeling of Government Coalition Formation: A Policy Based Approach with Interval Measurement." Ph.D. diss., University of Michigan, Ann Arbor, 1976.

Mortara, Vittorio. "The Italian Parliament's Role in Expenditure Decisions." In Coombes et al. (1976), 237–53.

Motta, Riccardo, "L'attivita legislativa dei governi." *Rivista Italiana di scienza politica* 15 (1985), 255–92.

Nanetti, Raffaella Y., Robert Leonardi, and Piergiorgio Corbetta. *Italian Politics: A Reader.* Vol. 2. London: Pinter, 1988.

Nilson, Sten Sparre. "Factional Strife in the Norwegian Labor Party 1918–1924." *Journal of Contemporary History* 16 (1981a), 691–704.

"Labor Insurgency in Norway: The Crisis of 1917–1920." *Social Science History* 5 (1981b), 393–416.

Nordal, Johannes, and Valdimar Kristinsson. *Iceland 1874–1974.* Reykjavik: Central Bank of Iceland, 1975.

Nordby, Trond, ed. *Storting og regjering 1945–1985.* Vol. 2. Oslo: Kunnskapsforlaget, 1985.

Nordisk Kontakt. Stockholm: Nordic Council, 1976.

Norton, Phillip. *The Commons in Perspective.* Oxford: Robertson, 1981.

Olsen, Johan P. *Organized Democracy: Political Institutions in a Welfare State: The Case of Norway.* Bergen: Universitetsforlaget, 1983.

"Governing Norway: Segmentation, Anticipation, and Consensus Formation." In Rose and Suleiman (1980), 203–55.

Olson, Mancur. *The Logic of Collective Action: Public Goods and the Theory of Groups.* Cambridge, Mass.: Harvard University Press, 1971.

Ordeshook, Peter C. *Game Theory and Political Theory.* Cambridge: Cambridge University Press, 1986.

Ordeshook, Peter C., and Mark Winer. "Coalitions and Spatial Policy Outcomes in Parliamentary Systems: Some Experimental Results." *American Journal of Political Science* 24 (1980), 730–52.

Ornstein, Norman J., ed. *The Role of the Legislature in Western Democracies.* Washington, D.C.: American Enterprise Institute, 1981.

Ørvik, Nils. *Kampen on Arbeiderpartiet: Venstrefløyen og vestorienteringen.* Oslo: Grøndahl, 1977.

Østerud, Øyvind. *Det planlagte samfunn.* Oslo: Gyldendal, 1979.

Pappalardo, Adriano. *Partiti e governi di coalizione in Europa.* Milan: Angeli, 1978.

Parisi, Arturo, and Gianfranco Pasquino. *Continuità e mutamento elettorale in Italia.* Bologna: Il Mulino, 1977.

"Changes in Italian Electoral Behavior: The Relationship between Parties and Voters." In Lange and Tarrow (1980), 6–30.

Pasquino, Gianfranco. "Le radici del frazionismo e il voto di preferenza." In Sartori (1973a), 75–91.

"The Italian Socialist Party: An Irreversible Decline?" In Penniman (1977a), 183–227.

"Per un'analisi delle coalizioni di governo in Italia." In Parisi and Pasquino (1977b), 251–79.

"Alla ricerca dell'elettore d'opinone: Il caso del PSI." In Parisi (1980a), 102–32.

"In Search of a Stable Governmental Coalition: The Italian Parliamentary Elections of 1979." Occasional Paper no. 35. Bologna: Johns Hopkins University Research Institute, 1980b.

"The Italian Socialist Party: Electoral Stagnation and Political Indispensability." In Penniman (1981), 141–71.

"Sources of Stability and Instability in the Italian Party System." *West European Politics* 6 (1983), 93–110.

Pedersen, Mogens N. "The Dynamics of European Party Systems: Changing Patterns of Electoral Volatility." *European Journal of Political Research* 7 (1979), 1–26.

"Changing Patterns of Electoral Volatility in European Party Systems, 1948–1977: Explorations in Explanation." In Daalder and Mair (1983), 67–94.

"The Danish 'Working Multiparty System': Breakdown or Adaptation?" In Daalder (1987), 1–60.

Penniman, Howard R., ed. *Italy at the Polls: The Parliamentary Elections of 1976.* Washington, D.C.: American Enterprise Institute, 1977.

Ireland at the Polls: The Dáil Election of 1977. Washington, D.C.: American Enterprise Institute, 1978.

Italy at the Polls, 1979: A Study of the Parliamentary Elections. Washington, D.C.: American Enterprise Institute, 1981.

Italy at the Polls, 1983: A Study of the National Elections. Washington, D.C.: American Enterprise Institute, 1987.

Penniman, Howard R., and Brian Farrell, eds. *Ireland at the Polls, 1981, 1982, and 1987.* Washington, D.C.: American Enterprise Institute, 1987.

Pesonen, Pertti, and Alastair Thomas. "Coalition Formation in Scandinavia." In Bogdanor (1983), 59–96.

Pettersen, Per Arnt. "Konfliktlinjer og partistrategi: En analyse av partiprogrammene foran stortingsvalget i 1969." Unpublished graduate thesis, University of Oslo, 1973.

Polsby, Nelson W. "Legislatures." In Greenstein and Polsby (1975), 257–319.

Pondaven, Philippe. *Le Parlement et la politique exterieure sous la IVe Republique.* Paris: Presses universitaires de France, 1973.

Powell, G. Bingham, Jr. "Voting Turnout in Thirty Democracies: Partisan, Legal, and Socio-Economic Influences." In Rose (1980), 5–34.

"Party Systems and Political System Performance: Participation, Stability and Violence in Contemporary Democracies." *American Political Science Review* 75 (December 1981a), 861–79.

"Party Systems as Systems of Representation and Accountability." Paper prepared for presentation at the Annual Meeting of the American Political Science Association, New York, September 3–6, 1981b.

Contemporary Democracies: Participation, Stability and Violence. Cambridge, Mass.: Harvard University Press, 1982a.

"Representative or Accountable Party Systems in Parliamentary Democracies." Paper prepared for presentation at the Western European Studies Conference on Representation and the State, Stanford University, October 11–16, 1982b.

Pridham, Geoffrey, ed. *Coalitional Behaviour in Theory and Practice: An Inductive Model for Western Europe*. Cambridge: Cambridge University Press, 1986.

Przeworski, Adam. "Institutionalization of Voting Patterns, or Is Mobilization the Source of Decay?" *American Political Science Review* 69 (1975), 49–67.

Putnam, Robert. *The Beliefs of Politicians: Ideology, Conflict, and Democracy in Britain and Italy*. New Haven, Conn.: Yale University Press, 1973.

Putnam, Robert, Robert Leonardi, and Raffaella Y. Nanetti. "Polarization and Depolarization in Italian Politics 1968–1981." Paper delivered to the Annual Meeting of the American Political Science Association, New York, September 3–6, 1981.

Rae, Douglas W. *The Political Consequences of Electoral Laws*. Rev. ed. New Haven, Conn.: Yale University Press, 1971.

Ramsøy, Natalie Rogoff, and Mariken Vaa, eds. *Det Norske Samfunn*. Oslo: Gyldendal, 1975.

Regini, Marino. "The Conditions for Political Exchange: How Concertation Emerged and Collapsed in Italy and Great Britain." In Goldthorpe (1984), 124–42.

Riker, William H. *The Theory of Political Coalitions*. New Haven, Conn.: Yale University Press, 1962.

"Political Theory and the Art of Heresthetics." In Finifter (1983), 47–67.

Riker, William H., and Peter Ordeshook. *An Introduction to Positive Political Theory*. Englewood Cliffs, N.J.: Prentice-Hall, 1973.

Robertson, David. *A Theory of Party Competition*. London: Wiley, 1976.

Rokkan, Stein. "Norway: Numerical Democracy and Corporate Pluralism." In Dahl (1966), 70–115.

"Geography, Religion, and Social Class: Crosscutting Cleavages in Norwegian Politics." In Lipset and Rokkan (1967), 367–444.

Citizens, Elections, Parties. New York: McKay, 1970.

Rokkan, Stein, and Derek Urwin, eds. *The Politics of Territorial Identity: Studies in European Regionalism*. London: Sage, 1982.

Rommetvedt, Hilmar. *Sprikende staur eller laftet tømmer?* Oslo: Universitetsforlaget, 1984.

Roness, Paul G. *Reorganisering av departmenta – Eit politisk styringsmiddel?* Bergen: Universitetsforlaget, 1979.

Rose, Richard. *The Problem of Party Government*. London: Macmillan, 1974b.

Rose, Richard, ed. *Electoral Behavior: A Comparative Handbook*. New York: Free Press, 1974a.

Electoral Participation: A Comparative Analysis. Beverly Hills: Sage, 1980.

Rose, Richard, and Thomas T. Mackie. "Incumbency in Government: Asset or Liability?" In Daalder and Mair (1983), 115–37.

Rose, Richard, and Ezra Suleiman, eds. *Presidents and Prime Ministers.* Washington, D.C.: American Enterprise Institute, 1980.

Rose, Richard, and Derek W. Urwin. "Persistence and Change in Western Party Systems Since 1945." *Political Studies* 18 (1979), 287–319.

Sanders, David, and Valentine Herman. "The Stability and Survival of Governments in Western Democracies." *Acta Politica* 12 (1977), 346–77.

Sani, Giacomo. "Le elezioni degli anni settanta: terremoto o evoluzione?" In Parisi and Pasquino (1977a), 67–102.

"The Italian Electorate in the Mid-1970's: Beyond Tradition?" In Penniman (1977b), 81–122.

"Amici-Nemici, Parenti-Serpenti: Communists and Socialists in Italy." In Brown (1979), 105–42.

"The Political Culture of Italy: Continuity and Change." In Almond and Verba (1980), 293–324.

Sani, Giacomo, and Giovanni Sartori. "Frammentazione, Polarizzazione e Cleavages: Democrazie Facili e Difficili." *Rivista Italiana di Scienza Politica* 8 (1978), 339–61.

"Polarization, Fragmentation, and Competition in Western Democracies." In Daalder and Mair (1983), 307–40.

Särlvik, Bo. "Coalition Politics and Policy Output in Scandinavia: Sweden, Denmark, and Norway." In Bogdanor (1983), 97–152.

Sartori, Giovanni. "European Political Parties: The Case of Polarized Pluralism." In LaPalombara and Weiner (1966), 137–76.

ed. *Correnti, frazionismo e fazioni nei partiti politici italiani.* Bologna: Il Mulino, 1973a.

"Un epilogo." In Sartori (1973b), 119–27.

Parties and Party Systems: A Framework for Analysis. Cambridge: Cambridge University Press, 1976.

Teoria dei partiti e caso italiano. Milan: Sugar, 1982.

Schlesinger, Joseph A. "On the Theory of Party Organization." *Journal of Politics* 46 (1984), 369–400.

Schmitter, Philippe C., and Gerhard Lehmbruch, eds. *Trends toward Corporatist Intermediation.* Beverly Hills, Calif.: Sage, 1979.

Schofield, Norman. "The Kernel and Payoffs in European Government Coalitions." *Public Choice* 26 (1976), 29–49.

"Bargaining Set Theory and Stability in Coalition Governments." *Mathematical Social Science* 3 (1982), 120–9.

Schofield, Norman, and Michael J. Laver. "Bargaining Theory and Portfolio Payoffs in European Coalition Governments 1945–83." *British Journal of Political Science* 15 (1985), 143–64.

Schwarz, John E. "Exploring a New Role in Policy Making: The British House of Commons in the 1970s." *American Political Science Review* 74 (1980), 23–37.

Seip, Jens Arup. *Fra embedsmannsstat til ettpartistat og andre essays.* Oslo: Universitetsforlaget, 1963.

Seliktar, Ofira. "Israel: Fragile Coalitions in a New Nation." In Browne and Dreijmanis (1982), 283–314.

Seton-Watson, Christopher. "Italy." In Bogdanor and Butler (1983), 110–21.

Shapley, Lloyd, and Martin Shubik. "A Method of Evaluating Power in a Committee System." *American Political Science Review* 48 (1954), 787–92.

Shepsle, Kenneth A. "Institutional Arrangements and Equilibrium in Multidimensional Voting Models." *American Journal of Political Science* 23 (1979), 27–59.

Sjöblom, Gunnar. *Party Strategies in a Multiparty System*. Lund: Studentlitteratur, 1968.

Sked, Alan, and Chris Cook. *Post-War Britain: A Political History*. New York: Barnes & Noble, 1979.

Skocpol, Theda. *States and Social Revolutions: A Comparative Analysis of France, Russia, and China*. Cambridge: Cambridge University Press, 1979.

Smelser, Neil. "The Methodology of Comparative Analysis." In Warwick and Osherson (1973), 42–86.

Spiro, Herbert J. *Government by Constitution: The Political Institutions of Democracy*. New York: Random House, 1959.

Stavang, Per. *Parlamentarisme og maktbalanse*. Oslo: Universitetsforlaget, 1968.

"Negativt fleirtal i norsk parlamentarisme." *Lov og Rett* (1971), 145–66.

"Parlamentarismen i Noreg." *Tidsskrift for Rettsvitenskap* 4 (1976), 423–63.

Stortrøen, O., Eikestøl, and J. Brotnov, eds. *Rotfeste og framtid: Senterpartiet i medgang og motgang 1920–1980*. Oslo: Cultura, 1980.

Strom, Kaare. "Party Goals and Government Performance in Parliamentary Democracies." *American Political Science Review* 79 (1985), 738–54.

"Deferred Gratification and Minority Governments in Scandinavia." *Legislative Studies Quarterly* 11 (1986), 583–605.

Strom, Kaare, and Jørn Y. Leipart. "Ideology, Strategy, and Party Competition in Postwar Norway." *European Journal of Political Research* 17 (1989), 263–88.

"Norway: Policy Pursuit and Coalition Avoidance." In Laver and Budge, forthcoming.

Strom, Kaare, and Seymour Martin Lipset. "Macroeconomics and Macropolitics." Paper prepared for presentation at the 1984 Annual Meeting of the American Political Science Association, Washington, D.C.

Suleiman, Ezra N. ed. *Parliaments and Parliamentarians in Democratic Politics*. New York: Holmes & Meier, 1986.

Tamburrano, Giuseppe. *Storia e cronaca del centro sinistra*. Milan: Feltrinelli, 1973.

Tarrow, Sidney. "Italy: Crisis, Crises or Transition?" In Lange and Tarrow (1980), 166–85.

Taylor, Charles L., and Michael Hudson, eds. *World Handbook of Political and Social Indicators*. 2nd ed. New Haven, Conn.: Yale University Press, 1972.

Taylor, Charles L., and David A. Jodice, eds. *World Handbook of Political and Social Indicators*. 3rd ed. New Haven, Conn.: Yale University Press, 1983.

Taylor, Michael, and Valentine Herman. "Party Systems and Government Stability." *American Political Science Review* 65 (1971), 28–37.

Taylor, Michael, and Michael J. Laver. "Government Coalitions in Western Europe." *European Journal of Political Research* 3 (1973), 205–48.

Thomas, Alastair H. "Denmark: Coalitions and Minority Governments." In Browne and Dreijmanis (1982), 104–41.

Urwin, Derek W. "Norway: Parties between Mass Membership and Consumer-Oriented Professionalism?" In Ware (1987), 183–204.

Valen, Henry. *Valg og politikk – et samfunn i endring*. Oslo: NKS-forlaget, 1981.

Valen, Henry, and Stein Rokkan. "Norway: Conflict Structure and Mass Politics in a European Periphery." In Rose (1974a), 315–70.

Valen, Henry, and Derek W. Urwin. "De politiske partiene." In Nordby (1985), 57–108.

Vassbotn, Per. *Lekkasje og forlis: Om regjeringen Bortens fall*. Oslo: Cappelen, 1971.

Von Beyme, Klaus. *Die parlamentarischen Regierungssysteme in Europa*. Munich: Piper, 1970.

Political Parties in Western Democracies. Aldershot: Gower, 1985.

Von Neumann, John, and Oskar Morgenstern. *The Theory of Games and Economic Behavior*. Princeton, N.J.: Princeton University Press, 1945.

Ware, Alan J., ed. *Political Parties: Electoral Change and Structural Response*. Oxford: Basil Blackwell, 1987.

Warwick, Donald P., and Samuel Osherson, eds. *Comparative Research Methods*. Englewood Cliffs, N.J.: Prentice-Hall, 1973.

Warwick, Paul. "The Durability of Coalition Governments in Parliamentary Democracies." *Comparative Political Studies* 11 (1979), 465–98.

Wertman, Douglas A. "The Italian Electoral Process: The Elections of June 1976." In Penniman (1977), 41–79.

"The Christian Democrats: The Big Losers." In Penniman (1987), 35–59.

"DC Congress: The End of Factions?" In Nanetti et al. (1988), 53–70.

Williams, Philip. *Crisis and Compromise: Politics in the Fourth Republic*. London: Longmans, 1964.

Wilson, James Q. *Political Organizations*. New York: Basic Books, 1973.

Zincone, Giovanna. "Partiti minori e alleanza laica." In Parisi and Pasquino (1977), 185–214.

Zuckerman, Alan S. *The Politics of Faction: Christian Democratic Rule in Italy*. New Haven, Conn.: Yale University Press, 1979.

Index

Action party (Italy), 165n
activists, 39, 53, 216, 221
aggregative majority systems, 239
Agrarian party (Norway), 191, 192, 193, 194, 204n, 205, 217–221, 224
Agudat Israel, 101, 102, 112
Almond, Gabriel A., 113, 147
alternation, 114, 123n, 130, 131, 238, 243
    captive government type and, 91, 92
    as measure of electoral performance, 125–127
alternative majority systems, 239
Andreotti, Giulio, 121, 142, 143, 170, 178
Arendal, 191
Arian, Alan, 132, 168, 187
Arrow, Kenneth J., 30
Austen-Smith, David, 26, 36, 44, 243
Austria, 64
Axelrod, Robert, 36, 38, 45, 53

Banks, Jeffrey S., 26, 36, 44, 243
bargaining power, 24, 46–47, 49, 50, 69, 70, 78, 81, 108, 109–110, 125–126, 237, 238, 243
Barnes, Samuel H., 132, 134, 168, 169, 187
Bartolini, Stefano, 153n, 154
Begin, Menachem, 58, 62, 76, 94, 96, 101, 102, 143
Belgium
    cabinet instability in, 63
    electoral decisiveness in, 70
    informateurs in, 26
    investiture in, 79
    majority and minority governments in, 58
    party system in, 239, 239n
    and political culture, 64
Belloni, Frank P., 161, 162
Berg, Ole, 216

Berger, Suzanne D., 2, 41
Beyme, Klaus von, 10, 15, 17, 18, 26, 62
Björnberg, Arne, 205, 217–219
Blaney, Neil, 104
Blondel, Jean, 3n, 21, 43, 58, 113, 115
Board of Presidents (Norwegian Storting), 207, 208, 208n
Bogdanor, Vernon, 2, 3, 20
Borten, Per, 198, 215, 234
Bratlie, Jens K. M., 198
Bratteli, Trygve, 210, 225, 235
Browne, Eric C., 3, 21, 25, 115
Brundtland, Gro Harlem, 225, 226
Budge, Ian, 3, 13, 36, 37, 40, 64, 171n
Butler, David, 2, 3
Bye, Ronald, 206n, 225

cabinet crisis duration, 68, 78, 79, 84
cabinet duration, 59, 114, 115, 117
Calise, Mauro, 138
Cantelli, Franca, 183, 183n, 185
captive government system, see Italy
caretaker government, 7, 13, 18, 50n, 80, 80n, 84
cause of resignation, 121
Cazzola, Franco, 162, 183, 185
Center Democrats (Denmark), 106
center-left, see Italy
Center party (Norway), 194, 224–226
centrifugal competition, 149–151, 168
centripetal competition, 240, 241
Chamber of Deputies (Italy), 134, 135, 142, 146n, 152
characteristic function, 34
Christian Democratic party (Italy), 119, 133, 134, 134n, 135, 137, 138, 142, 143, 148, 150, 151, 154, 155, 160–165, 165n, 167–169, 171, 171n, 173–176, 178, 182, 183, 185, 187
Christian People's party
    in Denmark, 106

Christian People's party (*cont.*)
  in Norway, 192, 193, 194, 204, 204n,
    206n, 212, 224, 225
Christophersen, Jens A., 212, 214, 223,
  234
Churchill, Winston S., 119
clientelism, 158–161, 164, 176
Cold War, 148, 153n, 165, 193
Communist party
  in Italy, 133, 134, 134n, 135, 137,
    146, 146n, 147, 148, 150, 151, 153,
    153n, 154, 159, 160, 162, 165, 167,
    168, 174, 178
  in Norway, 192–194, 203, 204, 204n,
    221
competitive solution, 36
Conservative party
  in Britain, 1
  in Denmark, 106
  in Norway, 190, 193, 194, 205, 208,
    212, 217, 217n, 218, 220–222, 224–
    226, 234
consociational democracy, 11
Constituent Assembly (Italy), 135,
  139n, 165n
constructive vote of no confidence, 4
Corbetta, Piergiorgio, 155, 156
core party, 171, 171n
corporate pluralism, 202, 206
corporatism, 2, 41
corporatist institutions, 41, 207
Cotta, Maurizio, 134
Craxi, Bettino, 143, 144, 163, 169, 172,
  179
crisis accord, 218, 224

Daalder, Hans, 8, 11, 19, 61, 63, 159
D'Alimonte, Roberto, 17
Damgaard, Erik, 189
De Mita, Ciriaco, 163
de Valera, Eamon, 103
decision point, 20, 38, 39, 69
decline of parliament, *see* Norway
decree laws, 185
Della Sala, Vincent, 185
Denmark
  electoral volatility in, 107
  government concessions in, 105–108
  government instability in, 107
  inclusionary politics (oppositional in-
    fluence) in, 190
  Justice party (Retsforbundet) in, 66n
  legislative coalitions in, 99, 100, 105–
    108
  majority and minority governments

in, 58, 59, 59n, 63, 87, 96, 96n,
  132, 138, 189, 240
and sovereignty over Greenland, 202n
DeSwaan, Abram, 36, 61
Dodd, Lawrence C., 13–17, 20, 31, 32,
  36, 38, 60, 63–66, 79, 115–117, 164,
  215
Downs, Anthony, 39, 45
Duverger, Maurice, 7

Eckstein, Harry, 54, 113, 202
Egeberg, Morten, 211
Elder, Neil, 108
electoral competitiveness, 46
  defined, 47, 73
electoral decisiveness, 52, 54, 70, 81,
  84, 86, 240
  defined, 46–48, 72–74
electoral proximity, 48, 74, 74n, 154
electoral responsiveness, 47–48, 74, 76,
  79, 81, 82, 241, 244
  as indicator of decisiveness, 73, 154
electoral salience, 74, 74n, 76, 79–82, 84
electoral success, 45, 56, 73, 86, 114,
  126, 127, 129–131, 194
  defined, 123
electoral systems, 2, 14, 112
Eliassen, Kjell A., 206
Elster, Jon, 29, 32, 33
Eriksen, Erik, 106
European Community, 107, 122, 193,
  225, 226
external support, 20, 60n, 95, 95n, 96,
  96n, 97, 109, 127
  defined, 61–62
  republicanism and, 111
extremist parties, 241, 242
  concept operationalized, 78
  defined, 65–66

Fanfani, Amintore, 121, 139n, 143, 144,
  161, 175, 176, 178, 179
Farneti, Paolo, 137, 138
Farrell, Brian, 103, 104
Fianna Fáil, 50, 103, 104, 110
Fine Gael, 103, 104, 125n
Finer, Samuel E., 2, 24, 60, 91n, 113
Finland
  cabinet stability in, 63
  electoral decisiveness in, 157
  majority and minority government in,
    58, 89, 96
  party system in, 66n
Finstad, Hans C., 221, 234
Fitzgerald, Garret, 104